Autism Spectrum Disorders

Inclusive Community for the Twenty-First Century

A Volume in
Contemporary Perspectives in Special Education

Series Editors:
Anthony F. Rotatori, *Saint Xavier University*
Festus E. Obiakor, *University of Wisconsin-Milwaukee*

Contemporary Perspectives in Special Education
Anthony F. Rotatori and Festus E. Obiakor, Series Editors

Autism Spectrum Disorders:
Inclusive Community for the Twenty-First Century (2012)
edited by Julie A. Deisinger, Sandra Burkhardt, Timothy J. Wahlberg,
Anthony F. Rotatori, and Festus E. Obiakor

Autism Spectrum Disorders

Inclusive Community for the Twenty-First Century

Edited by

Julie A. Deisinger and Sandra Burkhardt
Saint Xavier University

Timothy J. Wahlberg
Wahlberg and Associates

Anthony F. Rotatori
Saint Xavier University

and

Festus E. Obiakor
University of Wisconsin-Milwaukee

IAP

Information Age Publishing, Inc.
Charlotte, North Carolina • www.infoagepub.com

Library of Congress Cataloging-in-Publication Data

Autism spectrum disorders : inclusive community for the twenty-first century / edited by Julie A Deisinger.... [et al.].
p. cm. — (Contemporary perspectives in special education)
ISBN 978-1-61735-780-0 (paperback) — ISBN 978-1-61735-781-7 (hardcover) — ISBN 978-1-61735-782-4 (ebook) 1. Autism spectrum disorders. I. Deisinger, Julie A.
RC553.A88A8747 2012
616.85'882—dc23

2012003205

Printed in the United States of America

CONTENTS

PREFACE

Almost 100 years have passed since the term autism was first coined by a Swiss psychiatrist named Eugen Bleuler to describe a person's behavior that included significant retreat into a self-absorbed idiosyncratic mental state of fantasy. Unfortunately, the term became connected with childhood schizophrenia. While the current concept of autism was first described by Leo Kanner in a 1943 paper entitled "Autistic Disturbances of Affective Content" there was little advancement in the causes, prevalence, identification, diagnosis, education, and treatment of this disorder due to the disorder being confused with childhood schizophrenia. In the 1980s, the Diagnostic and Statistical Manual of Mental Disorders (DSM-III) helped advance what autism is by describing a group of conditions labeled pervasive developmental disorders. This advancement was followed by the 1990 federal legislation "Individuals with Disabilities Educational Act" which recognized the disorder as a disability category eligible for special education services. These latter advancements have lead to an explosion in: finding causes for the disorder; accurate identification and diagnosis of the disorder; best practices in educating children with this disorder; and social, emotional, and behavioral treatment of individuals with this disorder.

While this explosion of information added to the body of knowledge regarding this disorder, there is much more to be learned and discovered. A critical goal for the future of this disorder is to provide educators, clinicians, parents, and mental health professionals with accurate information to counter misinformation that exists among the general public and clinical professionals. This is the primary purpose of *Autism Spectrum Disorders: Inclusive Community for the Twenty-First Century*. The first chapter provides the reader a blueprint for systems of care for persons with autism spectrum disorders (ASD) and their families. The blueprint will assist profes-

Autism Spectrum Disorders: Inclusive Community for the Twenty-First Century, pp. vii–ix

sionals in unlocking the many advocacy puzzle pieces to yield a more meaningful picture for successful system care. Chapter 2 provides the reader with critical information that will assist professionals in tackling the challenge of employability for those adults with high functioning ASD. Key to this challenge is the realization that for adults with ASD to be successful in the workplace, business professionals in human resources must play an innovative part in providing access opportunities and systematic resources designed to provide these workers with programmatic support. Obtaining an accurate ASD diagnosis is imperative in educating and treating individuals with ASD. However, the ASD research indicates that there is a critical need to increase training of professionals who assess individuals with ASD. Chapter 3 discusses the process of obtaining an affirmative ASD diagnosis using reliable and valid screening and diagnostic devices by a variety of professionals (physicians, clinical and school psychologists, mental health clinicians). Examined are the use of cost-effective ASD instruments, demographic factors that may influence the course of evaluation, and the advantages of such a diagnosis. Since the 1990s, genetic researches have been examining the heritability of ASDs which indicate that genetic endowment strongly influences the etiology of these disorders. Chapter 4 provides a comprehensive and current synopsis of genetic factors associated with ASD. The chapter provides the reader with content on terminology, candidate genes, genetic disorders associated with ASDs, and implications for genetic counseling. Individuals with ASDs have siblings who themselves may be challenged socially and emotionally by the behavior of a brother or sister with ASD. Chapter 5 highlights for the reader adjustment challenges that may be present for a sibling of an individual with ASD. The chapter provides a summary of recent investigations about the adjustment of siblings of individuals with ASD which may provide critical information on the nature of ASDs and effective adjustment methods that can be used across the lifespan to meet the challenges these siblings encounter. Because of society's inclusive philosophy, individuals with ASD are spending more time in the community interacting in a variety of situations. These individuals and their families need community-based services to meet their social, behavioral, educational and mental health needs. Chapter 6 describes an innovative community-based clinic that addresses these elements via a broad array of services (diagnostic, social intervention, supportive outreach to family members, dissemination efforts, and the use of technology to search for information). Chapters 7, 8, and 9 are chapters reprinted with permission from *Finding the Gray: Understanding and Thriving in the Black and White World of Autism and Asperger's* (Wahlberg, 2010). Chapter 7 delineates effective treatment strategies and techniques (visualization, sensory breaks, the use of lead time, making choices more concrete, adjusting boundaries when necessary, planning ahead, and presenting information in a linear fashion) that can be used to help parents and teachers work effectively with children with ASDs. Chapter 8 discusses and illustrates emotional self-regulation strategies (finding the gray) via strategies such as managing the tendency to overreact, realizing calming down is a choice, breaking the cycle when individuals get stuck, intervening at the point of an emotional meltdown, and developing one's ability to read the emotions of others. Last, Chapter 9 provides the reader with information for understanding and assisting individuals with ASDs to cope with life challenges that they face such as friendship and relationship challenges, dealing with siblings, amount of time spent on video and screen time, handling homework, preparing for transitions, bullying, being overloaded, and dating.

REFERENCES

American Psychiatric Association, Task Force on Nomenclature and Statistics. (1980). *Diagnostic and statistical manual of mental disorders* (DSM III). Washington, DC: Author.

Individuals with Disabilities Education Act. (1990). Washington, DC: U.S. Government Printing Office.

Kanner, L. (1943). Autistic disturbances of affective contact. *The Nervous Child, 2*, 217-250.

Wahlberg, T. J. (2010). *Finding the grey: Understanding and thriving in the black and white world of autism and Asperger's.* Geneva, IL: Wahlberg & Associates.

CHAPTER 1

SYSTEMS OF CARE FOR PERSONS WITH AUTISM SPECTRUM DISORDERS AND THEIR FAMILIES

From Puzzle to Blueprint

Sandra Burkhardt

Autism spectrum disorders (ASD) are pervasive developmental disorders that warrant the "puzzle piece" symbol associated with autism advocacy (Autism Society, 2010). The characteristics of ASD affect communication, motor skills, learning, and social functioning in varied combinations to varying degrees. Similarly, the complexity of service provision for persons with ASD and their families warrants additional puzzle pieces. The etiology and prevention of ASD has received considerable attention and support in the form of millions of research dollars (American Medical Association, 2009). Currently, a lifespan treatment plan for ASD does not exist, therefore, persons with ASD, their families and their service providers are challenged at each stage of development to find care.

The needs of persons with ASD and their families begin in infancy and continue across the lifespan (Centers for Disease Control and Prevention (CDC), 2010). Updates regarding "best practices" related to the identifi-

Autism Spectrum Disorders: Inclusive Community for the Twenty-First Century, pp. 1–25

cation, diagnosis, treatment and support of persons with ASD and their families are available (e.g., Buttel, 2006; California Department of Developmental Services, 2002; Posserud, Lundervold, Lie, & Gillberg, 2010). Positive approaches, and obstacles, to progress in addressing the complex communication, socioemotional, behavioral, educational and vocational needs of this group have been discussed (Dymond, Gilson, & Myran, 2007; Schreiber, 2011; Simpson, 2008). Persons at the high functioning end of the autism spectrum may remain unidentified and underserved by the educational system (Safran, 2008).

Assistance and support for the current population of persons with ASD, their caregivers and their service providers are essential. Acknowledging the puzzlement of those who love and treat and teach persons with ASD does not provide immediate guidance for their care. Key elements of successful community-based services can be identified; creating a "blueprint" for success is a goal. The need to create *systems of care* (SOC) for persons with ASD and their families remains.

SOC refer to "community-based services that are accessible, accountable, comprehensive, coordinated, culturally competent, and family focused" (Brown, 2010, p.1). SOC are particularly relevant to children with special needs (CDC, 2007) and benchmarks for the evaluation of SOC have emerged. Advancement from the puzzle that is ASD to a "blueprint for progress" will necessarily rely upon SOC that include evidence-based practices related to identification, diagnosis, intervention and support of persons with ASD and their families. So while the engagement of the person with ASD and the family is paramount, building a network of accessible services and service providers is similarly important.

The exemplary standards for SOC can be applied to the pursuit of SOC for persons with ASD and their families. However, some of the unique features of ASD may constitute challenges to the development of SOC for ASD. Thus, the puzzle of ASD is not only relevant to understanding the condition, but also to identifying the means of serving persons with ASD and their families. "Systems" of care for ASD may be predated by "programs" of care that have not, as yet, become systematized.

The current chapter reviews the characteristics of ASD and SOC. Transdisciplinary management of ASD at the community level is discussed, with an emphasis upon existing key elements of community-based management for children with special needs, including special education services. Criteria for exemplary SOC are applied to ASD with an emphasis upon access to information and support. Finally, *Project Respect*, a pilot outreach program of the Psychology Department of Saint Xavier University for persons with ASD and their families, is described; the project's vision and shortfalls serve as a case study.

ASD CHARACTERISTICS: THE PUZZLE

National reports indicate that 1% of children have ASD (CDC, 2010), suggesting a major impact on society, including families and schools. The autism spectrum includes conditions with observable deficits in the developmental domains of communication, socioemotional functioning, behavior and attention (Interactive Collaborative Autism Network, 2011). Socially awkward behavior, unusual preoccupations, physical withdrawal and avoidance as well as inappropriate emotional expression accompany communication deficits that are verbal, nonverbal, receptive and/or expressive (Mesibov, Shea, & Adams, 2001). Motor oddities, including clumsiness, unusual gait, tics and self-stimulatory actions, such as rocking and spinning, are frequently in evidence (American Psychiatric Association, 2000).

Individuals with Asperger's disorder often interpret language literally (Attwood, 1998). Similarly, odd, pedantic, repetitive, monotonic speech patterns, often with unusual rhythms (prosody) are common (Attwood, 1998; Moyes, 2002). Although the relative importance of such characteristics in terms of functional communication capabilities may be unresolved, these "core deficits" serve as indicators of the presence of the disorder (Gotham, Risi, Pickles, & Lord, 2007).

The pressing goal for prevention and cure involves deciphering etiology (Volker & Lopata, 2008). Courchesne and Pierce (2005) describe some of the anatomical features of ASD which are presumed to be associated with neurodevelopmental abnormality and dysfunction: excessive neural connection in local regions of the brain in the presence of limited connections between more distant brain regions. The coexisting conditions of seizure disorder and cognitive impairment as well as comorbidity with Fragile X and tuberous sclerosis indicate the biological etiology of ASD (Volker & Lopata, 2008). Abnormal inhibitory neurotransmission, abnormal neuronal migration, both maternal and paternal chromosomal markers (deletions and duplications), abnormal serotonin levels, abnormal head size, unusual brain growth trajectories and abnormal anatomical features of the cerebral cortex, cerebellum and amygdala have each been associated with a diagnosis of ASD (Volker & Lopata, 2008).

As such, prevention and cure of ASD are not currently on the horizon. Lakes et al. (2009) suggest that in many cases families with the highest need for services may be the least likely to access such services or to use them. A closer look at the ASD community may contribute to increased understanding of the challenges associated with ASD intervention.

ASD: A UNIQUE "COMMUNITY"?

SOC, both actual and model, emphasize community-based services. MacQueen et al. (2001) surveyed over 100 individuals from four distinct, presumed "communities" to determine if there were commonalities in defining that term. Essential to the concept of community was the existence of a connection among people who were diverse but shared social ties, common perspectives, joint activities and location.

The quest for SOC that provide community-based ASD services is informed by the above description. The ASD "community" may have three distinct but related groups: families of persons with ASD, providers of service to persons with ASD and persons with ASD themselves. Each group has a pressing need to effectively manage ASD; however, groups may differ in key areas such as access to care, motivation for intervention and capacity to be an active partner in the care program.

First, it is evident that the families of persons with ASD are diverse, but often grow to share social ties, common perspectives, and joint activities, including establishing proximity to each other or networking via technology. Thus, families of persons with ASD may be a community who actively seek out ASD services. It is often family members who serve as the guardians and advocates for persons with ASD and as liaisons to service providers on behalf of persons with ASD.

A second segment of the ASD community, providers of services to persons with ASD and their families, also share social ties, common perspectives, joint activities and physical location in their efforts to treat persons with ASD and their families. The service providers may be a "community" of sorts based upon their interaction with persons with ASD and their families. Seldom are service providers primary members of the ASD community.

It might be hoped, or presumed, that persons with ASD themselves would constitute the most important and proactive segment of the ASD community. However, considering MacQueen et al.'s (2001) defining components of community, persons with ASD may not easily fill the role. Although persons with ASD share ASD characteristics, they typically fail to establish shared social ties, common perspectives, joint activities and willing physical proximity to each other. So, as such, the defining characteristics of ASD may be the antithesis of community and actually *interfere* with the identification and establishment of community-based services for this group. Thus, there may be unique service delivery obstacles in trying to help a group of persons who share a condition that is defined by the inability to easily establish a sense of connection to others. (Any service provider or parent who has ever tried to successfully engage persons with

ASD in group activities is reminded of the lessons regarding leading a horse to water.)

In sum, the development of SOC for persons with ASD and their families may be slow to emerge in part due to the difficulty with identifying the community to be served. Key questions include "Who is requesting the service?", "Who will benefit from the service?", and "Who will pay for the service?" Typically service providers discover that families are in the forefront. In general, parents are the first consumers in search of SOC for their children with ASD. The goal of eventually transferring responsibility for care to the person with ASD within the structure of an effective SOC that meets the unique needs of persons with ASD across the lifespan is envisioned, but generally unrealized (Hendricks & Wehman, 2009).

Systems of Care

The practice of medicine illustrates the progression from the public identifying and utilizing an individual skilled service provider (the family doctor, the pediatrician) to the public's reliance on organizations that provide medical service (Katz, Kessler, O'Connell & Levine, 2007). Similarly, services for children with special needs often begin with a family's trust in an individual teacher but frequently progress to reliance on public education services. Thus, there has been a trend away from the solitary guardian of care and toward the involvement of many service providers. This trend is not only difficult for the public, who still want the individual attention and concern of a trusted service provider, but also the service providers themselves who tend to "operate in uni-professional silos" with little interprofessional collaboration (Mitchell, Parker, Giles, & White, 2009, p. 1).

A description of exemplary SOC for children with special needs and their families has been proposed (CDC, 2007). The following components are endorsed: (a) availability of preventive care and screening for special needs; (b) shared decision-making between the family and the service providers; (c) continuous, coordinated and comprehensive care that identifies the source of care, the means for access to care, and communication among service providers; (d) readily available referral to qualified service providers; (e) good communication with parents, such as careful listening and adequate time spent with child and family; (f) culturally sensitive services, including the availability of interpreters as needed; (g) consumer friendly, accurate information for education and training; (h) affordability, including guaranteed access to care for insured individuals; (i) ongoing assessment of special needs conducted in a timely fashion; (j) grievance and appeal procedures on the child's behalf for addressing difficulty in accessing, using, maintaining or affording services; (k) planning and support programs for the child's transition to adult life including transition to adult SOC; and (l) a philosophy of care that promotes independence and self-reliance for the persons with special needs (CDC, 2007).

Many components of a model SOC for ASD exist. Services providers are developing ASD programs, strategies and evaluations that maximize interdisciplinary coordination and utilization of care. In sum, one hope for solving the puzzle that is ASD is to arrange the various puzzle pieces into an interlocking grid to constitute a blueprint for progress—ASD sensitive and specific SOC.

ASD CLINICAL SERVICES

The medical profession has made a major endorsement in support of increased awareness of ASD (e.g., Moyer, 2010). The American Psychiatric Association anticipates an evidence-based revision of the criteria for ASD in the 2014 edition, DSM-V, of its diagnostic manual (Swedo, 2009). The American Academy of Pediatrics has encouraged pediatricians to establish a "medical home" for all children and has tracked the increased incidence and prevalence of ASD to current estimates of 1% of all children in the United States (American Academy of Pediatrics, 2009). The academy specified guidelines to pediatricians and provides for ongoing, updated information to promote holistic care (Myers, Johnson, & Council on Children with Disabilities, 2007).

Clinical service providers related to the diagnosis and treatment of ASD, including speech pathologists, occupational therapists, physical therapists and clinical psychologists have, within the respective professions, attempted to identify good practices, and provide ASD-specific continuing education and training (American Speech-Language-Hearing Association, 2010; Case-Smith, 2010; Mieres & Kirby, 2009; Society of Clinical Child and Adolescent Psychology, 2010).

ASD EDUCATIONAL SERVICES

Special education service programs, particularly with an emphasis upon inclusion of the student with ASD in the general setting, are in the forefront of community-based services (e.g., Koenig, Bleiweiss, Brennan, Cohen, & Siegel, 2009). Still, there is no evidence of a formal mandate for coordination of services among educational and clinical service providers or their SOC (medicine, education, behavioral health, social services).

Although the ultimate goal of an ASD SOC would be guidelines for seamless interaction among the key service providers, no protocol for communication exists; rather, there is sometimes a territorial and/or adversarial conflict among those providing services for behavior, communication, learning and/or daily living skills (Carbone, Behl, Azor, & Murphy, 2010).

TRANSDISCIPLINARY ELEMENTS OF ASD CARE

Strategic areas of need for successful management of ASD include: identification of ASD characteristics, assessment and diagnosis, intervention and support. Identification involves awareness of the characteristics of a condition such that members of the community at large and members of the affected group know that a condition, and a need for treatment, exists. Diagnosis refers to the formal assessing and assigning a category of disorder. Intervention includes many forms of treatment drawn from various specialties as well as access to treatment services. Support may include information, respite, training and skills development. ASD care has encountered challenges in all strategic areas of need (Thomas, Ellis, McLaurin, Daniels, & Morrissey, 2007).

Key elements of ASD care that are needed across disciplines include: early and accurate identification of ASD characteristics; diagnostic clarity; evidence-based intervention; and effective education and support for families, service providers, and persons with ASD.

Early and Accurate Identification of ASD Characteristics. The characteristics of ASD have a history of confusing overlap with childhood behavioral disorders, although characteristics unique to ASD have been defined (Lecavalier, Gadow, DeVincent, & Edwards, 2008). There have been major efforts to heighten awareness of ASD characteristics. The American Academy of Pediatrics, the Centers for Disease Control and Prevention and several national autism awareness organizations spearheaded major campaigns to increase public awareness. Speech delay, hand flapping, and gaze avoidance have become recognizable markers of potential developmental difficulties. Circumscribed interests and one-sided conversations are emerging as recognizable features of Asperger's disorder (Lawrence, Alleckson, & Bjorklund, 2010).

For children with autism, early intervention often offers the promise of achieving "high functioning" status which includes acquisition of expressive verbal language and an IQ above 70. For children with other ASD, early and accurate identification offers the hope of minimal impairment in socioemotional development and activities of daily living. The underlying philosophy regarding identification is that the disordered aspect of a "developmental disorder" can be minimized by virtue of providing corrective intervention at the earliest possible stage of the developmental life span.

Diagnostic Clarity. Disorders beginning in childhood often share a common characteristic—failure to achieve and display age-appropriate self-regulation. Attention deficit hyperactivity disorder has as its core diagnostic features, the child's inability to self-regulate attention and impulsivity. Separation anxiety involves the child's inability to display age-appropriate emotions and behaviors associated with separation from an attachment figure. Obsessive compulsive disorder includes the inability to regulate interaction with the environment. Childhood tic disorders involve the inability of the developing motor system to inhibit nonfunctional motor activity.

ASD has experienced changing definitions that have expanded the "spectrum" to include Asperger's disorder and pervasive developmental disorder—not otherwise specified (PDD-NOS). The diagnoses often coexist with anxiety, mood regulation difficulties, poor sustained attention, tics, and obsessions (Buettel, 2006; Kutscher, Attwood, & Wolff, 2005). Additionally, due to the success of early childhood intervention for children with significant autistic characteristics, these successfully treated children will often proceed through middle and later childhood, adolescence and adulthood with greatly increased functioning, but residual, telltale deficits associated with the primary condition (Dawson, 2008).

The DSM-IV currently lists Asperger's disorder as one of five pervasive developmental disorder (PDD) subtypes; it is anticipated that DSM-V will eliminate confusing inclusionary and exclusionary criteria within the ASD spectrum (Swedo, 2009). There is debate regarding the differential diagnosis of PDD subtypes, especially among Asperger's disorder, high-functioning autism, and pervasive developmental disorder—not otherwise specified. Other neurodevelopmental disorders associated with ASD characteristics include personality disorders (schizoid, schizotypal, narcissistic), nonverbal learning disability, sensory-integration disorder and semantic-processing disorder (Volkmar et al., 1996), or are part of a spectrum that differs by social and cognitive impairment (Prior, 2003).

ASD as a pervasive developmental disorder is, by definition, a disorder that pervades domains of development and manifests itself as varied dysfunction at different stages of development. The young child with ASD may have difficulty with language acquisition. Early intervention results in language, however, by childhood the same youngster displays attention deficits, especially for low interest tasks or tasks requiring joint attention. With advancing age the same child may learn to attend but manifests increasing social awkwardness and peer rejection that creates social problems. By adolescence, the child with ASD who has acquired good instrumental social skills finds those scripted skills inadequate in the spontaneous world of teen social communication and culture. By adulthood, issues regarding sexual behavior, lack of reciprocity in relationships, and vocational stalemate frequently plague even the highest functioning persons with ASD.

Thus, valid, reliable diagnostic clarity for ASD is difficult to achieve. As a practical matter, ASD is often diagnosed based upon the most prominent features of difficulty in evidence *at the time of evaluation*. A person with ASD is likely to be diagnosed on the narrowest set of symptoms, with little consideration of the developmental history or future prognosis, similar to trying to decipher the plot of a movie by watching a short clip. Once the difficulties of the moment are reduced or resolved, the ongoing diagnosis of ASD is apt to be undetected, minimized or forgotten.

Assessment instruments that aid screening and diagnosis of ASD are available. In particular, the Autism Diagnostic Observation Schedule (ADOS) and Autism Diagnostic Interview-Revised (ADI-R) provide for in-depth information and structured observation of specific diagnostic characteristics of ASD across the lifespan and independent of cognitive development (Akshoomoff, Corsello, & Schmidt, 2006; National Research Council, 2001). These instruments serve to verify the extent of ASD characteristics by gathering detailed developmental history and creating a structured social setting to elicit key features of ASD communication and social cognition.

Ready Access to Evidence-Based Intervention. Intervention for ASD has proved to be a complex mixture of conventional treatments, modification of existing methods to suit ASD features, and discipline-specific protocols. Proposals for alternative treatments have emerged (e.g., Golnick & MacCabee-Ryavboy, 2010). Establishment of effective best practices that guide, cradle to grave, the care of persons with ASD has not been achieved by any specific discipline or SOC. In the interim, families and service providers continuously attempt to meet the needs of persons with ASD by using existing and modified community resources, by searching for emerging, unique, ASD-specific resources and by persevering in the absence of definitive outcome studies verifying the efficacy of helpful efforts.

Good or best practices related to the identification and diagnosis of ASD as well as treatment and support of persons with ASD and their families are available (Posserud et al., 2010). Evidence-based programs include: discrete trial training, Learning Experiences: an alternative program for preschoolers and parents; pivotal response training, and relationship development intervention (Hess, Morrier, Heflin, & Ivey, 2008; Simpson et al., 2005).

Behavioral intervention has been associated with prevention of cognitive limitations (Volker & Lopata, 2008). Although limited generalization of skills continues to be a concern with interventions, training that included teaching in the natural environment has been endorsed instead of, or in addition to, clinic based services (Schreibman & Ingersoll, 2005). A comprehensive report on educating children with ASD (National Research Council, 2001) concluded that both structured and naturalistic behavioral approaches were effective in increasing communication, peer interactions, and social interactions, and reducing problem behaviors.

Still, strategies for the teaching of students with ASD are often employed despite the lack of research support. Example of such strategies include gentle teaching, sensory integration, cognitive behavioral modification, assistive technology, and social stories (Hess et al., 2008).

Effective Education and Support for Families of Persons With ASD

Parental *involvement* on behalf of children with ASD has been widely endorsed, including enlisting parents for behavior management, generalization of skills, and relationship development (Iovannone, Dunlap, Huber, & Kincaid, 2003). Federal law mandates parental involvement even as schools struggle to determine how best to include parents (Iovannone et al., 2003).

Of equal importance is the concept of parental *support* for parents of children with ASD whose stress is considerable (Meadan, Halle, & Ebata, 2010). Online information for parents is plentiful. An Internet search of "parent's guide to autism spectrum disorders" yielded 240,000 sites. A few examples of commercial, consumer and public sites that provide evidence-based recommendations for families include AutismWeb: A Parent's Guide to Autism Spectrum Disorders (http://www.autismweb.com/), HELPGUIDE.org: A Trusted Non-Profit Resource (http://www.helpguide.org/mental/autism_spectrum.htm), the National Institute of Mental Health website (http://www.nimh.nih.gov/health/publications/autism/complete-index.shtml), and a guide recommended by the Autism Society of America (http://www.autism-society.org/site/DocServer/OCALI_Parent_Guide.pdf?docID=16143).

Additionally, referral to national, regional and state organizations as well as community-based support groups for parents can be located online and accessed via email or phone contact. The National Dissemination Center for Children With Disabilities (http://www.nichcy.org/Pages/Home.aspx) provides a list of informational and support resources by state (http://www.nichcy.org/Disabilities/Specific/Pages/autism.aspx). In general, service provider referral to family support services is not a formal component of treatment services. Most service providers, including pediatricians, special education teachers and speech pathologists readily endorse referral to support groups for parents, but do not necessarily facilitate the referral nor offer the support group services in conjunction with services for the child. Generally consumers surf and select at their own risk and it is presumed that local support group services are selected by families based upon location or knowing someone associated with the group

Systems of Care Criteria Applied to ASD

The CDC's criteria for SOC for children with special needs can be applied to ASD. Numerous elements of a model SOC exist: protocols for identification and early intervention; special education programs; and increased public and professional awareness of ASD (Boyd, Odom, Humphreys, & Sam, 2010; Carnahan, Hume, Clarke, & Borders, 2009). Emerging components of ASD SOC include increased training for service providers. Also, culturally sensitive services for ASD are being promoted (Arons, Katz-Leavy, Wittig, & Holden, 2002; Mandell & Novak, 2005).

Of concern are the elusive elements of SOC for ASD. Prevention and cure remain unattainable. Access to funding ASD services during a significant national economic downturn is concerning even as ASD prevalence continues to grow. It is uncertain whether mental health parity, nationalized health care insurance, and increased demands for funds for education will secure access to SOC for ASD. Help for adults with ASD is a pressing need.

Although both health care and public education continue to grapple with large scale issues related to SOC, some of the elements of a model SOC for ASD may be negatively impacted by unique features of the ASD community. For example, shared decision-making that involves the person with ASD and his or her family may be obstructed by the person's inability to communicate or to conduct social problem-solving. Persons with ASD often struggle with high levels of anxiety, opposition to change and resistance to new things. Thus, trying to engage a person in the decision-making process when the person becomes inordinately anxious at even the mention of change is likely to thwart many attempts at shared goal-setting. It is not uncommon for a family member to collaborate with an ASD service provider to identify the "help" they want for a person with ASD, only to have the person with ASD strenuously object to the help and sometimes actually regress in the face of increased opportunities for improvement.

Similarly, continuous, coordinated and comprehensive ASD services that are readily identified and easily accessed are unlikely in a climate in which discipline- and provider-specific practices seldom include the means for transdisciplinary case management, staffing and coordination of care. Access to qualified ASD service providers (teachers, physicians, therapists, respite workers, job coaches) who are trained, experienced and committed to serving persons with ASD lacks a logical and obvious point of entry. Waiting lists and closely guarded referrals are not uncommon.

The model SOC encourages quality communication with parents characterized by careful listening and adequate time spent with child and family. One difficulty associated with ASD that may interfere with progress toward this goal is evident: persons with ASD and their families often display limited and/or unusual communication characteristics that require extraordinary amounts of time and effort on the part of the service provider. Thus, the very constituents who are most in need of relaxed interviewing and coached communication are also the ones who may show the least amount of responsiveness to the provider's efforts.

Finally, of continuing concern are appropriate adult services and due process for persons with ASD. While families often continue to serve as both advocates and caregivers for adults with ASD, issues of civil rights and human rights emerge. Although independent living and full inclusion in society are desired outcomes, it is not uncommon for persons with high functioning ASD to succumb to the stress of their own success; marriage, parenting, employment and the daily activities of adult living often trigger episodes of depression, anxiety, thought-disorder and agitation that impact not only the person with ASD but his or her family, colleagues and community. Although it is typical for families and service providers of children with special needs to celebrate the child achieving the milestones needed to enter adult life, concerns regarding continued impaired social reasoning, judgment and personal responsibility for finances persist for adults with ASD, including those who have high levels of cognitive capability. The dilemma remains regarding how to promote the rights of adults who continue to display the social-emotional and communication deficits that define ASD.

In the vacuum of established SOC, advocacy and grass roots efforts typically emerge; ASD has been no exception. Without definitive best practice guidelines directed at families, the initial excitement regarding community-based services, alternative treatments, parent groups and pilot programs is understandable; families have experienced an almost desperate need to find appropriate and helpful care for their loved ones. With the prospect of many false starts and treatment detours, service providers from varying disciplines and sectors of the community might be expected to spearhead interim "programs of care" intended to meet an immediate community need. A description of a university-based program, Project Respect, will serve as an example of one such effort.

Project Respect: A University's Response to ASD

In 1999 at Saint Xavier University in Chicago, Illinois, this writer and two of her clinical colleagues, Anthony Rotatori, PhD (series editor of *Advances in Special Education*, published by Emerald Group Publishing Ltd.) and Julie Deisinger, PhD (contributing author to *Advances in Special Education* series) noted the increased incidence of children, teens and young adults with ASD. Many of these persons were referred for community counseling services to the on-campus outreach program established to train master's level counselors enrolled in a program of graduate studies at the university. Each of us knew something about ASD; none of us knew much. All of us recognized that a population of clients and families we had never seen before was emerging—not merely one child or one family, but numerous children and various families.

The university has a mission that allowed us to pursue our interest in the needs of the growing population of persons with ASD and their families in our community. Few services were readily available and the major research institutions and programs had long waiting lists and limited access for families in our location. Additionally, although early childhood services were in place, there were evident needs of children with Asperger's disorder and high-functioning autism who either aged-out of early intervention or were too high functioning to have ever qualified. Many families had children who were undiagnosed or misdiagnosed, students who were being educated in benevolent parochial school classrooms, intuitive alternative private schools or at home. Mothers called concerned about vaccinations, special diets, "mean" teachers and children who did not behave even when threatened with (or given) a spanking. Professors referred community college students: one had phoned the professor 50 times in a single day, insisting it was an urgent matter—suffice to say, it was not. Social service agencies sent uninsured families that other service providers had given up on because one or more family members either did not talk during counseling sessions, or conducted one-sided conversations without allowing any input from the counselor.

We administered tests to individuals with IQs in the 120s whose social skills were so atrocious we did not know whether to laugh or cry. We attended seminars and training workshops, using our professional development money to advance our knowledge and skills. We read, and published, articles. Most importantly, we continued to see community clients, finding new and exciting ways to identify the needs of persons with ASD, the needs of their families and, eventually, the needs of their service providers. The needs assessment led to a program proposal and the establishment of Project Respect, a community outreach program for persons with ASD and their families. *Respect* was a useful term. It was an acronym for research and education for spectrum disorders. But it also was symbolic of the university's core values: Respect, a value that calls upon us to understand and value the unique contributions of every person.

The overview of Project Respect was written in 1999 and has structured the program's progress since its inception. Three related components of the project were created: resource, research and response, with two tiers indentifying the immediate and long term goals for the project (see Table 1.1).

Resource Components

A needs assessment conducted at a Project Respect community information session in the late 1990s revealed an urgent need for family support in the immediate community. Four resource components were launched: an annual Information Session covering basic information about ASD (old news) and current findings (new views). Parent Partners involved the recruitment of four mothers of children with ASD who became board members of Parent Partners. Monthly parent support groups and information meetings were held on-campus with varying themes. Popular programs included "Thank goodness for grandma and grandpa: My grandchild has ASD," "Dad's night out," "Our children, our blessings," and "Mother's Miniretreat." Any session advertised as a "support group" was poorly attended.

Cougar Kids involved university student volunteers, trained to modify games and activities for children with ASD, sponsoring family activity nights, including a modified Halloween party for children with ASD and

Table 1.1. Project Respect: Program Components and Tiers

Program Components: Tier 1 (1999-2005)		
Resource	Research	Response
Information sessions	Publications	Service learning
Parent partners	Presentations	Professional training
Cougar kids	Attitude change	Resource center
Sibling support	Social coaching	Community partnerships
Program Components: Tier 2 (2006-2011)		
Ambassador program	Publications	Webpage
Delegate program	Presentations	Teacher/counselor CEU
Web friends/super Saturdays	Community screenings	Client services
	Instrument validation	

their families. A popular event was the Valentine party where each student volunteer created an individual valentine for each child who attended. The ritual of delivering the valentines and seeing the children delight in "making friends" with the university students was a program highlight, with one isolated youngster announcing loudly as he left ,"Dad, I made so many friends." In addition to the socioemotional benefits of the experience, students were given the opportunity to use concepts they were learning in psychology classes: modeling, positive reinforcement, and behavior management.

Sibling Support sessions were scheduled, although a complicating feature of the sessions emerged when it became evident that many siblings were actually on the spectrum themselves but had not been identified.

Advanced tier Project Respect resource components included an Ambassador Program, which identified and trained Project Respect community members to speak to other groups on behalf of persons with ASD and their families, and a Delegate Program, that identified members of the community who were considered ASD-friendly by Project Respect members.

Web Friends was launched as an effort to increase social interactions among persons with ASD. It will come as no surprise that these initial, and naïve, efforts were mostly unsuccessful, with no person with ASD ever ***spontaneously*** contacting anyone via email or voluntarily attending a Saturday social event held on campus.

Research Components

Dissemination of research findings and evidence-based diagnostic and treatment information was a key element of Project Respect's agenda. Quarterly Publications and Presentations were scheduled, and delivered. Faculty members, graduate students, community members, persons with ASD and university colleagues contributed various perspectives on the topic of ASD, service provision, training and the impact of ASD on families. Information presented at international, national and regional conferences was organized into community-friendly PowerPoint presentations for local groups, on-campus student orientation and monthly parent meetings for review and discussion. Thus, there was a continuous pipeline for disseminating current, high quality information regarding ASD to the local community.

Two research components initially identified in the needs assessments conducted at Information Sessions and Parent Partner meetings involved Attitude Change and Social Coaching. Family members consistently complained of the negative attitudes they encountered in their efforts to secure services for their loved ones with ASD. To address knowledge deficits and perhaps misconceptions about ASD as contributing factors to negative attitudes, Project Respect developed the *Charm and Challenge of ASD* series, brief multimedia presentations available to any and all community members who wished to learn more about ASD. The presentation includes video clips of Parent Partners discussing the impact of ASD on their families as well as the Top Ten Reasons Why You Should Know About ASD. (See Table 1.2 for an example for educators.)

The *Charm and Challenge* series currently includes the following versions: The Charm and Challenge of ASD in the Family, in the Classroom, in the Community, on Campus and in the Workplace.

Social skills training, including Carol Gray's Social Stories, was identified as programming that the Parent Partner families wanted. Training workshops for Writing Social Stories were conducted for parents and interested family members; faculty also researched Social Stories and had undergraduate students practice writing them for community clients.

As Project Respect became better known, adult members of the community were referred by family and friends due to concerns that the adult was on the autism spectrum but had never been diagnosed. *Community*

Table 1.2. Project Respect: Top Ten Reasons Educators Should Know About ASD

1.	Current and future cases: ASD affects 1% of children in the United States.
2.	Differential diagnosis: ASD characteristics resemble a number of childhood behavioral disorders including ADHD.
3.	Social concern: Many professions have questionable histories of helping parents, particularly mothers, of children with autism.
4.	Scope of services: Educators are important service providers.
5.	Expertise: Educators are experts in lifespan development, learning differences and accommodation of special needs.
6.	Call to action: Political advocacy and moral treatment are important aspects of serving Americans with disabilities.
7.	Support for caregivers: The stress for families of persons with ASD is considerable and chronic.
8.	Limited existing services: Few coordinated programs of care exist for intervention of ASD throughout the lifespan.
9.	Limited research: Many behavioral treatment studies formally exclude persons with PDD.
10.	Promising insights: Identifying the developmental pathways of ASD characteristics, such as language, sensory motor integration, cognition and attachment could shed light on other forms of developmental pathology.

Screenings were added as a research component to assist in identifying undiagnosed members of the community. Community screenings also provided opportunities to share information with families regarding the impact of ASD.

Instrument Validation is a planned research component that has not yet been conducted, a casualty of limited time and money. One benefit of the planned research, however, included the training of three Project Respect faculty members in ADOS administration and scoring, an essential component of the community screenings described above.

Response Components

From its inception Project Respect was designed to include a program evaluation that, on an annual basis, served to create subsequent years' program schedules and agendas.

Needs assessment and program evaluation were conducted at Information Sessions, Parent Partner monthly meetings, focus groups, Cougar Kids events, and audience evaluations of speakers' presentations. Surveys, interviews, group discussion with summary and written program evaluation forms served as sources of needs information. The most frequently identified needs included the following: a need for preprofessional training for college students regarding the characteristics of ASD and its impact on families; a need for professional training regarding ASD and its impact on families; a need for reliable information for parents and professionals; and a need for community-based access to information and support for parents, professionals and community organizations serving an increasing number of persons with ASD.

The Response component of Project Respect required analyzing the needs assessment data and devising program response that might meet the needs in a timely fashion, allowing for continuous, ongoing program evaluation. The need for preprofessional training for college students emerged in feedback from student volunteers and parents of children with ASD. The energy and enthusiasm of student volunteers as they worked Cougar Kids events and attended Parent Partner meetings was matched only by their patience and creativity. Service Learning became a ready response to the students' interests and training needs. Content of psychology course syllabi was matched to opportunities to witness key psychological concepts during Project Respect events. Thus, student volunteers could earn valuable experience tied to their academic coursework while providing valuable service to the community.

The Professional Training response component led the faculty to increase the number of presentations they applied to make at professional conferences at the regional and local level. Presentations for various disciplines were made: speech pathologists, school psychologists, general and special education teachers, clergy, school counselors, college administrators, day care workers, and the community planning council. Related to professional training, a print and digital Project Respect Resource Center was established to provide a central location for resources acquired through research and program development. Additionally, Community Partnerships were established to provide ongoing consultation, support and networking between Project Respect constituents and existing service providers and programs in the community.

The technical and staff supports needed for Webpage development and maintenance as well as the formal offering of Teacher and Counselor Continuing Education programming exceeded the resources available to Project Respect as a Psychology Department, faculty-initiated effort. Similarly, Project Respect programming to provide on-campus Client Services for persons with ASD and their families ended due to space restrictions and the closing of one of the campus clinics. Fortunately, persons with ASDs continue to receive services in the Communication Sciences and Disorders' clinic and an off-campus early intervention program affiliated with the university's School of Education.

PROJECT RESPECT: FROM PUZZLE TO BLUEPRINT

Project Respect and its resource, research and response components are considered here for their value as a case study in the attempt to move from the puzzle that is ASD to a blueprint for serving the existing population of persons with ASD, their families and their service providers as comprehensive SOC complete with evidence-based interventions is awaited.

Jones (2006) offers suggestions for what could be considered a blueprint for ASD evidence-based practice: staff training, specialists with knowledge of ASD, different teaching styles for students with ASD and a modified ASD-friendly environment. Racial, ethnic and socioeconomic disparities in access to prevention and early intervention ought to be given high priority. Parental vulnerability to the misguided albeit good intentions of practitioners trying to meet the needs of persons with ASD armed only with existing models of special education intervention needs to be addressed.

Recommendation were made that teachers have to be different in their work with children with ASD because the children with ASD have "particular and distinct needs from others" (Jones, 2006, p. 545). Interventions were endorsed that strive to improve the skills and strategies of the person with ASD, but while similarly endorsing a focus upon adapting the environment to enable the functioning of the person with ASD (Jones, 2006, p. 546).

Project Respect began with program staff hoping that identification of need would secure ASD services. We believed that sharing information would lead to program development. After 10 years of Project Respect programming we have witnessed the decreased need for Information Sessions and parent meetings, community screenings and professional training. These services are available in the community and families have more options. University students continue to enjoy learning about ASD; many come to classes already familiar with ASD. Research on ASD continues and best practices are being identified. Thus, there has been much progress in the past decade.

Still, true SOC that address the unique characteristics of ASD and the challenging features of ASD service delivery have not emerged. Parents of children, young and old, continue to experience relentless concern for their loved ones. The prognosis of adults with ASD remains guarded. At Project Respect we have witnessed a population of youngsters with ASD who received consistent care and tremendous support from family and service providers continue to struggle without promise that independent adult living will be achieved.

Lakes et al. (2009) makes recommendations to improve community-based services. For example, it is recommended that formal diagnosis not be required for family participation in a program. Indeed, formal diagnosis of ASD was not a requirement for enrollment in Project Respect. Similarly, barriers to access such as location of programs and lack of insurance coverage were minimized. Educating the community about children's psychosocial development and behavioral health, as well as deviations from typical development, was a central focus of programming. Minimal "red tape" such as registration forms, documentation and participant leadership was required. Instead, volunteer community leaders and group members, such as the Parent Partners, became spokespersons for less assertive community members. Additionally, hours and programs that appeal to working families with limited child care were established with the Cougar Kids program.

In many measurable ways, Project Respect has been a success: hours of services provided, program evaluation resulting in program improvement, university students involvement leading to careers in ASD treatment, articles published, presentations made, and careers advanced.

Uncomfortably lingering, however, is the lack of identified SOC for persons with ASD. There is no central referral source for ASD services. Misinformation continues to compete with sound sources of data regarding vaccines, diets, and potentially dangerous treatment methods. Teachers continue to be overwhelmed and underprepared for the plethora of behaviors and learning styles they encounter in the classroom, with students with ASD only one of many groups in need of their attention.

Finally, there are the persons with ASD themselves. Through Project Respect we have come to know many; we have watched them grow and mature. Although in many ways they develop, in many ways they remain the same. Each day they live their charming, challenging ASD lives. They experience continuing social confusion, like the teen with Asperger's disorder who remarked that it was not fair that the games of chess and checkers are played on a board that looks the same, an inadvertent insight into his confusion regarding his efforts to "play" the social games associated with adolescence. They grow weary in the face of continuous criticism and cajoling by their loved ones to become more social, make friends and join activities. For instance, there was the 30-year-old man whose mother brought him in for social skills training. He indicated he had had years of services; he looked her in the eye and stated, "Mother, you would change who I am behind my face." And there is the ongoing dilemma about how to measure success, as illustrated by the 50-year-old man with ASD, who has four children on the spectrum with three different wives. After attending numerous sessions with me, he admitted that he did not know my name but he did know the address of the clinic.

A blueprint for progress requires a notion of what will be built when the plans are completed. Benchmarks of success for Project Respect included stabilization or remission of symptoms, maintenance of community living, the self-reported comfort of the person with ASD and/or a reduction in the family's level of distress. Yet to be determined is if a blueprint for ASD service can lead to the building of a strong SOC.

CONCLUSION

The puzzle piece symbol associated with autism advocacy was identified as a relevant marker for the status of SOC for ASD—many interlocking pieces that are likely to yield a meaningful picture. The need for a blueprint for progress was articulated on behalf of families and service providers for persons with ASD who seek effective care and management even as society awaits prevention or cure for ASD. ASD characteristics and SOC were reviewed and issues related to identification, diagnosis, treatment and support of persons with ASD were discussed. Benchmarks for successful community-based services were enumerated and a model SOC identified by the CDC was applied to ASD services.

Barriers to development of SOC for ASD were identified, including those that may be unique to the ASD community. Program details and project outcomes of Project Respect, a university-based outreach program for persons with ASD and their families, served as a case study.

REFERENCES

Akshoomoff, N., Corsello, C., & Schmidt, H. (2006). The role of the autism diagnostic observation schedule in the assessment of autism spectrum disorders in school and community settings. *California School Psychologist, 11,* 7-19. Retrieved from http://www.education.ucsb.edu/school-psychology/CSP-Journal/CSP2006vol11.pdf

American Academy of Pediatrics. (2009). Autism spectrum disorders affect about one percent of U.S. children. *Healthy Children.* Retrieved from http://www.healthychildren.org/English/news/pages/Autism-Spectrum-Disorders-Affect-About-One-Percent-of-US-Children.aspx

American Medical Association. (2009). NIH awards grants to fund autism research. Retrieved from http://www.ama-assn.org/amednews/2009/11/23/prbf1123.htm

American Psychiatric Association. (2000). *Diagnostic and statistical manual of mental disorders: DSM-IV-TR.* Washington DC: Author.

American Speech-Language-Hearing Association. (2010). Evidence based practice compendium: Summary of clinical practice guideline. Retrieved from http://www.asha.org/Members/ebp/compendium/guidelines/National-Autism-Plan-for-Children-(NAPC)--Plan-for-the-Identification,-Assessment,-Diagnosis-and-Access-to-Early-Interventions-for-Pre-School-to-Primary-School-Aged-Children-with-Autism-Spectrum-Disor.htm

Arons, B.S., Katz-Leavy, J., Wittig, A. C., & Holden, E. W. (2002). Too young for ADHD: The potential role of systems of care. *Journal of Developmental and Behavioral Pediatrics, 23,* S57-S63. Retrieved from http://journals.lww.com/jrnldbp/pages/default.aspx

Attwood, T. (1998). *Asperger's syndrome: A guide for parents and professionals.* London, England: Jessica Kingsley.

Autism Society. (2010). Autism awareness puzzle ribbon. Retrieved from http://www.autism-society.org/site/PageServer?pagename=asa_ribbon

Boyd, B. A., Odom, S. L., Humphreys, B. P., & Sam, A. M. (2010). Infants and toddlers with autism spectrum disorder: Early identification and early intervention. *Journal of Early Intervention, 32*(2), 75-98. doi:10.1177/1053815110362690

Brown, J. D. (2010). Pediatric primary care as a component of systems of care. *Evaluation and Program Planning, 33,* 36-38. doi:10.1016/j.evalprogplan.2009.05.004

Buttel, M. P. (2006). Exploring current knowledge on Asperger syndrome and best practices for school-based intervention. *School Psychology Quarterly, 21*(3), 348-357. Retrieved from http://www.apa.org/pubs/journals/spq/index.aspx

California Department of Developmental Services. (2002). *Autistic spectrum disorders: Best practice guidelines for screening, diagnosis and assessment.* Sacramento, CA: Author.

Carbone, P. S., Behl, D. D., Azor, V., & Murphy, N. A. (2010). The medical home for children with autism spectrum disorders: Parent and pediatrician perspectives. *Journal of Autism and Developmental Disorders, 40*(3), 317-324. Retrieved from http://www.springer.com/psychology/child+%26+school+psychology/journal/10803

Carnahan, C. R., Hume, K., Clarke, L., & Borders, C. (2009). Using structured work systems to promote independence and engagement for students with autism spectrum disorders. *TEACHING Exceptional Children, 41,* 6-14. Retrieved from http://www.cec.sped.org/AM/Template.cfm?Section=Publications1

Case-Smith, J. (2010). Evidence-based review of interventions used in occupational therapy for children with autism spectrum disorder . *The American Occupational Therapy Association.* Retrieved from http://www.aota.org/CE/CEonCD/Autism.aspx

Centers for Disease Control and Prevention. (2007). Progress toward implementing community-based systems of services for children with special health care needs: Summary tables from the national survey of children with special health care needs, 2005-2006. Retrieved from http://www.cdc.gov/nchs/data/slaits/Summary_tables_NSCSHCN_0506.pdf

Centers for Disease Control and Prevention. (2010). Living with ASD: Family issues. Retrieved from http://www.cdc.gov/ncbddd/autism/living.html

Courchesne, E., & Pierce, K. (2005). Why the frontal cortex in autism might be talking only to itself: Local over-connectivity but long-distance disconnection. *Current Opinions in Neurobiology, 15,* 225-230. doi:10.1016/j.ijdevneu.2005.01.003

Dawson, G. (2008). Early behavioral intervention, brain plasticity, and the prevention of autism spectrum disorder. *Development and Psychopathology, 20,* 775-803. doi:10.1177/1073815110362690

Dymond, S. K., Gilson, C. L., & Myran, S. P. (2007). Services for children with autism spectrum disorders: What needs to change? *Journal of Disability Policy Studies, 18*(3), 133-147. Retrieved from http://dps.sagepub.com/

Golnick, A., & MacCabee-Ryavboy, N. (2010). Autism: Clinical pearls for primary care. *Contemporary Pediatrics, 27,* 42-60. Retrieved from http://contemporarypediatrics.modernmedicine.com/contpeds/issue/issueDetail.jsp?id=19610

Gotham, K., Risi, S., Pickles, A., & Lord, C. (2007). The Autism Diagnostic Observations Schedule: Revised algorithms for improved diagnostic validity. *Journal of Autism & Developmental Disorders, 37*(4), 613-627

Hendricks, D., & Wehman, P. (2009). Transition from school to adulthood for youth with autism spectrum disorders: Review and recommendations. *Focus on Autism and Other Developmental Disabilities, 24,* 77-88. doi:10.1177/1088357608329827

Hess, K. L., Morrier, M. J., Heflin, L. J., & Ivey, M. L. (2008). Autism treatment survey: Services received by children with autism spectrum disorders in public school classrooms. *Journal of Autism and Developmental Disorders, 38,* 961-971. doi:10.1007/s10803-007-0470-5

Interactive Collaborative Autism Network. (2011). Characteristics of autism spectrum disorder. *ICAN*. Retrieved at http://www.autismnetwork.org/modules/character/gen_char/index.html

Iovannone, R., Dunlap, G., Huber, H., & Kincaid, D. (2003). Effective educational practices for students with autism spectrum disorder. *Focus on Autism & Other Developmental Disabilities, 13*(3), 150-165. Retrieved from http://foa.sagepub.com/

Jones, G. (2006). Department for education and skills/department of health good practice guidance on the education of children with autistic spectrum disorder. *Child: Care, Health and Development, 32*(5), 543-552. doi:10.1111/j.1365-2214.2006.00680.x

Katz, J. N., Kessler, C. L., O'Connell, A., & Levine, S. A. (2007). Professionalism and evolving concepts of quality. *Journal of General Internal Medicine, 22,* 137-139. Retrieved from http://www.springer.com/medicine/internal/journal/11606

Koenig, K. P., Bleiweiss, J., Brennan, S., Cohen, S., & Siegel, D. E. (2009). The ASD nest program: A model for inclusive public education for students with autism spectrum disorders. *TEACHING Exceptional Children, 42,* 6-13. Retrieved from http://www.cec.sped.org/AM/Template.cfm?Section=Publications1

Kutscher, M. L., Attwood, T., & Wolff, R. R. (2005). *Kids in the syndrome mix of ADHD, LD, Asperger's, tourette's, bipolar, and more! The one stop guide for parents, teachers and other professionals.* London, England: Jessica Kingsley.

Lakes, K. D., Kettler, R. J., Schmidt, J., Haynes, M., Feeney-Kettler, K., Kamptner, ... Tamm, L. (2009). The CUIDAR early intervention parent training program for preschoolers at risk for behavioral disorders: An innovative practice for reducing disparities in access to service. *Journal of Early Intervention, 31*(2), 167-178. doi:1111/1053815109331861

Lawrence, D. H., Alleckson, D. A., & Bjorklund. (2010). Beyond the roadblocks: Transitioning to adulthood with asperger's disorder. *Archives of Psychiatric Nursing, 24* (4), 227-238. doi:10.1016/j.apnu.2009.07.004

Lecavalier, L., Gadow, K. D., DeVincent, C. J., & Edwards, M.C. (2008). Validation of DSM-IV model of psychiatric syndromes in children with autism spectrum disorders. *Journal of Autism and Developmental Disorders, 39*(2), 278-289. doi:10.1007/s10803-008-0622-2

MacQueen, K.M., McLellan, E., Metzger, D.S., Kegeles, S., Strauss, R., Scotti, R., ... Trotter II, R. T. (2001). What is community? An evidence-based definition for participatory public health. *American Journal of Public Health, 91,* 1929-1938. Retrieved from http://ajph.aphapublications.org/cgi/reprint/91/12/1929? maxtoshow=&hits=10&RESULTFORMAT=1&author1=MacQueen

Mandell, D. S., & Novak, M. (2005). The role of culture in families' treatment decision for children with autism spectrum disorders. *Mental Retardation and Developmental Disabilities Research Reviews, 11,* 110-115. doi:10.1002/mrdd.20061

Meadan, H., Halle, J. W., & Ebata, A. T. (2010). Families with children who have autism spectrum disorders: Stress and support. *Exceptional Children, 77,* 7-36.

Retrieved from http://www.cec.sped.org/AM/Template.cfm?Section=Publications1

Mesibov, G., Shea, V., & Adams, L. (2001). *Understanding Asperger syndrome and high functioning autism.* New York, NY: Plenum.

Mieres, A., & Kirby, R. S. (2009). Pediatrics: A primer for physical therapists on autism spectrum disorders. Part 1. *The American Physical Therapists Association.* Retrieved from http://iweb.apta.org/Purchase/ProductDetail.aspx?Product_code=LMS-86

Myers, S. M., Johnson, C. P., & Council on Children with Disabilities. (2007). Management of children with autism spectrum disorders. *Pediatrics, 120*(5), 1162-1182. doi:10.1542/peds.2007-2361

Mitchell, R., Parker, V., Giles, M., & White, N. (2009). An examination of the cognitive and psychosocial dynamics of interprofessional collaboration. *Medical Care Research and Review, 67,* 3-26. doi:10.1177/1077558709338478

Moyer, C. (2010). Autism increase may reflect greater awareness. *American Medical News.* Retrieved from http://www.ama-assn.org/amednews/2010/01/04/prl20104.htm

Moyes, R. (2002). *Addressing the challenging behavior of children with high functioning autism/Asperger syndrome in the classroom: A guide for parents and teachers.* London, England: Jessica Kingsley.

National Research Council. (2001). *Educating children with autism.* Washington, DC: National Academy Press.

Posserud, M., Lundervold, A. J., Lie, S. A., & Gillberg, C. (2010). The prevalence of autism spectrum disorders: Impact of diagnostic instrument and non-response bias. *Social Psychiatry and Psychiatric Epidemiology, 45*(3), 319-327. doi:10.1007/s00127-009-0087-4

Prior, M. (Ed.). (2003). *Learning and behavior problems in Asperger Syndrome.* New York, NY: The Guilford Press.

Safran, S. F. (2008). Why youngsters with autistic spectrum disorders remain underrepresented in special education. *Remedial & Special Education, 29*(2), 90-95. doi:10.1177/0741932507311637

Schreiber, C. (2011). Social skills interventions for children with high-functioning autism spectrum disorders. *Journal of Positive Behavior Intervention, 13,* 49-62. Retrieved from http://pbi.sagepub.com/content/by/year

Schreibman, L., & Ingersoll, B. (2005). Behavioral interventions to promote learning in individuals with autism. In F. R. Volkmar, R. Paul, A. Kiln, & D. Cohen (Eds.), *Handbook of autism and pervasive developmental disorders: Vol. 2. Assessment, interventions, and policy* (pp. 882-896). Hoboken, NJ: Wiley.

Simpson, R. L. (2008). Children and youth with autism spectrum disorders: The search for effective methods. *Focus on Exceptional Children, 40*(7), 1-14. doi:10.1080/09362830701653696

Simpson, R. L., de Boer-Ott, S. R., Griswold, D. E., Myles, B. S., Byrd, S. E., Ganz, J. B., … Adams, L. G. (2005). *Autism spectrum disorders: Interventions and treatments for children and youth.* Thousand Oaks, CA: Corwin Press.

Society of Clinical Child and Adolescent Psychology. (2010). Evidence-based mental health treatment for children and adolescents. Retrieved from http://www.abct.org/sccap/

Swedo, S. (2009). Report of the DSM-V neurodevelopmental disorders work group. *American Psychiatric Association.* Retrieved from http://www.psych.org/MainMenu/Research/DSMIV/DSMV/DSMRevisionActivities/DSM-V-Work-Group-Reports/Neurodevelopmental-Disorders-Work-Group-Report.aspx

Thomas, K. C., Ellis, A. R., McLaurin, C., Daniels, J., & Morrissey, J. P. (2007). Access to care for autism-related services. *Journal of Autism and Developmental Disorders, 37*(10), 1901-1912. doi:10.1007/s10803-006-0323-7

Volker, M. A., & Lopata, C. (2008). Autism: A review of biological bases, assessment, and intervention. *School Psychology Quarterly, 23*(2), 258-270. doi: 10.1037/1045-3830.23.2.258

Volkmar, F., Klin, A., Schultz, R. Bronen, R., Marans, W.D., Sparrow, S., & Cohen, D. J. (1996). Asperger's syndrome. *Journal of the American Academy of Child and Adolescent Psychiatry, 35*(1), 118-123. Retrieved from http://www.jaacap.com/

CHAPTER 2

ASD WORKFORCE

Workplace Access for Persons With Autism Spectrum Disorders

Sandra Burkhardt and Sandra Cardillo

Americans with disabilities struggle to achieve employment during difficult economic times. The U.S. Department of Labor estimates a 9% decline in jobs for Americans with disabilities during the current recession beginning in 2007, with men with disabilities experiencing a greater loss of jobs than females, and loss rates found even among college-educated workers with disabilities (Kaye, 2010). Workers with disabilities who were employed in high-skilled jobs experienced the greatest degree of job security during the recent economic reversal. Thus, it seems possible that persons with high functioning autism spectrum disorders (ASD) who find employment related to their talents may achieve a good fit for both themselves and their employers.

ASD are first evident in childhood and persist across the lifespan. Access to employment remains a substantial hurdle for workers with ASD who often report difficulty with obtaining and maintaining employment (Muller, Schuler, Burton, & Yates, 2003). Few vocational service programs at the federal, regional or state level are equipped to meet the needs of persons with high functioning ASD with priority in rehabilitative services often given to persons with cognitive impairment (Adreon & Durocher,

Autism Spectrum Disorders: Inclusive Community for the Twenty-First Century, pp. 27–45

2007; Muller et al., 2003). Postsecondary education as preparation for employment for students with ASD may require continued focus upon the social and communication deficits that are the defining features of the diagnosis (Adreon & Durocher, 2007). In order to increase access to employment for persons with ASD, at least two issues should be considered: how the worker with ASD adds value to the workplace and how the workplace values the worker with ASD.

The current chapter imagines an ASD Workforce made possible by business creating access to the workplace for persons with ASD. Estimates of the incidence and prevalence of adults with ASD are made and a review of the defining characteristics of ASD and its frequent comorbid conditions serves to highlight the unique features of the population of potential workers with ASD. Training considerations for workers with ASD and other disabilities are compared and contrasted, with a particular emphasis placed upon those persons with ASD that are cognitively capable and who often earn academic degrees beyond high school.

Human resources personnel are identified as crucial to creating access in the workplace for this category of talented workers. The authors incorporate valuable philosophy and practices from the Requisite Organization model of Eliot Jaques (1996) to guide the development of an ASD inclusive workplace. The chapter concludes with recommendations for the employment of a worker with high functioning ASD.

ASD WORKFORCE

Adults with high functioning ASD have expressive language capabilities and do not have cognitive impairment. VanBergeijk, Klin, and Volkmar (2008) estimate that there are nearly 500,000 individuals under 20 years of age who have ASD; the "overwhelming majority" of those individuals manifest a mild form of pervasive developmental disorder (VanBergeijk et al., 2008, p. 1). Thus, there is a sizable population of adults who have many capabilities, including average to above average intelligence, impressive vocabularies and a wealth of knowledge regarding their areas of interest. Still, these individuals continue to display a degree of social deficit, including awkwardness or avoidance, poor emotional regulation, and impaired social judgment that compromises their adaptive functioning at school, home and in the community (Adreon & Durocher, 2007).

At present, the core features of ASD appear to persist across the lifespan, even with the impressive improvements associated with early intervention and special education services. Some degree of deficit in communication, social interactions and range of interests remain. These core deficits include significant difficulties with pragmatic language,

Table 2.1. Conditions Frequently Associated With High Functioning ASD in Adulthood

- Depression and anxiety, possible in response to the fast pace of social demands associated with adult living (VanBergeijk et al., 2008)
- Tic disorder
- Obsessive-compulsive tendencies including rigidity and inflexible approaches to rules
- Social isolation
- Dependence upon parents and families for assistance with adult living
- Fine motor difficulties and slow motor response time
- Hypersensitive to sensory stimuli such as noise, heat, smells, and light

reciprocal social interactions and a reduced ability to sustain attention to low interest tasks. Thus, even with interventions that include behavior management, skills development and medication, the adult with ASD may continue to display communication and social skills deficits (Adreon & Durocher, 2007).

Additional features associated with ASD in adulthood include disturbances of affect, mood, attention and regulation (VanBergeijk et al., 2008). Table 2.1 lists coexisting conditions frequently associated with high functioning ASD.

For the prospective worker with ASD the demands of adult living increase, but the rate of developmental advancement slows. The young adult with ASD "ages out" of special education services. Thus, the adult with high functioning ASD continues to manifest many of the core deficits of the condition without the benefit of former support. For the highest functioning student with ASD, completion of a degree in higher education is the proof of successful intervention, although academic accomplishment may not yield suitability for employment (Schall, 2010).

DISABILITY AND WORK TRAINING

Adults with high functioning ASD may graduate with academic accomplishments that yield a high school diploma, an associate's degree from junior college and a bachelor's degree from a university and still experience considerable difficulty securing and sustaining employment. In general, persons with disabilities, particularly disabilities that affect behavior and emotional expression, have high rates of unemployment (Winn & Hay, 2009). Martz and Xu (2008) suggested that it is the attitudes of workers with disabilities that predict successful employment, such that having a "positive, forward-oriented perspective" improved the likelihood of employment (Martz & Xu, p. 1). In terms of adults with ASD, providing accommodations and creating access in the workplace remain unfulfilled goals. The adult with high functioning ASD who has attended school is presumed to be ready to work and is unlikely to receive essential guidance, support, training and accommodations in the workplace. Workers with ASD often display deficits in regards to understanding the work environment (Muller et al., 2003). Transition to postsecondary education and the workplace may be negatively impacted by even minor social behavioral deficits associated with ASD, such as poor hygiene, reluctance to drive or use public transportation, sensory sensitivity to smells and sounds, and avoidance of using public restrooms (Adreon & Durocher, 2007).

ASD-specific training suggestions provide promising approaches for the future. Although existing vocational programs, such as sheltered workshops and supported employment positions, are appropriate for workers with significant and permanent cognitive, motor and/or developmental disabilities, these programs are a poor fit for persons with high functioning ASD. Additionally, even with vocational training in the workshop, the demands of the actual workplace are often considerably different for the worker with a disability (Sartawi, Abu-Hilal, & Qaryouti, 1999). Gerhardt (2007) suggests that the concept of "work readiness" must be redefined to include workers with ASD. He indicates that education for students with ASD should ultimately result in the learners being "employment ready," with early jobs serving as sites for experiential learning. Job development and active ties between schools and the business community, including a Business Advisory Committee that serves as a liaison between schools and community businesses, are proposed. Finally, it is suggested that coworkers can be engaged as job trainers to provide environmental support for the worker with ASD.

Adults with high functioning ASD often appear to have employment potential but few demonstrated job skills, and skills acquired in one environment are not readily transferred to a new environment (Gerhardt, 2007). They would likely benefit from an opportunity to learn in the actual workplace rather than a vocational program in school or a workshop. Additionally, the employment prerequisite of already having a work ethic rather than acquiring one during actual employment is a challenge to conventional job training approaches that often favor employment placement of the most motivated trainees (Winn & Hay, 2009).

MOTIVATION AND WORKERS WITH ASD

Using structured interviews, Muller et al. (2003) identified distinctive attitudes and dispositions regarding work of 18 workers with high functioning ASD, several with advanced degrees. The interviews yielded a number of common themes among workers with ASD: lengthy periods of unemployment and underemployment; negative work experiences; difficulty applying for jobs; difficulty adapting to a new job routine; and difficulty communicating with coworkers, supervisors and customers. Interviewees made the following recommendations regarding their ability to secure and maintain employment: a good fit among their interests, abilities and the demands of the job; jobs that matched their savant capabilities; jobs that had minimal requirements for social competence; jobs with set routines; and flexible work schedules. A tolerant supervisor was identified as helpful (Muller et al., 2003).

The interviewees indicated that ASD-specific supports would be needed to find and maintain employment: on-site job coaching and mentoring as well as assistance with job applications and social interactions on the job were identified. The need for regular feedback from supervisors and explicit explanations of how the worker was doing on the job were noted. For example, interviewees indicated that vague instructions should be avoided and that tasks should be demonstrated rather than verbally explained.

Additionally, interviewees endorsed autism awareness training for vocational counselors and supervisors as well as coworkers. Themes were common across interviewees with younger workers with ASD (under 30 years of age) noting more positive work experiences than older workers with ASD. Thus, a good fit between worker and job as well as understanding supervisors and supportive coworkers seemed to be associated with positive experiences for workers with ASD (Muller et al., 2003).

Limited personal motivation may be one of the biggest challenges to employment of persons with high functioning ASD. Winn and Hay (2009) identify key differences between employed and unemployed workers with disabilities: motivation to work, effective time management, tolerance of criticism, initiative and concentration on task. Workers with disabilities who responded with increased anxiety in the face of job demands were most likely to establish a pattern of job losses. Thus, persons with high functioning ASD who are prone to display few of the desired traits and high levels of anxiety are likely to encounter numerous obstacles to finding and keeping jobs.

Motivation may also be affected by social demands of the workplace for persons with high functioning ASD. For example, workers with intellectual disabilities who were enrolled in sheltered workshops or employed in community settings liked the increased socialization and social status of community employment as compared to workers at a workshop training program (Hall & Kramer, 2009). Thus, workers with intellectual deficits *enjoy* the social benefits of working in a community setting. In contrast, workers with ASD dislike employment because socialization may be required or encouraged. This fundamental difference in the intrinsic rewards associated with working in the community may offer an insight into the reduced motivation of persons with ASD in community employment.

OBSTACLES TO ACCESS FOR WORKERS WITH ASD

In general, with coaching and supervision, many persons with other disabilities display suitable motivation and social competence in the workplace; workers with ASD may continuously struggle with limited motivation and significant social deficits. Thus, workers with ASD may experience particular employment challenges because they neither truly like work nor the workplace. Additionally, few workplaces are prepared for the inclusion of workers who appear both unmotivated and socially unresponsive.

Current training models for adults with cognitive impairment rely upon direct instruction and operant behavioral principles: reinforcement, extinction, rehearsal, chunking, scaffolding and shaping (Summers, Houlding, & Reitzel, 2004) as well as vocational training such as job coaching and on-site support (Muller et al., 2003).In terms of socialization patterns in the workplace, job coaches often needed to redirect workers with intellectual deficits to stop socializing and stay on task (Hall & Kramer, 2009). Workers with ASD are more likely to need direction and cues to attempt social interaction or communication on the job (Muller et al., 2003).

TRAINING CONSIDERATIONS FOR THE WORKER WITH ASD

Winn and Hays (2009) suggest that the existing approach to students with disabilities offers two avenues for transition to adulthood: learn or earn. Either a student pursues education as a prerequisite to employment or he or she gets a job and begins earning. For students with ASD these options may not be sufficient to support sustained employment or full inclusion in community living (Hendricks & Wehman, 2009). Thus, the availability of continuing support in the actual workplace may be an essential means of creating access to employment for persons with ASD. Indeed, supported employment emerged as the most successful form of employment for workers with ASD (Hendricks, 2011).

Cimera (2010) determined that community-based supported employment fostered modest, efficient transition to adulthood for high school students with disabilities compared to individuals receiving either in-school training experiences or no training. Supported employment typically involves paying a coworker to train and supervise a coworker with a disability. A good fit between the worker with ASD's areas of special interest and the job task is likely to enhance worker motivation and positive supervisor appraisal.

Persons with ASD display difficulty becoming independent even with education, training and practice (Carnahan, Hume, Clarke, & Borders, 2009). Factors that contribute to this difficulty for learners with ASD include deficits in attention, organization and initiation. In terms of attention, persons with ASD attend to details rather than "big picture" goals, often displaying inordinate attention to minutiae and "forgetting" the relevant task. Organizational problems stem from deficits in planning and sequencing with a limited ability to anticipate what will be needed to complete a task. Finally, persons with ASD frequently fail to initiate even routine, well-established tasks.

Positive behavior supports for learners with ASD may be pertinent to on-the-job training programs. For example, "work systems" promote independence for learners with ASD by organizing multistep tasks using visual cues to replace human prompts at strategic junctures in task completion (e.g., Carnahan et al., 2009; Keel, Mesibov, & Woods, 1997). On-site job coaching and support should include role plays to increase readiness and responsiveness to novel situations, such as expected and unexpected demands from customers, coworkers and supervisors (Carnahan et al., 2009). A "back-up" script that prepares the worker with ASD with an acceptable response when he or she encounters social situations that are beyond the ASD comfort zone may prove useful (VanBergeijk et al., 2008).

The nature of the work for workers with ASD should limit the need to make inferences or draw conclusions. Similarly, workers with ASD are likely to need work assignments and social situations reduced to an instrumental level. Engineering successful workplace access for persons with ASD requires understanding the core deficits of the condition; workers with ASD should not "be placed in jobs that are highly unpredictable and require the ability to discern complex social interactions" (VanBergeijk et al., 2008, p. 1367). Job coaches, supervisors and supportive coworkers can be encouraged to use direct, explicit literal guidance regarding tasks. Workplace organization can be enhanced by establishing a visual system of support: colored folders, visual planners, and posted office schedules. Workers with ASD may require extra time for taking workplace tests or conducting evaluative tasks. Such accommodations are available at college and can be adapted to the workplace (VanBergeijk et al., 2008).

HOSPITABLE WORKPLACES

Traditional approaches to employment for persons with disabilities typically involves preparing the persons with a disability for the workplace and finding a workplace that can provide adequate accommodations to support a mutually beneficial employment arrangement. To some extent the transition to work for persons with ASD will rely upon this established formula. Still, two unique challenges impact employment for persons with ASD: the persons themselves may display minimal motivation for success in the workplace and the workplace typically includes a covert social agenda that may undermine inclusion of the person with ASD into the required social milieu.

Thus, an overarching model to address the unique accommodations needed by adults with ASD in the workplace draws from varied literatures. Theories and research pertaining to defining work, including work for persons with disabilities, serve as traditional foundations: vocational rehabilitation, advocacy and the rights of persons with disabilities. However, a vast number of the most capable persons with ASD will not meet the criteria for rehabilitation; they are too intelligent and too educated to qualify for rehabilitation services. Thus, advocates for persons with high functioning ASD must look beyond existing models for transition to the world of work.

HUMAN RESOURCES AND THE HUMAN CAPITAL PERSPECTIVE

Since Adam Smith wrote *The Wealth of Nations* in 1776 (1776/2010), economists have believed that human productivity has value—as important as the capital value found in land, buildings or machines (see Cannan, 1976). *Human capital*, an economic term, centers on how the education, skills, talents and knowledge of the members of a society enable that society to be productive (Hershberg, 1996). As Dr. Julianne Malveaux, president of Bennet College for Women said in her 2009 address to the ICAN Omaha, Nebraska Women's Leadership Conference, "we cannot afford as a nation to sideline one working brain" (Malveaux, 2009). Today, economists continue to explore how best to identify and measure the value of what goes on in the hearts and minds of individuals as productive members of the workforce. Workers with high functioning ASD are likely to have both potential and value.

The challenge lies in creating greater access to and in the workplace for a category of worker whose disability is at odds with the neurotypical workplace. Innovative approaches to not only preparing the worker with ASD for the workplace but also preparing the workplace for the worker with ASD may begin with the incorporation of successful elements of human resources theory and practice. Workers with ASD have talents; those who identify, define and design the work of the workplace are strategically positioned to create access for such workers.

For example, Rhoads (2010) discusses the relative merits of face-to-face communication compared to computer-mediated communication. Social skills are needed to meet and interact with others face-to-face, conduct groups or answer questions. One might speculate that workers who excel at one communication modality might not perform as well at the other. Extrapolating from Rhoads, one might consider that workers with ASD, awkward in face-to-face interactions, might excel in online communication.

Human resources (HR) management has continuously served the needs of workers on behalf of organizations. HR grew out of the labor relations movement of the early industrial age, providing a workplace department to address worker issues such as child labor, fair wages, and worker safety. Concerns of the early twentieth century created the need for personnel management departments in organizations. At the outset, many of these personnel management departments were part of the accounting and finance areas with a focus on the legal and financial costs of the human capital of the organization.

Training and development departments grew out of the need to break down work tasks into small and easily understood assignments rendering humans as efficient as machines (Burke, 2006). Henry Ford, Frederick W. Taylor, and others created a vast workforce based upon this approach. Following World War II, and the continued education of the workforce, efficiency in the management of humans in the workplace gave way to the rise of the field of organization development. Organization development as a field of study encompasses the social dimensions of an organizational system, including the individual's role as a team member (Burke, 2006).

Today, HR in most organizations is a hybrid of payroll, staffing, recruiting, benefits management, training, and organization development. Although the complexity of managing the legal and regulatory components of HR often overshadows the recruitment, retention and development of talent, it lies within the job description and capabilities of HR personnel to manage human capital on behalf of the organization. Thus, HR becomes a strategically placed gatekeeper for access to the workplace.

At its core, the development of an employable workforce is both an economic and social issue. In the western world, the history of human capital or workforce development is intrinsically linked to the movement from the agrarian, guild and craftsman-working arrangements through the industrial age to the knowledge based economy. The fields of human capital development, HR management and organization development all focus on the economic and social issues of humans' participation in the workforce.

REQUISITE ORGANIZATION—A USEFUL THEORETICAL FRAMEWORK

Requisite organization, a theoretical framework for understanding how organizations are structured and how individuals work within those organizations, is based on over 50 years of study by Dr. Elliot Jaques and his colleagues. In the requisite organization careful consideration is made of what is required of the worker in the workplace. The study of requisite organization is composed of four interacting components: a system for understanding organization structure, a set of managerial principles and practices, a system for implementing fair compensation systems and a system for talent management in the organization (Jaques, 1996).

Relevant to workers with ASD, Gerhardt (2007) suggests that the degree of job match, or fit, between the employer and employee with ASD is essential. The requisite organization model provides a guide to creating that fit. Structuring an organization requisitely entails developing and defining tasks so that the right worker can be identified. The model is applicable in three areas that support a good job match: knowing how work is understood within an organization structure; defining the role of a manager in leading a group of individuals to use resources in completing assignments; and a clear understanding of "suitability for a role" which allows every individual in an organization to come to work every day and do his or her best.

Tasks, as work assignments, are best understood using the following simple analysis. What is the work that needs to be done? Who can do the work? With whom will workers work? When these dynamics are understood, tasks become clear at all levels of an organization. Tasks, appropriately understood, according to Dr. Jaques and his colleagues, enable a trust-building environment in the workplace.

Lee (2007) defines *task* as "an assignment to produce a specific output" (p. 41). Such specificity includes identifying the quality or quantity of the output needed, the time in which the assignment is to be completed, and what, if any, resources are available to assist in completing the assignment. Clarity of assignment for individuals in roles at all levels of the organization is important. For individuals with ASD this clarity of task assignment may be critical.

In its common usage, "work" has many definitions. It is work to go to work and do our work everyday. Throughout his career, Dr. Jaques sought to define the meaning of work, wanting deeply to put the precision of medical science into the science of organizational behavior and systems. Jaques (2002) defined work as "what the person has to do in order to achieve a task: use judgment and make decisions in overcoming obstacles" (p. 3). "Goal directed work," states Jaques "is a basic feature, perhaps the basic feature of all life. All humans need to do work that not only benefits oneself, but is at the same time of value to others. The opportunity to do such work is an important factor in self-actualization" (p. 22).

In sum, in the requisite organization work is considered fundamental to humans; there is a universal drive to be productive and move toward a goal. For individuals with ASD, these same basic needs are a part of their humanity. Channeling the talents and productivity potential of persons with ASD into meaningful work is a needed step toward the inclusion of persons with ASD in society. The requisite organization in the service of this goal involves finding managers and coworkers within the organization who are capable of creating a workplace that is hospitable to the worker with ASD. Only from within organizations can ways be found to define the work that can be done by workers with ASD in concert with coworkers, customers and supervisors.

THE STRATEGIC ROLE OF MANAGERS

In the workplace, managers have a primary role in setting direction and providing leadership through the assignment of tasks. Task assignment and feedback regarding those assignments are the fundamental work of a manager within an organizational system. Managers are accountable for the work output and the working behavior of their employees (Lee, 2007). Managers set direction, provide resources, and deal with those things that get in the way of getting work done in an organization.

Ellinger, Ellinger, Bacharach, Wang, and Bas (2011) identified managerial coaching as an important means of enhancing employee performance and promoting organizational learning; that is, learning that is accomplished through the organization's various social contexts. Thus, at all levels of an organization those accountable for managing the resources of the organization, including employees, should do so from a perspective of managerial leadership that fosters collegial relationships, trust, and collaboration as well as providing clarity in setting direction and giving feedback. Thus managerial coaching, presumed to be a positive attribute in any workforce, might prove particularly helpful to the worker with ASD.

For the worker with ASD, the manager is the gatekeeper of opportunities for successful adjustment in the workplace. The manager is the individual accountable for clarity of task assignment, feedback on that assignment and dissemination of resources needed to complete the assignments. Additionally, in the role of managerial coach, the manager provides a social context for workers, including workers with ASD, to learn and produce. A manager provides social cues, defining not only the work but setting the social milieu in which the work is conducted. A managerial coach with knowledge of ASD is likely to be quite capable of providing the essential social prompts and accommodations that will result in organizational learning for the worker with ASD.

In effect, the manager identifies and delivers the needed instrumental and social support for the worker with ASD in the workplace. That support comes in many forms: defining the tasks to be accomplished, outlining schedules and deadlines, and designing the social network that will provide support for the worker with ASD. Organizational support for workers with ASD may take the form of assigning another team member or coworker who is familiar with high functioning spectrum behaviors to provide worksite training and social support to coworkers with ASD.

In this way, team members become human "assistive technology" to the worker with ASD regarding completion of work assignments. The ambiguity of the social elements of the workplace is reduced. With competent leadership, managers understand the strategic supports that are needed and provide this "human resource" as a matter of course. Through training and development HR professionals identify and train capable managers to work in cooperation with job coaches, rehabilitation specialists, special educators, behavior analysts and even family members to render the worker with ASD a productive member of the organization.

UNDERSTANDING SUITABILITY FOR A ROLE

Jaques and Cason (1994) developed a model for understanding the potential found in each individual in carrying out the work of a specific role: the four true components of applicable capability or suitability for a role. *Applied capability,* as defined by Jaques and Cason is "the level of capability the individual is actually applying at a given moment in some specific work" (p.7). The relevance of applied capability to workers with ASD lies in the useful delineation between capability and productivity. Many individuals with high functioning ASD have demonstrated capability, as evidenced by good achievement scores and impressive skills. Still, when pressed to use their capabilities to produce, there can be significant delay, resistance, avoidance and opposition on the part of the person with ASD.

Individuals with high functioning ASD may possess impressive capabilities; however, their approach to productivity frequently lacks relevance and coherence. Although reduced productivity for persons with ASD may be attributed to lack of effort, it is possible that the ability to sustain joint

Table 2.2. Elements of Applicable Capability (Jaques & Cason, 1994)

1. Information processing ability: The necessary innate capability to process information related to the task that needs to be completed

   ASD application: Workers with high functioning ASD may have exceptional information processing capabilities, but may find task completion a low priority.

2. The worker's role: The knowledge, skill and experience required to assume the role of worker relative to the work.

   ASD application: Workers with ASD may have a limited understanding of the role of worker. Pairing a worker with ASD with a supportive model employee is likely to teach the appropriate demeanor for workplace success.

3. Attention to task: Being engaged in and valuing the work enough to bring one's full attention to the role of worker every day.

   ASD application: Workers with ASD may find attention to low interest tasks difficult to sustain. It is recommended that jobs related to areas of high interest be identified and cultivated for the worker with ASD.

4. Temperament: The ability to carry out the required behaviors of the role without temperament getting in the way of task completion.

   ASD application: Anxiety, frustration and negativity are common reactions for persons with ASD when they confront unexpected situations. Coworkers and managers can be instrumental in providing positive supports by providing schedules and scripts for handling changes in routine.

attention to low interest tasks and to process complex information create the real obstacles. Thus, preoccupation with special interests may yield impressive knowledge and the promise of capability, but the failure to apply that knowledge to meaningful work renders the capable person unemployable. Elements of applicable capability and their applications to workers with ASD are listed in Table 2.2.

Information Processing

Jaques and Cason (1994) believed that potential capability grows across an individual's lifetime, given appropriate opportunity for skill development and the individual's own valuing of the work. The capacity to process information relative to a task involves numerous elements. First, the numbers of factors that can be dealt with at any given time must be considered. Rote and repetitive assembly line action requires limited information processing; manning a call center for angry complainants may require addressing numerous tasks simultaneously.

A second element of information processing involves the rate of change of these factors. Some jobs involve a high degree of routine while others require flexibility and adaptability at every juncture. The ability to categorize information processing factors, recognize ambiguity in tasks, foresee problems, anticipate solutions and conceptualize future outcomes determines the capability of a worker for the demands of a particular job.

Careful consideration of the elements of information processing may facilitate access to the workplace for workers with ASD. Jaques and Cason's list is similar to a functional assessment, requiring an operational definition of the work to be done. Such specificity supports the concrete, literal approach to task preferred by persons with ASD with clear communication and minimal need to predict future consequences. Thus, frustration may be kept at a minimum for all workers in the well-planned workplace where antecedent management is practiced.

A capable manager or coworker may provide a template for a worker with ASD that outlines the information processing demands of a job. Antecedent management provides an index of the workplace conditions that lead to the productivity of the worker with ASD. Examples include specifying the job factors and the schedule with which such factors change, predicting common problems related to the job, identifying workplace resources for clarifying ambiguous or unpredicted job changes, and providing daily, weekly, monthly and quarterly concrete goals and objectives for the worker with ASD. The worker's productivity is observed and antecedent modifications are made. Only after careful refinement of antecedent management should contingency management become a major focus.

Suitability to a Role

For an individual to be suitable to a role as worker, the complexity of information processing must be considered. To be fully employed in meaningful work, an individual must be capable of meeting the processing needs of that work, have the needed skills and experience, value the work and be able to meet the behavior requirements of the role. Too often employers place workers in roles based primarily on the worker's skills and experience without understanding the full impact of what happens when the information processing requirements of the role are not in sync with what the individual brings to the role. For example, when the worker is more capable that the processing required in the role, boredom and lack of challenge will result in acting out behaviors. If the worker does not, at the present time, demonstrate the necessary problem solving needed in the role, the result is increased stress, lack of work completion, and over time, serious health consequences.

In addressing the needs of workers with ASD, understanding and balancing the elements related to suitability of role are most critical. Persons with ASD are often quite productive regarding their areas of special interest and find that indulging in those interests is quite relaxing. When bored, persons with ASD will seek out their interests and engage in them with what appears to be endless energy. Harnessing such energy in the workplace would no doubt result in considerable productivity for the worker with ASD assigned to the right role in the workplace.

Some of the features of ASD, such as social incompetence, literal thinking, and impoverished communication in the presence of superior knowledge and talent, present challenges to defining and assuming roles in the workplace. The requisite organization model for assisting workers with ASD endorses a job coach to bridge the gaps of understanding for workers in their pursuit of productivity. The job coach includes working with human resources professionals, managerial leaders, and workers with ASD to fully maximize the potential of those on the autistic spectrum. A job coach for workers with ASD would include the education of HR professionals on the unleashed capability of potential of individuals with ASD as well as the inherent social communication challenges associated with ASD. Socially competent managers in the workplace would provide clear task assignment, directions and feedback to workers with ASD, and skilled integration of workers with ASD into the workplace.

Workplaces that support and assist managers in the definition of tasks and appropriate assignments, at every level of the organization and level of task complexity, create workplace access for workers with ASD. Identification, training and development of socially competent coworkers provide ongoing, day-to-day support of the worker with ASD. By addressing both the work assignment and the social conditions in which work is conducted, it is predicted that social behaviors in the workplace that get in the way of completing the task or becoming a full member of the team would be reduced for the worker with ASD. Ongoing coaching of those identified coworkers to assist with day-to-day challenges in providing support to their team members with ASD would be considered a valued feature of the team and its manager.

ASD WORKFORCE MODEL: RIGHT PERSON, RIGHT ROLE FOR WORKERS WITH ASD

Organizations continue to grapple with human capital challenges of the twenty-first century workplace. The pace of global organizations, stunning advances in technology, the need for knowledge and skill never seen before and the increased complexity of tasks to manage it all provide significant challenges for leaders to find and develop needed talent. HR professionals assist and guide employers in ways that assure workplace productivity: defining work through job or role definition, recruiting talent, coaching and providing feedback to organization talent and ensuring that the right compensation and benefits systems are in place.

The challenge of employability for those adults with high functioning ASD continues to intersect with HR persons in search of talent, with or without the compliance frameworks that may be set forth by regulatory agencies. Workplaces need workers, particularly the right person for the right role. An aging workforce, unmet education needs and a seismic change in talent requirements in the competitive world of work reinforce Dr. Malvaux's challenge to not "waste one working brain." The considerable talents and unique capabilities that workers with high functioning ASD have to offer suggest there is both a responsibility and a benefit to bringing forth the humanness in others by fostering access to making meaning on a daily basis through work.

HR professionals, busy as they are with their traditional tasks of hiring, firing, managing benefits and compensation within the legal requirements of the state and federal jurisdiction, are uniquely positioned to create access for workers with ASD. By bridging the gap between organizational and individual needs, HR professionals can place and develop the talents of individuals with ASD in the workplace. HR professionals, using sound organizational theory and positive behavior support, can work in concert with social services professionals and families in meeting the needs of unique and talented workers with ASD. Indeed, universal design in the workplace promotes communication, technology and an environment that benefits all workers (Button, 2007).

STEPS TO SUCCESS FOR EMPLOYMENT OF WORKERS WITH ASD

Schall (2010) proposes a system of positive behavior supports (PBS) to support workers with ASD in the workplace. Functional assessment of behavior should occur in the work setting and can be accomplished using logs of antecedent-behavior-contingency documentation. A positive behavior support plan can be developed that provides for increased competence and independence for the worker with ASD by preventing unwanted behaviors, teaching substitution behaviors and reinforcing wanted behaviors. A good job match is considered one of the best strategies for prevention of problem behaviors; sensory stimuli, social demands and routine should be assessed and planned for. Providing for choices was identified as an effective strategy for reducing problem behaviors for workers with ASD. Strategies for successful engagement of workers with ASD appear in Table 2.3.

Table 2.3. ASD Workforce Strategies for Success

Preemployment preparation:

- Begin transition to work in high school for students with ASD (Hendricks & Wehman, 2009)
- Use structured work systems that promote independence and engagement (Carnahan et al., 2009).
- Provide a business advisory council to promote employment of workers with ASD in community businesses (Gerhardt, 2007).
- Access ASD informational sites to inform Human Resources personnel, manager and co-workers about ASD.

Recruitment of workers with ASD (Hendricks, 2011):

- Provide a supported job interview that allows the applicant to compensate for social communication deficits
- Interview the applicant with special consideration of the match between the applicant's areas of interests and work to be done
- Assess the applicant's likes, dislikes, and preferences as they may relate to the performance of the job to determine goodness of fit.
- Use concrete language to describe tasks.
- Describe the amount of interpersonal demands that will be placed upon the applicant.

Retention of workers with ASD (adapted from Muller et al., 2003):

- Expand the job description to identify explicit, step-by-step examples of the work to be done
- Encourage managers and supervisors to provide regular positive feedback to the worker with ASD.
- Inform coworkers to disregard benign idiosyncratic or unusual patterns of behavior that may occur on the job, such as failure to greet others, tics, pacing and one-sided conversations.
- Find community and on-line resources for education about ASD. Excellent information regarding reasonable accommodations for workers with ASD can be found at http://www.jan.wvu.edu/media/employmentASDfact.doc and http://askjan.org/media/downloads/AspergerA%26CSeries.doc
- Utilize current employees who are familiar with ASD to serve as job coaches
- Provide organizational supports such as visual schedules
- Establish and maintain routines
- Allow extra time for tests and evaluations
- Minimize sensory distractions
- Help worker to design a pre-planned, pre-approved list of strategies that can be relied upon during periods of unexpected changes in the workplace
- Provide advance notice and practice when changes to the workplace routine are planned

Workers with ASD are encouraged to consult the following site for recommendations regarding disclosure of their disability: http://askjan.org/ENews/2010/Enews-V8-I4.ht.htm

There are many reasons for limited access to employment for the ASD Workforce. There is a disconnection between the potential of adult learners with ASD and systemic resources designed to provide them with programmatic support. There is an absence of legislative entitlement to services for adults with ASD who are not intellectually impaired. Transition planning may be inadequate or inappropriate. Finally, there may be limited interest in supporting adult learners with social and behavioral challenges. Still, these features, while significant, are not insurmountable. Greater emphasis on the role of HR professionals to create access to employment for workers with high functioning ASD will provide insights for support and success, ultimately leading to new opportunities to harness the unconventional talents of adults with high functioning ASD. The task ahead then is to take this possibility and translate it into a certainty.

REFERENCES

Adreon, D., & Durocher, J. (2007). Evaluating the college transition needs of individuals with high-functioning autism spectrum disorders. *Intervention in School & Clinic, 42*(5), 271-279. Retrieved from EBSCO*host*.

Burke, W. W. (2006). Where did OD come from? In J. V. Gallos (Ed.), *Organization development* (pp. 13-38). San Francisco, CA: Jossey-Bass.

Button, C. (2007). *Universal design*. Washington, DC: United States Department of Labor, Office of Disability Employment Policy. Retrieved from http://www.dol.gov/odep/alliances/universal.htm

Cannan, E. (Ed.). (1976). *An inquiry into the nature and causes of the wealth of nations*. Chicago, IL: University of Chicago Press.

Carnahan, C. R., Hume, K., Clarke, L., & Borders, C. (2009). Using structured work systems to promote independence and engagement of students with autism spectrum disorders. *TEACHING Exceptional Children, 41*(4), 6-14. Retrieved from http://www.cec.sped.org

Cimera, R. (2010). Can community-based high school transition programs improve the cost-efficiency of supported employment? *Career Development for Exceptional Individuals, 33*(1), 4-11. doi:10.1177/0885728809346959

Ellinger, A. D., Ellinger, A. E., Bachrach, D., Wang, Y., & Bas, A. (2011). Organizational investment in social capital, managerial coaching and employee work-related performance. *Management Learning, 42*(1), 67-85. doi:10.1177/1350507610384329

Gerhardt, P. (2007). Effective transition planning for learners with ASD. *Exceptional Parent, 37*, 26-27. Retrieved from http://www.eparent.com/index.asp

Hall, A., & Kramer, J. (2009). Social capital through workplace connections: Opportunities for workers with intellectual disabilities. *Journal of Social Work in Disability & Rehabilitation, 8*(3/4), 146-170. doi:10.1080/15367100903200452

Hendricks, D. (2011). Employment and adults with autism spectrum disorders: Challenges and strategies for success. *Journal of Vocational Rehabilitation, 32*(2), 124-134. doi:10.3233/JVR-2010-0502

Hendricks, D. R., & Wehman, P. (2009). Transition from school to adulthood for youth with autism spectrum disorders: Review and recommendations. *Focus on Autism and Other Developmental Disabilities, 24*(2), 77-88. doi:10.1177/1088357608329827

Hershberg, T. (1996). Human capital development: America's greatest challenge. *The Annals of the American Academy of Political and Social Science, 43*, 544. doi: 10.1177/000271629654400100 4

Jaques, E. (1996). *Requisite organization: A total system for effective managerial organization and managerial leadership for the 21st century*. Arlington, VA: Cason Hall & Co.

Jaques, E. (2002). *Social power and the CEO: Leadership and trust in a sustainable free enterprise system.* Westport, CT: Quorum Books.

Jaques, E., & Cason, K. (1994). *Human capability: A study of individual potential and its application.* Arlington, VA: Cason Hall & Co.

Kaye, H. S. (October, 2010). The impact of the 2007–09 recession on workers with disabilities. *Monthly Labor Review,* 19-30. Retrieved from http://stats.bls.gov/opub/mlr/2010/10/art2full.pdf

Keel, J., Mesibov, G., & Woods, A. (1997). TEACCH-supported employment program. *Journal of Autism and Developmental Disorders, 27,* 3-9.

Lee, N.R. (2007). *The practice of managerial leadership*. Retrieved from http://www2.xlibris.com/bookstore/

Malveaux, J. (2009). Invited address at the ICAN Women's Leadership Conference, Omaha, Nebraska.

Martz, E., & Xu, Y.J. (2008). Person-related and service-related factors predicting employment of individuals with disabilities. *Journal of Vocational Rehabilitation, 28*(2), 97-104. doi:1052-2263/08/

Muller, E., Schuler, A., Burton, B., & Yates, G. (2003). Meeting the vocational support of individuals with Asperger syndrome and other autism spectrum disabilities. *Journal of Vocational Rehabilitation, 18*(3), 163-175. doi:1052-2263/03

Rhoads, M. (2010). Face-to-face and computer-mediated communication: What does theory tell us and what have we learned so far? *Journal of Planning Literature, 25*(2), 111-122. doi:10.1177/0885412210382984

Sartawi, A., Abu-Hilal, M., & Qaryouti, I. (1999). The causal relationship between the efficacy of training programs and the work environment for workers with disabilities. *International Journal of Disability, Development and Education, 46*(1). doi:0156-6555/99/010109-07.

Schall, C. (2010). Autism spectrum disorders: Transitions and employment. *Journal of Vocational Rehabilitation, 32,* 79-80. doi:10.3233/JVR-2010-0497

Smith, A. (2010). *An inquiry into the nature and causes of the wealth of nations*. Memphis, TN: General Books. (Original work published 1776)

Summers, J. A., Houlding, C. M., & Reitzel, J. M. (2004). Behavior management services for children with Autism/PDD: Program description and patterns of referral. *Focus on Autism & Other Developmental Disabilities, 19*(2), 95-101. Retrieved from EBSCO*host*.

VanBergeijk, E., Klin, A., & Volkmar, F. (2008). Supporting more able students on the autism spectrum: College and beyond. *Journal of Autism and Developmental Disorders, 38,* 1359-1370. doi:10.1007/s10803-007-0524-8

Winn, S., & Hay, I. (2009). Transition from school for youths with disability: Issues and challenges. *Disability & Society, 24*(1), 103-115. doi:10.1080/09687590802535725

CHAPTER 3

THE PROCESS OF OBTAINING AN AUTISM SPECTRUM DIAGNOSIS

Julie A. Deisinger

Most people would not welcome the prospect of receiving a psychiatric diagnosis. Being classified as having a mental health disorder signifies that a person's thoughts, emotions, and/or behaviors are considered abnormal, which often leads to the experience of stigmatization for the diagnosed individual and his or her family (Halgin & Whitbourne, 2010).

However, receiving an autism spectrum diagnosis may elicit both negative and positive emotions. Understandably, someone may feel sad, anxious, or even angry upon learning that he or she or a loved one has a pervasive developmental disorder (Elder & D'Alessandro, 2009). Yet in addition to these distressing feelings, the identification of an autism spectrum condition sometimes may lead to positive feelings such as relief, a sense of validation, and hope for the possibility of finding and accessing appropriate treatment (Anderson, 2007; Elder & D'Alessandro, 2009; Osborne & Reed, 2008; Siklos & Kerns, 2007).

This chapter will discuss the process of obtaining an autism spectrum diagnosis. Attention will be given to the types of professionals who may be involved, the use of assessment instruments, and demographic factors that may influence the course of evaluation, as well as the advantages of receiving such a diagnosis.

Autism Spectrum Disorders: Inclusive Community for the Twenty-First Century, pp. 47–74

THE IMPETUS FOR SEEKING A DIAGNOSIS

Autism spectrum disorders (ASDs) are pervasive developmental disorders that occur on a continuum of severity (Anderson, 2007; Rosenberg, Daniels, Law, Law, & Kaufmann, 2009) and are of lifelong duration (Elder & D'Alessandro, 2009; Lord, 2010). Symptoms of these conditions include impairments in communication and social functioning, as well as behavioral rigidity and restricted interests (Cashin & Barker, 2009; Dover & Le Couteur, 2007; Elder & D'Alessandro, 2009; Ellis, Lutz, Schaefer, & Woods, 2007; Gonzalez, Cassel, & Boutot, 2011; Hoffman, 2009; Landa, 2008; Lord, 2010; Samms-Vaughan & Franklyn-Banton, 2008; Wicks-Nelson & Israel, 2009).

Many children with ASDs do not appear physically unusual (Farrugia, 2009; Wicks-Nelson & Israel, 2009). Instead, differences or delays in a child's behavior, rather than in his or her appearance, may lead parents to suspect that the child's development is not proceeding appropriately (Dover & Le Couteur, 2007; Landa, 2008). With regard to ASDs, the types of problems that might trigger parents' concerns could include lags in speech or language acquisition, abnormalities in social responsiveness, or unusual eating or sleeping habits (Gaspar de Alba & Bodfish, 2011; Volkmar, Chawarska, & Klin, 2008). A slowing in the child's rate of development, or a regression in vocabulary, pretend play, imitation, or interactive capacity also might elicit parental misgivings (Hoffman, 2009; Landa, 2008; Volkmar et al., 2008). Regression of previously acquired skills occurs in about 20% to 35% of cases of ASDs. Although regression is not observed among all individuals with ASDs, it seems to be specifically associated with these kinds of disorders (Volkmar et al., 2008). In addition, coexisting medical problems such as seizures (Hoffman, 2009) or psychiatric difficulties such as anxiety, depression, or attention deficits (Gaspar de Alba & Bodfish, 2011; Gonzalez et al., 2011) might foster parents' worries.

According to Boutot and Wahlberg (2011), parents' initial concerns often pertain to a child's language difficulties. In some children, communicative delays may be noticeable even in the preverbal period before 2 years of age, as shown by less frequent use of gaze, pointing, and vocalizing in comparison to neurotypical children (Boyd, Odom, Humphreys, & Sam, 2010; Hoffman, 2009; Paul & Wilson, 2009). Also, preverbal children who eventually are diagnosed with an ASD may use atypical gestures to convey their wishes (Paul & Wilson, 2009). Some children with ASDs will begin to talk later than the age when most neurotypical children begin speaking (Halgin & Whitbourne, 2010; Wicks-Nelson & Israel, 2009). More than one third of children with ASDs who are over 2 years of age have no expressive language (Paul, 2008). Among children who do acquire expressive language at the expected time, they may speak in a strange rhythm or pitch, demonstrate unusual repetition of what they hear spoken to them (i.e., echolalia), or express ideas using peculiar words or grammar (Paul & Wilson, 2009; Wicks-Nelson & Israel, 2009).

A child's interpersonal deficits also may signal to parents that something is amiss and in need of evaluation. Social impairments in a young child that might cause alarm could include infrequent eye contact, a lack of social smiles, and/or failure to respond to his or her own name (Gamliel & Yirmiya, 2009; Hoffman, 2009).

Atypical behaviors might serve as red flags for parents. For example, a child may be much more likely than other children of his or her age to place objects in his or her mouth. He or she also might be more likely than other same-aged children to engage in repetitive behaviors or intense temper tantrums, or to have an unusual gait or posture (Baranek, Wakeford, & David, 2008; Boyd et al., 2010; Osborne & Reed, 2008).

Sensory sensitivities are not among the formal criteria for ASDs that are listed in the revised fourth edition of the *Diagnostic and Statistical Manual of Mental Disorders* (*DSM-IV-TR*; American Psychiatric Association, 2000). However, the *DSM-IV-TR* does cite unusual reactions to sensory stimuli as an associated feature of autistic disorder, and parents may observe odd responses to sensory stimuli in young children who later receive an ASD diagnosis. Either sensory oversensitivity or undersensitivity may be evident; for example, a child may be excessively disturbed by certain noises or tactile sensations, or may exhibit an unusually high threshold for pain (Baranek et al., 2008).

Retrospective studies of parents whose children eventually were diagnosed with ASDs found that 30% to 50% of parents reported concerns before their children reached the age of 1 (Volkmar et al., 2008), and 80% to 90% of parents noticed developmental differences before their children were 2 years old (Jonsdottir, Saemundsen, Antonsdottir, Sigurdardottir, & Olason, 2011; Volkmar et al., 2008). It is encouraging that many parents are able to detect developmental warning signs so early, because earlier identification of ASDs has been shown to lead to earlier intervention and better outcomes for affected individuals (Finke, Drager, & Ash, 2010; Landa, 2008; Le Couteur, Haden, Hammal, & McConachie, 2008; Matson, Nebel-Schwalm, & Matson, 2007; Pandey et al., 2008; Samms-Vaughan & Franklyn-Banton, 2008; Turner, Stone, Pozdol, & Coonrod, 2006; van Daalen et al., 2009; Volkmar et al., 2008).

PROFESSIONALS WHO IDENTIFY ASDS

Once parents have become concerned that their child's development is not progressing as expected, they may seek an evaluation for the child to obtain information and assistance. Often, the first professional whom parents will consult is the child's physician (Allen, Robins, & Decker, 2008; Anderson, 2007; Dover & Le Couteur, 2007; Hoffman, 2009; Lord & Bishop, 2010; Osborne & Reed, 2008; Richard, 2008; Samms-Vaughan & Franklyn-Banton, 2008). This doctor most likely is a general practitioner, family practitioner, or primary care pediatrician, but a specialized physician such as a developmental pediatrician, neurologist, or psychiatrist also might be sought (Dover & Le Couteur, 2007; Heidgerken, Geffken, Modi, & Frakey, 2005; Lord & Bishop, 2010; Osborne & Reed, 2008; Rhoades, Scarpa, & Salley, 2007).

Although seeking evaluation from a pediatrician would seem to be a sensible first step toward identifying the nature of a child's unusual symptoms, some research suggests that this approach sometimes might not be as beneficial as one might otherwise assume. A 2005 survey conducted by Heidgerken and colleagues found that primary care providers (e.g., family practitioners and pediatricians) were likely to harbor outdated beliefs about the characteristics of ASDs and did not feel comfortable diagnosing these disorders. In a more recent qualitative study, Finke et al. (2010) interviewed five general pediatricians to learn about their role in diagnosing ASDs. All five doctors stated that the amount of training about ASDs which they had received in medical school was minimal. They also claimed that few opportunities existed to undergo formal continuing education about ASDs. Some of them further admittedly candidly that they were not strongly interested in pursuing in-depth continuing education on ASDs (Finke et al., 2010). Of course, it is not possible to make broad generalizations on the basis of so few respondents. Still, the possibility does exist that these five pediatricians' views and experiences may mirror those of at least some others in their field.

Clinical psychologists also might become involved in evaluating a child for the possible presence of ASDs (Heidgerken et al., 2005; Osborne & Reed, 2008). Unfortunately, and similar to what has already been observed about physicians, many of these mental health professionals may have had insufficient training concerning how to assess and identify ASDs. As noted by Egger and Emde (2011), clinical diagnoses "will be only as good as the systems of care and individual clinicians who apply them" (p. 103). With regard to the identification of ASDs, many clinical psychologists may not have undergone formal training to recognize and assess for the presence of ASDs in their clients. Weiss, Lunsky, and Morin (2010) wrote, "Psychology graduate student training in developmental disability has received very little attention in North America" (p. 177). These authors pointed out that while both the American Psychological Association and the Canadian Psychological Association emphasize the need for diversity training in clinical psychology, training geared specifically toward knowledge about developmental disability is not required of clinical psychology graduate programs. When Weiss et al. (2010) surveyed Canadian graduate students in clinical psychology, counseling psychology, and clinical neuropsychology, they discovered that 70% of the 303 respondents had not taken either a required course or an elective course on developmental disabilities. More than half of this sample rated their education concerning developmental disorders as poor. These results pertained to students who eventually planned to work mainly with youth, and were even more likely to be true for students who eventually planned to work mostly with adult clients. As Weiss et al. (2010) correctly observed, the latter finding is disturbing due to the lifelong nature of developmental disorders.

By virtue of their employment in early childhood centers and their involvement in preschool screenings, speech-language pathologists (SLPs) may be among the first to evaluate a child exhibiting possible symptoms of ASDs (Boyd et al., 2010; Richard, 2008). The American Speech-Language Hearing Association has asserted that appropriately trained SLPs may diagnose ASDs (Richard, 2008; Schwartz & Drager, 2008). However, some speech-language pathologists may not have obtained such training. Schwartz and Drager (2008) conducted a survey of 67 speech-language pathologists working in 33 different states in the United States, 94% of whom had earned a master's degree. The remaining participants had obtained a doctoral degree. Sixty percent of the respondents in this study reported that their graduate coursework devoted only 1 week to information about ASDs. Although all of these participants had worked with at least one person with an ASD, more than half of them indicated that they had worked with 20 or fewer individuals on the autism spectrum during their careers. On the basis of their survey, Schwartz and Drager (2008) concluded that "some professionals in the field of speech-language pathology do not demonstrate a clear understanding of what autism is and how it is diagnosed" (p. 72).

Others who may be involved in the initial identification of ASDs include school psychologists (Allen et al., 2008; Volker & Lopata, 2008), school nurses (School nurses can help, 2010; Strunk, 2009), social workers (Dababnah, Parish, Brown, & Hooper, 2011) and teachers (Samms-Vaughan & Franklyn-Banton, 2008). Yet these professionals also may have had inadequate training about how to recognize ASDs (Allen et al., 2008; School nurses can help, 2010). Allen and colleagues (2008) surveyed 117 school psychologists and interpreted their findings to show "gaps between what would be considered best practices of ASD assessment and current practice" (p. 915). Similarly, Strunk's (2009) survey of 231 school nurses found that 57% of these respondents claimed to be only "minimally familiar" with the symptoms of ASDs (p. 451). Dababnah et al. (2011) asserted that most social workers have not been trained to identify ASDs and further claimed that many social workers harbor erroneous beliefs about the characteristics of ASDs and the methods used to diagnose them. Regarding teachers' familiarity with ASDs, Barnhill, Polloway, and Sumutka (2011) contacted higher education institutions throughout the United States to inquire about teacher preparation for working with students who have ASDs. They learned that 36 of the 87 responding institutions (i.e., 41% of their sample) did not offer coursework specifically about ASDs to their education majors.

As suggested by the research cited in this section, "most pediatricians, general practitioners, teachers, social workers, clinical psychologists, and psychiatrists who are in practice on the 'frontline', are not familiar with the clinical presentation of autism in children" (Matson et al., 2007, p. 43). The widespread lack of familiarity with ASDs among professionals in health care and education complicates the diagnostic process and often leads to delays or errors in identification.

THE USE OF INSTRUMENTS TO IDENTIFY ASDS

The process of making an ASD diagnosis may include the use of such measures as structured interviews, questionnaires, checklists, and standardized behavioral observations (Deisinger, 2008; Sapp, 2008). It is beyond the scope of this chapter to describe these instruments in detail. To learn about the psychometric properties and administration procedures for such measures, the interested reader is directed to Deisinger (2008) and Sapp (2008). This section will discuss whether professionals who are involved in the identification of ASDs typically incorporate such assessment methods in the course of making a diagnosis.

As mentioned earlier in this chapter, pediatricians and family physicians are among the professionals who most often are expected to identify ASDs. However, anywhere from 50% to 75% of physicians fail to regularly use developmental screening tests during examinations of infants and toddlers (Lord & Bishop, 2010). Gillis (2009) examined the ASD screening practices of family physicians and pediatricians in Alabama and Mississippi and found that 78% of the 51 respondents in the study performed general developmental screenings. In contrast, only 28% of them (all pediatricians) reported that they used screening tools devised specifically for the identification of ASDs, such as the Modified Checklist for Autism in Toddlers (M-CHAT; Robins, Fein, Barton, & Green, 2001). Furthermore, only one pediatrician in this study reportedly conducted routine screening for ASDs at well-child visits for 18-month-old and 24-month-old children. The participants who did not routinely screen for ASDs cited lack of familiarity with ASD screening instruments and lack of time as barriers to including ASD screening as part of their regular examination procedures (Gillis, 2009).

A 2010 qualitative study conducted by Finke et al. pointed out that the American Academy of Pediatrics recommends the use of standardized checklists during a pediatric assessment for the presence of an ASD. However, none of the five pediatricians who participated in this study reported using any of the formal screening measures that have been suggested by the American Academy of Pediatrics. In another qualitative study involving nine pediatricians (Carbone, Behl, Azor, & Murphy, 2010), most of them expressed a belief that they should engage in ASD screening through the use of the M-CHAT or another empirically validated measure. However, these doctors also reported conflicted feelings about the expectation to provide an early diagnosis, due to a perceived lack of treatment options once a diagnosis has been assigned.

When considering psychologists' use of psychometric instruments to identify ASDs, Akshoomoff, Corsello, and Schmidt (2006) compared ASD assessment procedures used by clinical psychologists and school psychologists. These investigators learned that the clinical psychologists in their sample had completed more ASD evaluations per year than the school psychologists. Akshoomoff et al. found that both groups were equally likely to include parent interview data, developmental history-taking, and a review of clients' records as part of the assessment. However, they also discovered that school psychologists were significantly more likely than clinical psychologists to include the use of teacher questionnaires, teacher interviews, and observations of the client at home or in school as components of an ASD assessment. Both school psychologists and clinical psychologists in this study reported that they used standardized measures such as the Childhood Autism Rating Scale (Schopler, Reichler, De Vellis, & Daly, 1980), the Gilliam Autism Rating Scale (Gilliam, 1995), or the Autism Diagnostic Observation Schedule (ADOS; Lord, Rutter, DiLavore, & Risi, 2001) .

Akshoomoff et al. (2006) noted that the findings of their study might not be typical of most psychologists. Instead, psychologists may tend to rely on unstructured clinical interviews and informal behavioral observations, with the format of these assessments varying on the basis of the training and theoretical perspective of the psychologist. Akshoomoff et al. cited a 2006 study conducted by another research team which revealed that "professionals assigning an initial ASD diagnosis used a standardized diagnostic tool in only 30% of evaluations" (p. 15).

Another survey of 117 school psychologists (Allen et al., 2008) indicated that more than half of them never included the results of medical examinations among the data that they used to make a diagnosis. Sixteen percent of these survey respondents further reported that they never used developmental questionnaires to identify ASDs, and 13% said that they never included interviews with parents or guardians as part of the assessment process.

Matson et al. (2007) identified several factors which might limit professionals' use of psychometric devices to diagnose ASDs. As already cited by physicians, one barrier is the time required to give and score such tests, some of which may take more than an hour to administer. Another issue that may interfere with the use of formal diagnostic measures is that some of them require fairly extensive training before they can be used. For example, clinicians are not supposed to administer the ADOS unless they have either completed a 2-day training workshop or have viewed more than 7 hours of training videotapes (Western Psychological Services, 2011). According to Matson et al. (2007), "Most clinicians are not going to do that" (p. 49). Yet another factor that may discourage the use of standardized test instruments is the caveat issued by the test developers stating that such instruments should not be used to diagnose ASDs, even though that is the purpose for which they were created. Matson et al. argued that because standardized measures have known reliability and validity, they should be employed in ASD evaluations until such time when more accurate diagnostic methods exist.

AGE OF INITIAL DIAGNOSIS

The age at which someone might receive an ASD diagnosis varies considerably. Because early recognition leads to more rapid treatment and improved outcomes, diagnostic professionals are being encouraged to identify individuals who have ASDs as early as possible.

Preterm infants comprise a population that has received increased attention in recent years. Medical advancements have progressed to the point that some infants born at as young as 22 weeks' gestation are able to survive (Zlatohlavkova et al., 2010). However, several studies have determined that preterm infants are at heightened risk for ASDs (Johnson et al., 2010; Kuban et al., 2009).

The prevalence of ASDs among children who were born very prematurely has not yet been fully established (Johnson et al., 2010), but two recent studies employed the M-CHAT as a screening measure to examine ASD prevalence rates in children who had been born preterm. In the first study of its kind (Limperopoulos et al., 2008), the researchers obtained a participant sample of 91 children who had weighed less than 1,500 grams at birth, and whose gestational age at the time of delivery ranged from 23 to 30 weeks of age. These children's developmental progress was evaluated at a mean age of around 21 months, using raters who were unaware of the children's prior medical history. Twenty-six percent of this sample yielded positive results on the M-CHAT, suggesting that they might have an ASD. Statistical analyses revealed that variables such as earlier gestational age, smaller birth weight, male gender, prenatal infection, illness at the time of birth, and the presence of structural abnormalities in the child's brain were associated with positive scores on the M-CHAT. In addition, these authors found that positive M-CHAT scores were linked with internalizing behavioral problems such as withdrawal and emotional reactivity, as well as difficulties with communication and socialization.

Following the Limperopoulos (2008) study, Kuban et al. (2009) sought to clarify the extent to which developmental delays resulting from extreme prematurity, rather than from an ASD, might elevate the likelihood of obtaining a positive score on the M-CHAT. These investigators recruited 988 participants from an ongoing study of infants who were born before 28 weeks of gestation, and found that children with visual, hearing, and/or motor deficits were significantly more likely to receive a positive score on the M-CHAT. Kuban et al. stated that they could not be sure whether these youngsters who scored positive on the M-CHAT would later have a confirmed ASD diagnosis. They speculated that perhaps the positive screening results might have been due to behaviors that are actually the consequences of vision impairments (e.g., lack of eye contact), hearing deficits (e.g., failure to respond to others' vocal utterances), or motor problems (e.g., unusual play behavior), rather than symptoms of an ASD. Kuban et al. concluded that a modified form of the M-CHAT might be needed when conducting ASD screenings for children with physical or sensory deficits as a result of extreme prematurity at birth.

Using a prospective approach, a 2010 study by Johnson and colleagues tracked all infants in the United Kingdom and Ireland who had been born in 1995 at less than 26 weeks' gestation. These children were evaluated at 2.5, 6, and 11 years of age, and were compared with a group of randomly selected, same-aged peers who were similar to the participants in terms of sex, age, and ethnicity. Of the 219 children in this study who had been born extremely preterm, 16 of them (i.e., approximately 8% of the sample) eventually received an ASD diagnosis, while none of the children in the comparison group were so diagnosed. Johnson et al. reported that in their study, "the prevalence of narrowly defined autistic disorder is approximately 65 times higher than community populations, and the prevalence of ASD are four to 12 times higher" (p. 528). These scientists concluded that "autism spectrum symptoms and disorders are highly prevalent in extremely preterm children" (p. 530) and identified extreme prematurity as an environmental factor that may have an important causal role with regard to ASDs.

However, Moore, Johnson, and Marlow (2010) urged caution when conducting ASD screenings for children who had been born at extremely early gestational ages. Similar to Kuban et al. (2009), Moore et al. suggested that the use of the M-CHAT in this population leads to a large number of false positive results that are by-products of these children's deficits in cognitive functioning, vision, hearing, or motor skills.

Infants and toddlers who have older siblings already diagnosed with an ASD constitute another group that is being examined closely for early signs of ASDs. Prevalence rates of ASDs among siblings of individuals previously identified with ASDs are 20 times higher than the rates found in the general population (Constantino, Zhang, Frazier, Abbacchi, & Law, 2010), indicating that these youngsters are at increased risk for themselves having an ASD (Landa, 2008). Furthermore, infants who have more than one older sibling with an ASD have significantly greater risk for developing an ASD than infants with only one affected older sibling (Schwichtenberg, Young, Sigman, Hutman, & Ozonoff, 2010).

An instrument called the Autism Observation Scale for Infants (Bryson, Zwaigenbaum, McDermott, Rombough, & Brian, 2008) can be used to evaluate infants and toddlers ranging in age from 6 to 18 months. The Autism Observation Scale for Infants seeks to detect early signs of ASDs by examining an infant's abilities for orienting to his or her name, visual tracking, shifting of attention, making eye contact, social smiling, babbling, imitation, and other behaviors (Bryson, Zwaigenbaum, et al., 2008). Brian et al. (2008) employed both the Autism Observation Scale for Infants and the ADOS in a prospective study of 18-month-olds who had older siblings with ASDs and found that each instrument contributed unique information toward the identification of ASDs. When the 155 infants in this study were evaluated again at 36 months of age, 35 of them (21 boys) were diagnosed with an ASD. The Brian et al. (2008) investigation stated that the following behaviors were early markers for an eventual ASD diagnosis: response to name, abilities for eye contact, social smiling, and shared enjoyment, and unusual sensory and motor characteristics.

Using another instrument called the Communication and Symbolic Behavior Scales Developmental Profile (Wetherby & Prizant, 2002), Shumway and Wetherby (2009) assessed 125 children in the 18-to-24-month age range. Fifty of these children later received an ASD diagnosis. They were found to communicate at a significantly lower rate when compared to children with other forms of developmental delay, or to neurotypical children. In addition, the ASD children engaged in significantly less joint attention and were less likely than the children in the two comparison groups to point at people or things for the purpose of shared attention. Based on their results, Shumway and Wetherby cited impairments in communication rate, use of communicative gestures, and joint attention as indications of ASDs in 18- to 24-month-old children.

Recently a new module of the ADOS was devised for the purpose of evaluating children younger than 30 months of age (Luyster et al., 2009). The ADOS Toddler Module reportedly can be used with children from age 15 months to age 30 months, provided that they have a nonverbal mental age of at least 12 months and are able to walk unaided. Similar to the Autism Observation Scale for Infants, use of the ADOS Toddler Module involves observations of a child's communication skills, social interactions, and play behaviors. However, Luyster et al. (2009) stated that some children who meet diagnostic cut-offs on the ADOS Toddler Module may not receive an ASD diagnosis if they do not meet other formal criteria for ASDs that are listed in the *DSM-IV-TR* (American Psychiatric Association, 2000). Also, some children who fail to meet the cut-offs for this new ADOS module may still receive an ASD diagnosis if it is a clinician's expert judgment that such a diagnosis is warranted (Luyster et al., 2009). As suggested by these findings, the ADOS Toddler Module may require further refinement before it can be used on a widespread scale for the identification of toddlers with ASDs.

The M-CHAT also has been employed to evaluate young children for the possible presence of ASDs. Pandey et al. (2008) compared the positive predictive power of the M-CHAT when evaluating younger versus older toddlers. Results indicated that when using the M-CHAT with toddlers who are presumed to be at low risk for having an ASD, its predictive power is better for 24-month-olds than for 18-month-olds. However, for toddlers who are suspected of being at risk for an ASD, the predictive power of the M-CHAT is relatively high, even when they are less than 2 years of age.

Landa (2008) discussed the stability of ASD diagnoses that are assigned to children prior to their third birthday. She noted that such diagnoses may be unstable for children who are less than 30 months old and for young children whose cognitive functioning is relatively good. Landa further mentioned that ASD diagnoses in young children tend to be more stable when they are assigned by an experienced clinician who includes multiple sources of information in the decision-making process, rather than relying solely on scores from standardized diagnostic measures.

A prospective study by van Daalen et al. (2009) examined the stability of ASD diagnoses in 131 children who had been identified with an ASD via screening at age 18 months. These toddlers were reevaluated at ages 23 months and 42 months. The research team found that diagnostic stability held for 63% of those whose diagnosis was autistic disorder, for 54% of those with a diagnosis of pervasive developmental disorder not otherwise specified (PDD-NOS), and for 91% of cases when considering ASDs as a general category. When a diagnosis changed from one category assigned at 23 months to another category at 42 months, it usually shifted from autistic disorder to PDD-NOS as a result of decreases in the severity of ASD symptoms. van Daalen et al. concluded that the stability of ASD diagnoses in their sample of toddlers was good.

Despite efforts to identify ASDs in infants and toddlers, it is more common for children to be diagnosed with ASDs during the preschool years, particularly for children with more severe symptoms. Several recent studies (e.g., Boyd et al., 2010; Brian et al., 2008; Dababnah et al., 2011; Finke et al., 2010; Jonsdottir et al., 2011; Landa, 2008; Rhoades et al., 2007) have reported that the typical age for an initial ASD diagnosis is from 3 to 6 years old. Jonsdottir et al. (2011) compared children who were diagnosed with ASDs before 6 years of age versus those who were diagnosed later than that. They found that children who were diagnosed earlier than age 6 were more likely to receive a diagnosis of autistic disorder, to have lower levels of intelligence and verbal ability, and to have had a history of regression, most often with regard to vocabulary.

Unfortunately, many children are not diagnosed with ASDs until they are school aged or older (Dababnah et al., 2011; Dover & Le Couteur, 2007). Some of these youngsters may have less severe symptoms (Finke et al., 2010; Jonsdottir et al., 2011; Yirmiya & Charman, 2010), thereby enabling family members to manage them up to that time (Dover & Le Couteur, 2007). Once they enter school, however, increasingly complex academic and social challenges may call their problems to the attention of parents and teachers (Dover & Le Couteur, 2007). In other cases, these children simply may not have come into contact with professionals who were familiar enough with ASDs to recognize symptoms and assign a diagnosis.

Some individuals with ASDs may not receive an initial diagnosis until adolescence. For example, Conti-Ramsden, Simkin, and Botting (2006) evaluated 76 teens who had a previous diagnosis of language impairment, using a caregiver interview, the ADOS, and the Autism Diagnostic Interview-Revised (Lord, Rutter, & Le Couteur, 1994). They found that almost 4% of the participants also met diagnostic criteria for an ASD, a prevalence rate that is 10 times higher than what would be expected in the general population. Another study (Bryson, Bradley, Thompson, & Wainwright, 2008) located 171 adolescents with intellectual disabilities and evaluated them using the Autism Diagnostic Interview-Revised. They identified 43 teens in their sample who met criteria for an ASD diagnosis on the basis of results from the Autism Diagnostic Interview-Revised, yet discovered that less than half of them had previously been diagnosed with an ASD.

In other instances a person with an ASD might not be diagnosed until adulthood. A 2001 study by Nylander and Gillberg involved the screening of more than 1300 adults who were undergoing outpatient psychiatric care. Although 19 individuals in this sample met criteria for having an ASD, only two of these patients had previously been diagnosed as such. A more recent study (Ketelaars et al., 2008) examined 36 adults who had been referred to an autism clinic in the Netherlands for further evaluation. Based on data from the Autism Diagnostic Interview-Revised, the ADOS, and parental interviews, 15 of them were found to have a mild form of ASD. Ketelaars and colleagues noted that client self-report alone did not yield enough information to make an ASD diagnosis for these adults, because more than half of their original sample had reported symptoms suggestive of an ASD but were found not to have an ASD when formally evaluated. As stated by these researchers, "the prevalence of patients with less severe ASD is relatively high compared to the more severe ASD categories" (p. 180). Thus, there is a strong possibility that many adults with mild forms of ASD may have gone undiagnosed during childhood and adolescence.

REASONS WHY THE DIAGNOSTIC PROCESS MAY GO ASTRAY

The previously cited investigations show that numerous cases of ASDs fail to be identified in early childhood, at a time during which treatment subsequently might lead to enhanced functioning throughout life. One factor that may contribute to delays in the diagnosis of ASDs is their heterogeneity (Lord & Bishop, 2010; Siklos & Kerns, 2007). These conditions make up "a spectrum of disorders, along which individuals can present problems ranging from those that cause almost total impairment to others that allow some but not optimal function" (Goldstein & Ozonoff, 2009, p. 5). Variation in the types of symptoms that are evident, and in their severity, makes ASDs harder to correctly identify. "When a child does not seem to meet all of the criteria for an ASD but meets some of the criteria, the clinician must consider the possibility of developmental delay, mental retardation, or communication disorder, as well as PDD-NOS" (Overton, Fielding, & de Alba, 2007, p. 2005).

Some cases of ASDs may escape early detection due to the absence of extreme symptoms. However, when Jonsdottir et al. (2011) compared children with ASDs who were diagnosed before 6 years of age with those who received diagnoses later than age 6, they discovered no difference between the two groups in terms of the child's age when parents first expressed developmental concerns. Therefore, it seems that parents became concerned about their children's development at around the same age, regardless of symptom severity. Despite this finding, the length of time between parents' first expressions of worry and the receipt of an ASD diagnosis may be anywhere from 34 to 48 months (Dababnah et al., 2011; Rhoades et al., 2007). As Dababnah et al. (2011) commented, "This trend of late detection is alarming" (p. 266).

Unfortunately, some cases of ASDs are not identified soon enough due to certain clinicians' misguided belief that the best way to proceed is to "adopt a 'wait and see' approach" regarding lags in development (Finke et al., 2010, p. 260; also see Boyd et al., 2010; Roth, 2010). Pediatricians in the Finke et al. (2010) study claimed that waiting to assign an ASD diagnosis was acceptable due to individual differences in children's development or evidence of delay in only one realm of development, as well as their own desire to avoid upsetting parents through the delivery of alarming news.

Difficulty in recognizing so-called negative symptoms of ASDs also may hamper the early identification of ASDs. Negative symptoms of a psychological condition are "those that involve functioning below the level of behavior regarded as normal" (Halgin & Whitbourne, 2010, p. 282). With regard to ASDs, negative symptoms include "decreases in the frequency of or lack of social and communicative behaviors" (Pandey et al., 2008, p. 515). Failure to respond to one's name, lack of gazing at other people, blunted facial expressivity, social avoidance, and minimal speech output are examples of negative symptoms of ASDs (Deprey & Ozonoff, 2009; Rogers, 2000; Woodbury-Smith, Boyd, & Szatmari, 2010; Wouters & Spek, 2011). Such behaviors are harder for parents and evaluators to notice because they require the detection of actions that are not being performed, or that are performed but at greatly diminished levels. Because negative symptoms are more common than positive symptoms in infants and toddlers who have ASDs (Rogers, 2000), failure to recognize them may account for some instances when ASDs are not diagnosed in early childhood.

In addition, diagnostic errors may delay the eventual assignment of an ASD diagnosis. Depending on the symptoms present, ASDs often are mistaken for other conditions such as cognitive impairment, language disorders (Gibson, 2007; Jonsdottir et al., 2011), attention-deficit/hyperactivity disorder (Gibson, 2007; Mandell, Ittenbach, Levy, & Pinto-Martin, 2007; Mandell et al., 2009; Mayes et al., 2009), adjustment disorder, conduct disorder (Gibson, 2007; Mandell et al., 2007), oppositional defiant disorder (Gibson, 2007; Mandell et al., 2009), obsessive-compulsive disorder, social phobia, schizoaffective disorder (Ritvo et al., 2008), or schizophrenia (Woodbury-Smith et al., 2010). Among children who display an oversensitivity to pain, physicians may wrongly assume that the pain is due to a medical problem rather than an ASD, and spend time looking for a medical cause for the pain (Mandell, Novak, & Zubritsky, 2005).

These kinds of errors also may occur due to the comorbidity of ASDs with other medical or psychiatric conditions (Deprey & Ozonoff, 2009). For example, children with ASDs who also suffer from impaired hearing usually are diagnosed 10 months later than other children (Mandell et al., 2005). Significant intellectual deficits may occur in 50% to 70% of people with ASDs (Corbett, Carmean, & Fein, 2009), and from 28% to 78% of people with ASDs also may have attention-deficit/hyperactivity disorder (Ronald, Edelson, Asherson, & Saudino, 2010). Mood disorders, anxiety disorders, psychotic disorders, and tic disorders are other conditions that may coexist with ASDs (Deprey & Ozonoff, 2009). It sometimes may happen that only comorbid conditions are identified while ASD symptoms are overlooked.

Expansion of the diagnostic criteria for ASDs may further explain the delays that take place during the process of identifying ASDs. The diagnostic categories of Asperger's disorder, childhood disintegrative disorder, Rett's disorder, and PDD-NOS did not enter the *DSM* until 1994 (Feinstein, 2010). As a consequence of a broadened definition for ASDs, more individuals are now classified as having an ASD (Rosenberg et al., 2009; Seltzer et al., 2003). Thus, as Matson and Neale (2009) pointed out, some adults who now might be considered to have an ASD would not have been diagnosed during their childhoods.

Related to the expansion of ASD diagnostic criteria is the phenomenon of diagnostic substitution, in which some individuals with ASDs may have received alternative diagnoses in the past (Bishop, Whitehouse, Watt, & Line, 2008; Grether, Rosen, Smith, & Croen, 2009). For example, Bishop et al. (2008) located 38 adults who had been diagnosed with developmental language disorders in childhood and reevaluated them using current diagnostic criteria. These authors discovered that "a high proportion of people who were regarded as language-impaired rather than autistic when seen in childhood were deemed to meet contemporary diagnostic criteria for ASD in adulthood" (p. 342). Intellectual impairment and childhood schizophrenia are other diagnoses that might have been applied to people with ASDs in the past (Grether et al., 2009; Rosenberg et al., 2009).

DEMOGRAPHIC FACTORS THAT INFLUENCE ASD DIAGNOSIS

A number of demographic factors may influence the timing and accuracy of an initial ASD diagnosis, one of which may be the profession of the evaluator. One study (Wiggins, Baio, & Rice, 2006) indicated that initial

ASD diagnoses most often were assigned by clinical psychologists who held the doctor of philosophy (PhD) degree, followed by neurologists, developmental pediatricians, psychiatrists, educational specialists, and psychologists holding the doctor of psychology (PsyD) degree. In another study (Siklos & Kerns, 2007), most of the participating families obtained an ASD diagnosis from clinical psychologists and pediatricians, with fewer families receiving such diagnoses from a multidisciplinary team or a child psychiatrist. Results of an investigation by Rhoades et al. (2007) indicated that developmental pediatricians tended to diagnose children with ASDs about 1 year earlier than psychologists and neurologists, and approximately 2.5 years sooner than other kinds of physicians. More recently, Rosenberg et al. (2009) determined that children with Asperger's disorder were significantly more likely to be identified by psychiatrists and clinical psychologists than by school-based evaluation teams.

Racial or ethnic background also affects the ASD diagnostic process. As Gibson (2007) observed, "autism knows no racial, ethnic, or social boundaries" (p. 34), yet several recent studies have reported that members of racial and ethnic minority groups routinely are underdiagnosed or misdiagnosed with regard to ASDs (Becker, Seay, & Morrison, 2009; Begeer, Bouk, Boussaid, Terwogt, & Koot, 2009; Gibson, 2007; Lord & Bishop, 2010; Mandell et al., 2007; Mandell et al., 2009; Overton et al., 2007; Palmer, Walker, Mandell, Bayles, & Miller, 2010; Rosenberg et al., 2009). The racial or ethnic group membership of both the clinician and the client are relevant here. If clinicians do not share the same race or ethnicity as their clients, they may be unfamiliar with the norms and typical behaviors of their clients' culture and consequently may misinterpret their clients' behavior (Becker et al., 2009; Gibson, 2007; Overton et al., 2007). Additionally, clinicians may harbor erroneous stereotypes that may inject biases into the diagnostic process (Mandell et al., 2007; Mandell et al., 2009). When clients are recent immigrants, language barriers also might hinder professionals' ability to make accurate diagnoses (Begeer et al., 2009).

Delayed diagnosis of ASDs is common for African American youngsters (Mandell et al., 2009); an ASD diagnosis tends to be assigned approximately 1.5 years later for African American children in comparison to White children (Gibson, 2007; Theus, 2008). Often, these children are initially misdiagnosed as having some other psychological disorder. Mandell et al. (2007) found that African American children with ASDs "were nearly three times more likely than White children to receive another diagnosis first" (p. 1798), most often obtaining an initial diagnosis of attention-deficit/hyperactivity disorder. Other incorrect diagnostic labels that are frequently given to African American children with ASDs include obsessive-compulsive disorder and oppositional defiant disorder (Gibson, 2007), as well as schizophrenia (Theus, 2008).

Parental behaviors also might contribute to delayed identification of ASDs among African American youth. In general, African Americans are less likely than Whites to request mental health services; thus, they may not see a need to pursue diagnostic evaluations for their children (Theus, 2008). Furthermore, given a cultural history of having experienced discriminatory treatment due to their race, these parents understandably might dismiss suggestions made by physicians or teachers that the behavior of a child with an ASD appears abnormal and requires professional examination. Some African American parents may assume that such recommendations stem from racial bias and may view them with skepticism. As a result, some African American children who have ASDs may not be evaluated and diagnosed in early childhood (Theus, 2008).

Similarly, Hispanic American children with ASDs may go undiagnosed or misdiagnosed. These children are less likely than either White or African American children to be diagnosed with an ASD (Becker et al., 2009; Liptak et al., 2008), with rates two to three times lower than among non-Hispanic White youngsters (Palmer et al., 2010). Also, Hispanic children who eventually are diagnosed with ASDs are identified at older ages than either White or African American children (Overton et al., 2007; Palmer et al., 2010). For example, a study of children who were eligible for Medicaid revealed that Hispanic children with ASDs typically were diagnosed around 8 years of age, which was 1 year older than for African American children and 2 years older than for White children (cited in Overton et al., 2007). Palmer et al. (2010) hypothesized that factors such as low income, lack of health insurance, lack of access to both regular and specialized medical care, and possible difficulties in communicating with diagnostic professionals could contribute to lower-than-expected rates for the identification of ASDs among Hispanic-American children.

Mothers' level of educational attainment is another variable that may affect the likelihood of receiving an ASD diagnosis during childhood. Mandell et al. (2009) discovered that children with ASDs were more likely to have been identified as such if their mothers had completed some portion of a college education. Goin-Kochel, Mackintosh, and Myers (2006) also stated that "higher levels of parental education and income were associated with earlier diagnosis" (p. 439).

In addition, whether a child is adopted may delay the diagnosis of an ASD. Mandell et al (2005) reported that adopted children tend to be diagnosed approximately 10 months later than children living with their biological parents.

Residential location influences the diagnostic process as well. Living in an urban setting makes it easier to obtain an ASD diagnosis locally, while individuals who live in rural communities may need to travel to ASD specialty centers in cities to obtain a diagnosis (Rosenberg et al., 2009). For example, a study involving Canadian families of children with ASDs found that 42% of them had to travel away from their own city in order to receive an ASD diagnosis (Siklos & Kerns, 2007).

The region of the United States in which one lives also makes a difference with regard to the type of ASD diagnosis that one receives. Rosenberg et al. (2009) examined trends in ASD diagnosis from 1994 through 2007 and learned that diagnostic labels appear to be applied differently in different parts of the country. These authors noted that although individuals with a diagnosis of PDD-NOS comprise roughly 30% to 40% of all persons with ASDs, the diagnosis of PDD-NOS was significantly more likely to be assigned in the Northeast and significantly less likely to be given in the West. Instead, autistic disorder was the initial diagnosis assigned in almost 50% of cases in the West (Rosenberg et al., 2009).

PARENTS' VIEWS ABOUT THE DIAGNOSTIC PROCESS

Studies examining parents' perceptions about having a child diagnosed with an ASD reveal that many of them find the process very distressing (Siklos & Kerns, 2007). One source of stress is the delay in obtaining an ASD diagnosis for a child (Osborne & Reed, 2008). As Goin-Kochel et al. (2006) noted, "parents are frequently faced with a slow and frustrating period of uncertainty and worry and find themselves in the position of trying to convince their children's doctors that there is a need for a specialist assessment" (p. 439). In fact, another study (Harrington, Patrick, Edwards, & Brand, 2006) surveyed 75 parents of youngsters with ASDs and learned that 75% of them had very little confidence in their primary care physician's ability to identify ASDs.

When Goin-Kochel and colleagues (2006) surveyed 494 parents of children with ASDs, they found that on average, parents saw four to five clinicians before their child received a diagnosis, with some parents seeing as many as 29 different professionals before a diagnosis was finally obtained. Siklos and Kerns (2007) similarly reported that families in their study typically saw four to five diagnostic professionals before getting a diagnosis, with 41% of their sample requiring visits to more than five professionals. "Parents describe the process of having to repeat the family history and retell their child's story to one professional after another as exhausting and frustrating" (Roth, 2010, p. 250). As the number of clinicians that were seen in order to obtain a diagnosis increases, there is a corresponding decrease in the level of parents' satisfaction with the diagnostic process (Goin-Kochel et al., 2006).

A related source of stress for parents of children with ASDs is the nature of their communication with diagnostic professionals. When Osborne and Reed (2008) asked parental focus groups about their experience of the diagnostic process, this question evoked emotional answers. Fifty percent of the parents in their sample whose children were diagnosed during the preschool years, 11% of parents of elementary school children, and 25% of parents of high school students complained that nothing about the process seemed helpful to them. This finding was echoed in the results of the investigation by Goin-Kochel et al. (2006), in which 40% of parents expressed dissatisfaction with the diagnostic process.

One study (Carbone et al., 2010) reported that parents were upset about what they perceived to be professionals' lack of concern for them following their children's ASD diagnosis. Parents would have appreciated being asked how they themselves were feeling in response to the diagnosis, or how having a child with an ASD might impact their marriage or their other children. In another study (Osborne & Reed, 2008), parents claimed that they did not receive sufficient information about the implications of the ASD diagnosis, and as many as 40% of participating parents stated that they did not receive any offers of help. However, some parents in this study also indicated that the diagnostic process helped them by confirming their suspicions that something was wrong, and by modifying their expectations for their children.

Upon learning that one's child has been diagnosed with an ASD, the issue of stigma also must be managed (Farrugia, 2009). Because children with ASDs often exhibit odd or inappropriate behavior and impaired social functioning, their parents may experience feelings of embarrassment and may become socially isolated (Farrugia, 2009). In the absence of a diagnosis, outsiders may make hurtful, inaccurate assumptions about the causes of a child's inappropriate behavior; for example, they may mistakenly assume that incompetent parenting is to blame (Farrugia, 2009; Roth, 2010). Having received a formal diagnosis may help to reduce the painful experience of stigmatization because parents can use the diagnosis to educate family members, friends, and acquaintances about the biological causes of ASDs.

In spite of the many frustrations that accompany the process of obtaining an ASD diagnosis, the cost of not receiving one is tremendous. Not having a diagnosis blocks a family from accessing vital services and resources for a loved one who has an ASD, and prevents the affected person's behavior from being viewed with compassionate understanding (Roth, 2010).

CONCLUDING RECOMMENDATIONS

As demonstrated by the research cited in this chapter, there is a definite need for increased training of professionals who evaluate people with ASDs. According to Barnhill et al. (2011), ASDs constitute "the fastest growing group of students served through special education" (p. 75), yet a review of the literature suggests that currently too few physicians, clinical psychologists, and other diagnosticians have undergone sufficient training to be proficient in identifying these conditions. Medical schools, doctoral programs in clinical psychology, and other institutions that educate healthcare providers should incorporate more information about ASDs into their curricula and offer more opportunities for ASD-specific training.

Another important future direction is the development of ASD assessment instruments that can provide accurate classifications rapidly, easily, and cost-effectively. Presently a variety of instruments exist for the screening and diagnosis of ASDs. However, as mentioned earlier, some professionals are reluctant to use these measures because they require lengthy training before use or because they take too much time to administer. Perhaps in the future some form of medical testing will be capable of identifying people with ASDs, but until such a time when these medical tests are discovered and implemented, there will be a continued need for assessment tools that can detect ASDs quickly and correctly.

Finally, an ongoing challenge is the need to educate the general public about early warning signs of ASDs. Early diagnosis should not be a luxury that can be accessed only by those with higher incomes or higher levels of education. Nowadays parents are routinely told about the importance of positioning a sleeping infant on its back, rather than on its side or stomach, to reduce the likelihood of sudden infant death syndrome (Ostfield, Esposito, Perl, & Hegyi, 2010). Perhaps in similar fashion, healthcare providers routinely should inform parents about symptoms that may be early indicators of an ASD. By making such information more widely available, more children with ASDs may obtain early diagnoses, which in turn may lead to a better quality of life for themselves and their families as well as reductions in societal costs of healthcare.

REFERENCES

Akshoomoff, N., Corsello, C., & Schmidt, H. (2006). The role of the Autism Diagnostic Observation Schedule in the assessment of autism spectrum disorders in school and community settings. *The California School Psychologist, 11*, 7-19. Retrieved from http://web.ebscohost.com

Allen, R. A., Robins, D. L., & Decker, S. L. (2008). Autism spectrum disorders: Neurobiology and current assessment practices. *Psychology in the Schools, 45*(10), 905-917. doi:10.1002/pits.20341

American Psychiatric Association. (2000). *Diagnostic and statistical manual of mental disorders* (4th ed., text rev.) Arlington, VA: Author.

Anderson, M. (2007). Autistic spectrum disorders in children. *Practice Nurse, 33*(6), 14-18. Retrieved from http://web.ebscohost.com

Baranek, G. T., Wakeford, L., & David, F. J. (2008). Understanding, assessing, and treating sensory-motor issues. In K. Chawarska, A. Klin, & F. R. Volkmar (Eds.), *Autism spectrum disorders in infants and toddlers: Diagnosis, assessment, and treatment* (pp. 104-140). New York, NY: The Guilford Press.

Barnhill, G. P., Polloway, E. A., & Sumutka, B. M. (2011). A survey of personnel preparation practices in autism spectrum disorders. *Focus on Autism and Other Developmental Disabilities, 26*(2), 75-86. doi:10.1177/1088357610378292

Becker, H., Seay, P., & Morrison, J. (2009). Differences in the prevalence of autism among Black, Hispanic, and White students. *Multicultural Learning and Teaching, 4*(1), 45-57. doi:10.2202/2161-2412.1043

Begeer, S., Bouk, S. E., Boussaid, W., Terwogt, M. M., & Koot, H. M. (2009). Underdiagnosis and referral bias of autism in ethnic minorities. *Journal of Autism and Developmental Disorders, 39*(1), 142-148. doi:10.1007/s10803-008-0611-5

Bishop, V. M., Whitehouse, J. O., Watt, H. J., & Line, E. A. (2008). Autism and diagnostic substitution: Evidence from a study of adults with a history of developmental language disorder. *Developmental Medicine & Child Neurology, 50*, 341-345. doi:10.1111/j.1469-8749.2008.02057.x

Boutot, E. A., & Wahlberg, J. L. (2011). Working with families of children with autism. In E. A. Boutot & B. S. Myles (Eds.), *Autism spectrum disorders: Foundations, characteristics, and effective strategies* (pp. 93-117). Upper Saddle River, NJ: Pearson Education.

Boyd, B. A., Odom, S. L., Humphreys, B. P., & Sam, A. M. (2010). Infants and toddlers with autism spectrum disorder: Early identification and early intervention. *Journal of Early Intervention, 32*(2), 75-98. doi:10.1177/1053815110362690

Brian, J., Bryson, S. E., Garon, N., Roberts, W., Smith, I. M., Szatmari, P., & Zwaigenbaum, L. (2008). Clinical assessment of autism in high-risk 18-month-olds. *Autism, 12*, 433-456.

Bryson, S. E., Bradley, E. A., Thompson, A., & Wainwright, A. (2008). Prevalence of autism among adolescents with intellectual disabilities. *Canadian Journal of Psychiatry, 53*(7), 449-459. doi:10.1177/1362361308094500

Bryson, S. E., Zwaigenbaum, L., McDermott, C., Rombough, V., & Brian, J. (2008). The Autism Observation Scale for Infants: Scale development and reliability data. *Journal of Autism and Developmental Disorders, 38*, 731-738. doi:10.1007/s10803-007-0440-y

Carbone, P. S., Behl, D. D., Azor, V., & Murphy, N. A. (2010). The medical home for children with autism spectrum disorders: Parent and pediatrician perspectives. *Journal of Autism and Developmental Disorders, 40*(3), 317-324. doi:10.1007/s10803-009-0874-5

Cashin, A., & Barker, P. (2009). The triad of impairment in autism revisited. *Journal of Child and Adolescent Psychiatric Nursing, 22*(4), 189-193. doi:10.1111/j.1744-6171.2009.00198.x

Constantino, J. N., Zhang, Y., Frazier, T., Abbacchi, A. M., & Law, P. (2010). Sibling recurrence and the genetic epidemiology of autism. *American Journal of Psychiatry, 167*(11), 1349-1356. doi:10.1176/appi.ajp.2010.09101470

Conti-Ramsden, G., Simkin, Z., & Botting, N. (2006). The prevalence of autistic spectrum disorders in adolescents with a history of specific language impairment (SLI). *Journal of Child Psychology and Psychiatry, 47*(6), 621-628. doi:10.1111/j.1469-7610.2005.01584.x

Corbett, B. A., Carmean, V., & Fein, D. (2009). Assessment of neuropsychological functioning in autism spectrum disorders. In S. Goldstein, J. A. Naglieri, & S. Ozonoff (Eds.), *Assessment of autism spectrum disorders* (pp. 253-289). New York, NY: Guilford Press.

Dababnah, S., Parish, S. L., Brown, L. T., & Hooper, S. R. (2011). Early screening for autism spectrum disorders: A primer for social work practice. *Children and Youth Services Review, 33*(2), 265-273. doi:10.1016/j.childyouth.2010.09.009

Deisinger, J. A. (2008). Recent developments in the diagnosis and assessment of autism spectrum disorders. In A. F. Rotatori, F. E. Obiakor, & S. Burkhardt (Eds.), *Autism and developmental disabilities: Current practices and issues* (pp. 85-108). London, England: Emerald.

Deprey, L., & Ozonoff, S. (2009). Assessment of comorbid psychiatric conditions in autism spectrum disorders. In S. Goldstein, J. A. Naglieri, & S. Ozonoff (Eds.), *Assessment of autism spectrum disorders* (pp. 290-317). New York, NY: Guilford Press.

Dover, C. J., & Le Couteur, A. (2007). How to diagnose autism. *Archives of Disease in Childhood, 92*, 540-545. doi:10.1136/adc.2005.086280

Egger, H. L., & Emde, R. N. (2011). Developmentally sensitive diagnostic criteria for mental health disorders in early childhood: The *Diagnostic and Statistical Manual of Mental Disorders-IV*, the Research Diagnostic Criteria-Preschool Age, and the Diagnostic Classification of Mental Health and Developmental Disorders of Infancy and Early Childhood-Revised. *American Psychologist, 66*(2), 95-106. doi:10.1037/a0021026

Elder, J. H., & D'Alessandro, T. (2009). Supporting families of children with autism spectrum disorders: Questions parents ask and what nurses need to know. *Pediatric Nursing, 35*(4), 240-245, 253. Retrieved from http://web.ebscohost.com

Ellis, C. R., Lutz, R. E., Schaefer, G. B., & Woods, K. E. (2007). Physician collaboration involving students with autism spectrum disorders. *Psychology in the Schools, 44*(7), 737-747. doi:10.1002/pits.20262

Farrugia, D. (2009). Exploring stigma: Medical knowledge and the stigmatisation of parents of children diagnosed with autism spectrum disorder. *Sociology of Health & Illness, 31*(7), 1011-1027. doi:10.1111/j.1467-9566.2009.01174.x

Feinstein, A. (2010). *A history of autism: Conversations with the pioneers*. Malden, MA: Wiley-Blackwell.

Finke, E. H., Drager, K. D. R., & Ash, S. (2010). Pediatricians' perspectives on identification and diagnosis of autism spectrum disorders. *Journal of Early Childhood Research, 8*, 254-268. doi:10.1177/1476718X10366773

Gamliel, I., & Yirmiya, N. (2009). Assessment of social behavior in autism spectrum disorders. In S. Goldstein, J. A. Naglieri, & S. Ozonoff (Eds.), *Assessment of autism spectrum disorders* (pp. 138-170). New York, NY: The Guilford Press.

Gaspar de Alba, M. J., & Bodfish, J. W. (2011). Addressing parental concerns at the initial diagnosis of an autism spectrum disorder. *Research in Autism Spectrum Disorders, 5*, 633-639. doi:10.1016/j.rasd.2010.07.009

Gibson, D. D. (2007). Racial disparities in the age of diagnosis of autism spectrum disorder: Examining factors that may contribute to delayed diagnosis in African-American children. *Praxis, 7*, 34-38. Retrieved from http://scholar.google.com

Gilliam, J. E. (1995). *Gilliam Autism Rating Scales*. Austin, TX: Pro-Ed.

Gillis, J. M. (2009). Screening practices of family physicians and pediatricians in 2 Southern states. *Infants & Young Children, 22*(4), 321-331. Retrieved from http://web.ebscohost.com

Goin-Kochel, R. P., Mackintosh, V. H., & Myers, B. J. (2006). How many doctors does it take to make an autism spectrum diagnosis? *Autism, 10*(5), 439-451. doi:10.1177/1362361306066601

Goldstein, S., & Ozonoff, S. (2009). Historical perspective and overview. In S. Goldstein, J. A. Naglieri, & S. Ozonoff (Eds.), *Assessment of autism spectrum disorders* (pp. 1-17). New York, NY: Guilford Press.

Gonzalez, K., Cassel, T., & Boutot, E. A. (2011). Overview of autism spectrum disorders. In E. A. Boutot & B. S. Myles (Eds.), *Autism spectrum disorders: Foundations, characteristics, and effective strategies* (pp. 1-33). Upper Saddle River, NJ: Pearson Education.

Grether, J. K., Rosen, N. J., Smith, K. S., & Croen, L. A. (2009). Investigation of shifts in autism reporting in the California Department of Developmental Services. *Journal of Autism and Developmental Disorders, 39*(10), 1412-1419. doi:10.1007/s10803-009-0754-z

Halgin, R. P., & Whitbourne, S. K. (2010). *Abnormal psychology: Clinical perspectives on psychological disorders* (6th ed.). New York, NY: McGraw-Hill.

Harrington, J. W., Patrick, P. A., Edwards, K. S., & Brand, D. A. (2006). Parental beliefs about autism: Implications for the treating physician. *Autism, 10*(5), 452-462. doi:10.1177/1362361306066609

Heidgerken, A. D., Geffken, G., Modi, A., & Frakey, L. (2005). A survey of autism knowledge in a health care setting. *Journal of Autism and Developmental Disorders, 35*(3), 323-330. doi:10.1007/s10803-005-3298-x

Hoffman, E. J. (2009). Clinical features and diagnosis of autism and other pervasive developmental disorders. *Primary Psychiatry, 16*(1), 36-44. Retrieved from http://web.ebscohost.com

Johnson, S., Hollis, C., Kochhar, P., Hennessy, E., Wolke, D., & Marlow, N. (2010). Autism spectrum disorders in extremely preterm children. *The Journal of Pediatrics, 156*(4), 525-531.e2. doi:10.1016/j.jpeds.2009.10.041

Jonsdottir, S. L., Saemundsen, E., Antonsdottir, I. S., Sigurdardottir, S., & Olason, D. (2011). Children diagnosed with autism spectrum disorder before or after the age of 6 years. *Research in Autism Spectrum Disorders, 5*(1), 175-184. doi:10.1016/j.rasd.2010.03.007

Ketelaars, C. Horwitz, E., Sytema, S., Bos, J., Wiersma, D., Minderaa, R., & Hartman, C. A. (2008). Brief report: Adults with mild autism spectrum disorders (ASD): Scores on the Autism Spectrum Quotient (AQ) and comorbid psychopathology. *Journal of Autism and Developmental Disorders, 38*(1), 176-180. doi:10.1007/s10803-007-0358-4

Kuban, K. C. K., O'Shea, M., Allred, E. N., Tager-Flusberg, H., Goldstein, D. J., & Leviton, A. (2009). Positive screening on the Modified-Checklist for Autism in Toddlers (M-CHAT) in extremely low gestational age newborns. *Journal of Pediatrics, 154*(4), 535-540. doi:10.1016/j.jpeds.2008.10.011

Landa, R. J. (2008). Diagnosis of autism spectrum disorders in the first 3 years of life. *Nature Clinical Practice Neurology, 4*(3), 138-145. doi:10.1038/ncpneuro0731

Le Couteur, A., Haden, G., Hammal, D., & McConachie, H. (2008). Diagnosing autism spectrum disorders in pre-school children using two standardised assessment instruments: The ADI-R and the ADOS. *Journal of Autism and Developmental Disorders, 38*, 362-372. doi:10.1007/s10803-007-0403-3

Limperopoulos, C., Bassan, H., Sullivan, N. R., Soul, J. S., Robertson Jr., R. L., ... du Plessis, J. (2008). Positive screening for autism in ex-preterm infants: Prevalence and risk factors. *Pediatrics, 121*(4), 758-765. doi:10.1542/peds.2007-2158

Liptak, G. S., Benzoni, L. B., Mruzek. D. W., Nolan, K. W., Thingvoll, M. A., ... Fryer, G. E. (2008). Disparities in diagnosis and access to health services for children with autism: Data from the National Survey of Children's Health. *Journal of Developmental & Behavioral Pediatrics, 29*(3), 152-160. doi:10.1097/DBP.0b013e318165c7a0

Lord, C. E. (2010). Autism: From research to practice. *American Psychologist, 65*(8), 815-826. doi:10.1037/0003-066X.65.8.815

Lord, C., & Bishop, S.L. (2010). Autism spectrum disorders; Diagnosis, prevalence, and services for children and families. *Social Policy Report, 24*(2), 3-21. Retrieved from http://scholar.google.com

Lord, C., Rutter, M., DiLavore, P. C., & Risi, S. (2001). *Autism Diagnostic Observation Schedule.* Los Angeles, CA: Western Psychological Services.

Lord, C., Rutter, M., & Le Couteur, A. (1994). Autism Diagnostic Interview-Revised: A revised version of a diagnostic interview for caregivers of individuals with possible pervasive developmental disorders. *Journal of Autism and Developmental Disorders, 24*(5), 659-685. doi:10.1007/BF02172145

Luyster, R., Gotham, K., Guthrie, W., Coffing, M., Petrak, R., Pierce, K., ... Lord, C. (2009). The Autism Diagnostic Observation Schedule-Toddler Module: A new module of a standardized diagnostic measure for autism spectrum disorders. *Journal of Autism and Developmental Disorders, 39*, 1305-1320. doi:10.1007/s10803-009-0746-z

Mandell, D. S., Ittenbach, R. F., Levy, S. E., & Pinto-Martin, J. A. (2007). Disparities in diagnoses received prior to a diagnosis of autism spectrum disorder. *Journal of Autism and Developmental Disorders, 37*(9), 1795-1802. doi:10.1007/s10803-006-0314-8

Mandell, D. S., Novak, M. M., & Zubritsky, C. D. (2005). Factors associated with age of diagnosis among children with autism spectrum disorders. *Pediatrics, 116*(6), 1480-1486. doi:10.1542/peds.2005-0185

Mandell, D. S., Wiggins, L. D., Carpenter, L. A., Daniels, J., DiGiuseppi, C., Durkin, M. S., ... Kirby, R. S. (2009). Racial/ethnic disparities in the identification of children with autism spectrum disorders. *American Journal of Public Health, 99*(3), 493-498. doi:10.2105/AJPH.2007.131243

Matson, J. L., & Neal, D. (2009). Diagnosing high incidence autism spectrum disorders in adults. *Research in Autism Spectrum Disorders, 3*(3), 581-589. doi:10.1016/j.rasd.2009.01.001

Matson, J. L., Nebel-Schwalm, M., & Matson, M. L. (2007). A review of methodological issues in the differential diagnosis of autism spectrum disorders in children. *Research in Autism Spectrum Disorders, 1*, 38-54. doi:10.1016/j.rasd.2006.07.004

Mayes, S. D., Calhoun, S. L., Murray, M. J., Morrow, J. D., Yurich, K. K. L., ... Petersen, C. (2009). Comparison of scores on the Checklist for Autism Spectrum Disorder, Childhood Autism Rating Scale, and Gilliam Asperger's Disorder Scale for children with low functioning autism, high functioning autism, Asperger's disorder, ADHD, and typical development. *Journal of Autism and Developmental Disorders, 39(*12), 1682-1693. doi:10.1007/s10803-009-0812-6

Moore, T., Johnson, S., & Marlow, N. (2010). Screening for autism in extremely preterm infants: Potential pitfalls. *Archives of Disease in Childhood, 95* (Suppl. 1), A5-A6. doi:10.1136/adc.2010.186338.13

Nylander, L., & Gillberg, C. (2001). Screening for autism spectrum disorders in adult psychiatric outpatients: A preliminary report. *Acta Psychiatrica Scandanavica, 103*(6), 428-434. Retrieved from http://web.ebscohost.com

Osborne, L. A., & Reed, P. (2008). Parents' perceptions of communication with professionals during the diagnosis of autism. *Autism, 12*(3), 309-324. doi:10.1177/1362361307089517

Ostfield, B. M., Esposito, L., Perl, H., & Hegyi, T. (2010). Concurrent risks in sudden infant death syndrome. *Pediatrics, 125*(3), 447-453. doi:10.1542/peds.2009-0038

Overton, T., Fielding, C., & de Alba, R. G. (2007). Differential diagnosis of Hispanic children referred for autism spectrum disorders: Complex issues. *Journal of Autism and Developmental Disorders, 37*, 1996-2007. doi:10.1007/s10803-006-0349-x

Palmer, R. F., Walker, T., Mandell, D., Bayles, B., & Miller, C. S. (2010). Explaining low rates of autism among Hispanic schoolchildren in Texas. *American Journal of Public Health, 100*(2), 270-272. Retrieved from http://web.ebscohost.com

Pandey, J., Verbalis, A., Robins, D. L., Boorstein, H. Klin, A., Babitz, T., ... Fein, D. (2008). Screening for autism in older and younger toddlers with the Modified Checklist for Autism in Toddlers. *Autism, 12*, 513-535. doi:10.1177/1362361308094503

Paul, R. (2008). Communication development and assessment. In K. Chawarska, A. Klin, & F. R. Volkmar (Eds.), *Autism spectrum disorders in infants and toddlers:*

Diagnosis, assessment, and treatment (pp. 76-103). New York, NY: The Guilford Press.

Paul, R., & Wilson, K. P. (2009). Assessing speech, language, and communication in autism spectrum disorders. In S. Goldstein, J. A. Naglieri, & S. Ozonoff (Eds.), *Assessment of autism spectrum disorders* (pp. 171-208). New York, NY: The Guilford Press.

Rhoades, R. A., Scarpa, A., & Salley, B. (2007). The importance of physician knowledge of autism spectrum disorder: Results of a parent survey. *BMC Pediatrics, 7*, 37-46. doi:10.1186/1471-2431-7-37

Richard, G. J. (2008, September 23). Autism spectrum disorders in the schools: Assessment, diagnosis, and intervention pose challenges for SLPs. *The ASHA Leader*, 26-28. Retrieved from http://www.asha.org/Publications/leader/2008/080923/080923d.htm

Ritvo, R. A., Ritvo, E. R., Guthrie, D., Yuwiler, A., Ritvo, M. J., & Weisbender, L. (2008). A scale to assist the diagnosis of autism and Asperger's disorder in adults (RAADS): A pilot study. *Journal of Autism and Developmental Disorders, 38*(2), 213-223. doi:10.1007/s10803-007-0380-6

Robins, D. L., Fein, D., Barton, M. L., & Green, J. A. (2001). The Modified Checklist for Autism in Toddlers: An initial study investigating the early detection of autism of autism and pervasive developmental disorders. *Journal of Autism and Developmental Disorders, 31*(2), 131-151. doi:10.1023/A:1010738829569

Rogers, S. J. (2000). Diagnosis of autism before the age of 3. In L. M. Glidden (Ed.), *International review of research in mental retardation* (Vol. 23, pp. 1-31). San Diego, CA: Academic Press.

Ronald, A., Edelson, L. R., Asherson, P., & Saudino, K. J. (2010). Exploring the relationship between autistic-like traits and ADHD behaviors in early childhood: Findings from a community twin study of 2-year-olds. *Journal of Abnormal Child Psychology, 38*(2), 185-196. doi:10.1007/s10802-009-9366-5

Rosenberg, R. E., Daniels, A. M., Law, J. K., Law, P. A., & Kaufmann, W. E. (2009). Trends in autism spectrum disorder diagnoses: 1994-2007. *Journal of Autism and Developmental Disorders, 39*(8), 1099-1111. doi:10.1007/s10803-009-0723-6

Roth, I. (2010). *The autism spectrum in the 21st century: Exploring psychology, biology and practice*. Philadelphia, PA: Jessica Kingsley.

Samms-Vaughan, M., & Franklyn-Banton, L. (2008). The role of early childhood professionals in the early identification of autistic disorder. *International Journal of Early Years Education, 16*(1), 75-84. doi:10.1080/09669760801892318

Sapp, M. (2008). Assessment of autism spectrum disorders. In A. F. Rotatori, F. E. Obiakor, & S. Burkhardt (Eds.), *Autism and developmental disabilities: Current practices and issues* (pp. 59-84). London, England: Emerald.

School nurses can help identify children with undiagnosed autism. (2010). *Paediatric Nursing, 22*(2), 7. Retrieved from http://web.ebscohost.com

Schopler, E., Reichler, R. J., DeVellis, R. F., & Daly, K. (1980). Toward an objective classification of childhood autism: Childhood Autism Rating Scale (CARS). *Journal of Autism and Developmental Disorders, 10*(1), 91-103. doi:10.1007/BF02408436

Schwartz, H., & Drager, K. D. R. (2008). Training and knowledge in autism among speech-language pathologists: A survey. *Language, Speech, and Hearing Services in Schools, 39*, 66-77. Retrieved from http://scholar.google.com

Schwichtenberg, A. J., Young, G. S., Sigman, M., Hutman, T., & Ozonoff, S. (2010). Can family affectedness inform infant sibling outcomes of autism spectrum disorders? *Journal of Child Psychology and Psychiatry, 51*(9), 1021-1030. doi:10.1111/j.1469-7610.2010.02267.x

Seltzer, M. M., Krauss, M. W., Shattuck, P. T., Orsmond, G., Swe, A., & Lord, C. (2003). The symptoms of autism spectrum disorders in adolescence and adulthood. *Journal of Autism and Developmental Disorders, 33*(6), 565-581. doi:10.1023/B:JADD.0000005995.02453.0b

Shumway, S., & Wetherby, A. M. (2009). Communicative acts of children with autism in the second year of life. *Journal of Speech, Language, and Hearing Research, 52*(5), 1139-1156. doi:10.1044/1092-4388(2009/070280)

Siklos, S., & Kerns, K. A. (2007). Assessing the diagnostic experiences of a small sample of parents of children with autism spectrum disorders. *Research in Developmental Disabilities, 28*, 9-22. doi:10.1016/j.ridd.2005.09.003

Strunk, J. A. (2009). School nurses' knowledge of autism spectrum disorders. *The Journal of School Nursing, 25*(6), 445-452. doi:10.1177/1059840509348221

Theus, F. C. (2008). Asperger syndrome in the African American community: Barriers to diagnosis. In A. F. Rotatori, F. E. Obiakor, & S. Burkhardt (Eds.), *Autism and developmental disabilities: Current practices and issues* (pp. 109-133). Bingley, England: Emerald.

Turner, L. M., Stone, W. L., Pozdol, S. L., & Coonrod, E. E. (2006). Follow-up of children with autism spectrum disorders from age 2 to age 9. *Autism, 10*(3), 243-265. doi:10.1177/1362361306063296

van Daalen, E., Kemner, C., Dietz, C., Swinkels, S. H. N., Buitelaar, J. K., & van Egeland, H. (2009). Inter-rater reliability and stability of diagnoses of autism spectrum disorder in children identified through screening at a very young age. *European Child and Adolescent Psychiatry, 18*, 663-674. doi:10.1007/s00787-009-0025-8

Volker, M. A., & Lopata, C. (2008). Autism: A review of biological bases, assessment, and intervention. *School Psychology Quarterly, 23*(2), 258-270. doi:10.1037/1045-3830.23.2.258

Volkmar, F. R., Chawarska, K., & Klin, A. (2008). Autism spectrum disorders in infants and toddlers: An introduction. In K. Chawarska, A. Klin, & F. R. Volkmar (Eds.), *Autism spectrum disorders in infants and toddlers: Diagnosis, assessment, and treatment* (pp. 1-22). New York, NY: The Guilford Press.

Weiss, J. A., Lunsky, Y., & Morin, D. (2010). Psychology graduate student training in developmental disability: A Canadian survey. *Canadian Psychology, 51*(3), 177-184. doi:10.1037/a0019733

Western Psychological Services. (2011). *Autism Diagnostic Observation Schedule (ADOS)*. Retrieved from http://portal.wpspublish.com/

Wetherby, A., & Prizant, B. (2002). *Communication and Symbolic Behavior Scales Developmental Profile* (1st ed.). Baltimore, MD: Paul H. Brookes.

Wicks-Nelson, R., & Israel, A. C. (2009). *Abnormal child and adolescent psychology* (7th ed.). Upper Saddle River, NJ: Pearson/Prentice Hall.

Wiggins, L. D., Baio, J., & Rice, C. (2006). Examination of the time between first evaluation and first autism spectrum diagnosis in a population-based sample. *Journal of Developmental and Behavioral Pediatrics, 27*(2), S79-S87. Retrieved from http://scholar.google.com

Woodbury-Smith, M. R., Boyd, K., & Szatmari, P. (2010). Autism spectrum disorders, schizophrenia and diagnostic confusion. *Journal of Psychiatry and Neuroscience, 35*(5), 360. doi:10.1503/jpm.100130

Wouters, S. G. M., & Spek, A. A. (2011). The use of the Autism-spectrum Quotient in differentiating high-functioning adults with autism, adults with schizophrenia and a neurotypical adult control group. *Research in Autism Spectrum Disorders, 5*(3), 1169-1175. doi:10.1016/j.rasd.2011.01.002

Yirmiya, N., & Charman, T. (2010). The prodrome of autism: Early behavioral and biological signs, regression, peri- and post-natal development and genetics. *Journal of Child Psychology and Psychiatry, 51*(4), 432-458. doi:10.1111/j.1469-7610.2010.02214.x

Zlatohlavkova, B., Kytnarova, J., Kubena, A., Fleishnerova, A., Dokoupilova, M., & Plavka, R. (2010). Five-year survival without major disability of extremely preterm infants born at 22-27 weeks' gestation admitted to a NICU. *Acta Paediatrica, 99*(11), 1618-1623. doi:10.1111/j.1651-2227.2010.01895.x

CHAPTER 4

GENETIC FACTORS ASSOCIATED WITH AUTISM SPECTRUM DISORDERS

Julie A. Deisinger

Autism spectrum disorders (ASDs) are a group of pervasive developmental disorders that include the diagnostic categories of autistic disorder, Asperger's disorder, Rett's disorder, childhood disintegrative disorder, and pervasive developmental disorder not otherwise specified (American Psychiatric Association, 2000). From the 1940s through the mid-1960s it was believed that these conditions resulted from poor parenting (Bumiller, 2009; Rutter, 2000). Yet even during that time, pioneering autism researchers Leo Kanner and Hans Asperger noticed that ASDs seemed to run in families (Freitag, 2007; Rutter, 2000). Their observations prompted speculation that genetics might be relevant to the etiology of ASDs, but genetic factors were discounted as possible causes of these conditions until the mid-1970s (e.g., see Hanson & Gottesman, 1976). Since the late 1970s, however, numerous investigations have shown that genetics do play an important causal role with regard to ASDs (Deisinger, 2011). This chapter will discuss what is currently known about the genetics of ASDs, based on the findings of various research methods that have been used to examine these issues. The implications of this information for genetic counseling also will be presented.

Autism Spectrum Disorders: Inclusive Community for the Twenty-First Century, pp. 75–111

EARLY GENETIC INVESTIGATIONS OF ASDS

Past research had indicated that the prevalence of ASDs among siblings of children diagnosed with autism was 50 times greater than the rate of ASDs in the general population. As a result, scientists began to consider that genetic factors might be involved in the etiology of ASDs (Folstein & Rutter, 1977a, 1977b). The first research method used to learn about the genetics of ASDs was the twin study (Rutter, 2000). When conducting this kind of investigation, scientists locate identical twin pairs and fraternal twin pairs in which at least one twin in each pair has the disorder being examined. Both members of an identical twin pair derive from a single fertilized ovum and have an identical genetic endowment. In contrast, fraternal twins originate from two ova, each fertilized by a different sperm cell. Thus, fraternal twins are only as genetically similar as any two siblings, having approximately 50% of their genes in common. Next, the researchers determine the rate of concordance for the twin pairs, that is, how often both twins in a pair have the same disorder. Because identical twins share all of the same genes, a disorder that is strongly determined by genetic factors will have a much higher rate of concordance among identical twins than among fraternal twins (Roth, 2010).

Performing the first study of its kind, Folstein and Rutter (1977a, 1977b) found 21 same-sex twin pairs in Great Britain in which at least one twin had a diagnosis of autism. Eleven of these twin sets contained identical twins; the other 10 pairs were fraternal twins. Folstein and Rutter discovered that four of the 11 identical twin pairs were concordant for autism, whereas none of the fraternal twin pairs were concordant. In other words, the rate of concordance was 36% for the identical twin pairs in comparison to 0% for the fraternal twin pairs. When these authors used a broader definition of autism that included some form of cognitive impairment, they noted that nine of the 11 identical twin pairs were concordant while only one of the 10 fraternal twin pairs was concordant. Thus, employing a broader definition of autism yielded an 82% rate of concordance for identical twins in comparison to a concordance rate of only 10% for fraternal twins. On the basis of these results, Folstein and Rutter (1977a, 1977b) concluded that genetic factors are highly relevant to the etiology of ASDs. However, they also wrote, "Both the mode of inheritance and exactly what is inherited remain uncertain" (Folstein & Rutter, 1977a, p. 728).

Another early twin study performed in the United States (Ritvo, Freeman, Mason-Brothers, Mo, & Ritvo, 1985) compared 23 pairs of identical twins versus 17 pairs of fraternal twins in which at least one twin per pair met diagnostic criteria for autism. This study yielded a concordance rate of 95.7% for the identical twin pairs, while the rate of concordance for the fraternal twin pairs was only 23.5%.

Similar findings were reported by Steffenburg et al. (1989), using a sample comprised of same-sex twin pairs from five Nordic countries. Eleven identical twin pairs and 10 fraternal twin pairs, each of which contained at least one twin with autism, participated in the study by Steffenburg et al. Rates of concordance in this Scandinavian study were 91% for identical twins but 0% for fraternal twins.

The initial twin study by Folstein and Rutter (1977a, 1977b) was replicated and extended in 1995 by Bailey and colleagues, who reexamined the twins from the 1977 study. In addition, Bailey et al. (1995) conducted a total population screening of all twins in Great Britain to recruit a second sample of twins with autism, which they combined with the first twin sample. According to Rutter (2005), the 1995 study by Bailey et al. made several improvements over the 1977 study, beyond simply increasing the sample size. The 1995 study used standardized measures to verify autism diagnoses and excluded participants who had neurological conditions known to be due to chromosomal abnormalities. This screening process enabled investigators to look more closely at genetic factors in autism which were not linked with known medical conditions. Furthermore, the research team performed blood tests to verify whether twins in each pair were identical or fraternal. Once again, significant differences were noted regarding the rates of concordance for autism. Among the 25 identical twin pairs, 60% were concordant for autism, whereas none of the 20 fraternal twin pairs were concordant. Bailey and colleagues concluded, "The findings indicate that autism is under a high degree of genetic control and suggest the involvement of multiple genetic loci" (p. 63).

Taken together, these four early twin studies yielded estimates about the heritability of autism in excess of 90% (Freitag, 2007). Heritability is defined as "the proportion of observed variation in a particular trait ... that can be attributed to inherited genetic factors in contrast to environmental ones" (Merriam-Webster, 2011).

Family studies are another method of exploring psychological disorders that may have genetic origins. These studies require investigators to collect detailed medical histories of extended families in which one or more members have the condition being studied. The purpose of gathering these data is to determine the prevalence of the disorder among biological relatives. If the condition is genetically based, the more likely it becomes that multiple family members who are blood relatives will have the same disorder (Halgin & Whitbourne, 2010). The value of family studies is that they allow researchers to examine the roles of both genetic and environmental factors in the etiology of a disorder (Hopper, Bishop, & Easton, 2005). Family studies also enable researchers to check whether a condition might be transmitted via a single gene; this cannot be accomplished with a twin study (Rutter, 2005).

One of the earliest family studies of autism (DeLong & Dwyer, 1988) involved gathering family histories from 929 first- and second-degree relatives of 51 individuals who were diagnosed with an ASD. Three of the second-degree relatives were found to have autism and 17 relatives were identified as having Asperger's disorder. Based on their findings, DeLong and Dwyer (1988) believed that high-functioning ASDs were familial in nature but that more severe forms of ASDs might be primarily the result of neurological damage rather than genetics.

Another early study (Bolton et al., 1994) located 99 families who had a member with autism and compared them with 36 families of individuals with Down syndrome. All first-degree relatives in each of these families underwent a family history interview and tests of cognitive functioning. Analyses of these data revealed that 5.8% of siblings in the autism group had some form of ASD, while none of the siblings in the Down syndrome group had an ASD. When Bolton and colleagues (1994) considered whether participants might exhibit milder problems with communication, social interaction, and repetitive behavior, they found significant differences between the two groups. The autism relatives were much more likely to manifest difficulties in these three kinds of problems that are characteristic of ASDs. As a result, Bolton et al. (1994) concluded that autism is a genetically heterogeneous condition with an etiology that most likely involves multiple genes.

Also in 1994, Spiker and colleagues located 37 so-called multiplex families throughout the United States in which two or more children were identified as having an ASD. Among these, 33 of the families had two children with autism, two families had four children with autism, and two families had five children with autism. Twenty-six nonautistic siblings also were evaluated. A few of them exhibited slightly elevated scores on the Autism Diagnostic Interview (Le Couteur et al., 1989) despite meeting none of the diagnostic criteria on the Autism Diagnostic Interview. This research team drew two general conclusions from their data. First, they noted that within multiplex families, it was possible to unambiguously classify children as either having or not having an ASD. Second, they observed symptom variability within multiplex families. Siblings with autism were not highly similar in terms of intellectual functioning, verbal ability, or other features of ASD, although they were similar with regard to behavioral rituals and deficits in recognizing the emotional meaning associated with various facial expressions (Spiker et al., 1994).

In 1995, Pickles et al. performed a family study of ASDs using a statistical method called latent class analysis. This research team employed latent class analysis in order to avoid the limitations that they perceived to be associated with a family history-gathering approach. According to Pickles and colleagues, the family history-gathering method may have inadequate measurement sensitivity because reports about cases of ASDs within a family are affected by the amount of first-hand knowledge that family members possess about affected relatives. As a result, only more severe cases might be remembered when reporting about distant relatives. Pickles et al. (1995) analyzed the data from the sample that had originally been gathered in the Bolton et al. (1994) study and found that among persons previously diagnosed with an ASD, their "only relatives with autism/[pervasive developmental disorder] were male sibs … and MZ co-twins" (p. 721). In other words, only identical twins and brothers of individuals with ASDs could be identified as also having an ASD. None of the family members who were parents, fraternal twins, sisters, or second- or third-degree relatives of persons with an ASD diagnosis could be classified as having an ASD. Based on these observations and on the results from a series of latent class analyses, Pickles et al. (1995) estimated that three genetic sites might best account for the heritability in ASDs but they hypothesized that anywhere from two to 10 gene loci might be implicated.

A question that arose from the preceding studies concerned whether or not autism and Asperger's disorder arose from similar genetic factors. Recruiting 46 multiplex families of children with ASDs, MacLean et al. (1999) sought to investigate this issue. Ninety-four children were evaluated to learn whether ASD children within the same family received the same ASD diagnosis. However, the only similarity found among family members was a comparable level of deficit in nonverbal communication; otherwise, results indicated that family members differed in terms of the ASD diagnostic categories that were assigned to them. MacLean et al. (1999) speculated that at least three different genetic models could account for the differences that they observed within families. They further surmised that the genetic mechanisms associated with low-functioning ASDs are different from those that give rise to high-functioning ASDs.

RECENT TWIN AND FAMILY STUDIES OF ASDS

Recently published twin and family studies have sought to further elucidate the genetics of ASDs. The purpose of one such study (Hoekstra, Bartels, Hudziak, Van Beijsterveldt, & Boomsma, 2007a) was to measure traits that are commonly associated with ASDs in a general population, and to determine the extent to which these traits genetically overlapped with ASDs. Hoekstra and colleagues solicited the participation of 18-year-old twins and their siblings from 424 families in the Netherlands. The sample included 166 identical twin pairs, 153 fraternal twin pairs, and 206 siblings. These adolescents completed a Dutch version of an instrument called the Youth Self-Report (Verhulst, Van der Ende, & Koot, 1997), which assesses the nature and severity of behavioral problems that respondents may have experienced during the prior 6 months. They also completed the Autism Quotient (AQ; Baron-Cohen, Wheelwright, Skinner, Martin, & Clubley, 2001), a 50-item self-report questionnaire that measures ASD features in people with normal levels of intellectual functioning.

Using a statistical procedure called multiple regression, Hoekstra and colleagues (2007a) found that two scales of the Youth Self-Report called the Withdrawn Behavior scale and the Social Problems scale were significant predictors of overall scores on the AQ. Next, AQ scores and scores from the Withdrawn Behavior and Social Problems scales were analyzed using multivariate structural equation modeling to determine what proportion of variance in these scores could be attributed to genetic factors. These investigators discovered that overlap between AQ scores and scores on the Withdrawn Behavior and Social Problems scales of the Youth Self-Report could be explained by genetic effects, while the effects of shared environment on their results were nonsignificant. However, the Withdrawn Behavior and Social Problems scores could explain only 23% of the variance in AQ scores. Therefore, Hoekstra et al. (2007a) concluded that characteristics such as withdrawn behavior and social problems share some common genetic causal factors with ASDs, but ASD traits also seem to be genetically independent from these two particular forms of behavioral difficulty.

Hoekstra, Bartels, Verweij, and Boomsma (2007b) conducted another twin study about the genetics of ASDs, involving 370 twins from the general population in Netherlands who were 18 years old. Eighty-one pairs of identical twins and 113 pairs of fraternal twins, as well as 94 siblings and 128 couples who were parents of twins, participated in this investigation. Participants completed a Dutch version of the AQ, described above in the study by Hoekstra et al. (2007a); their AQ responses were then subjected to structural equation modeling. Results indicated that ASD traits are continuously distributed in the general population and that the genes which affect such traits are similar for both men and women. In this study it appeared that ASD traits are heritable, with little evidence of shared environmental influences. This study also looked for evidence of assortative mating in connection with ASDs. The term *assortative mating* refers to "nonrandom partner choice" and "partner resemblance for personality traits" (Hoekstra et al., 2007b, p. 373). Assortative mating involving the presence of ASD traits at subclinical levels in both parents has been suggested as a possible risk factor for an increased likelihood of ASDs among their offspring (Hoekstra et al., 2007b); however, findings from this study did not reveal assortative mating in this sample.

A similarly designed study (Ronald, Simonoff, Kuntsi, Asherson, & Plomin, 2008) examined the degree of genetic overlap between ASDs and attention-deficit/hyperactivity disorder in a sample of twins gathered from a general population. Participants came from a longitudinal study being conducted in the United Kingdom, known as the Twins Early Development Study. Ronald et al. (2008) recruited families of 8-year-old twins, resulting in data from more than 6,000 families. The twins' parents completed a questionnaire called the Childhood Asperger Syndrome Test (Scott, Baron-Cohen, Bolton, Brayne, 2002) to report on their children's ASD symptoms. They also filled out the Revised Conners' Parent Rating Scale (Conners, Sitarenios, Parker, & Epstein, 1998), which measures symptoms of attention-deficit/hyperactivity disorder. When the twins reached 9 years of age, their families were asked whether the children's teachers could be contacted to submit additional data; 95% of the parents gave permission for teacher contact. Seventy-six percent of these instructors completed a shortened version of the Childhood Asperger Syndrome Test as well as an instrument called the Strengths and Difficulties Questionnaire (Goodman, 2001). The data from all of these questionnaires underwent multivariate structural equation model-fitting and liability threshold model-fitting, among other types of statistical analyses. Ronald and colleagues found moderate overlap between ASDs and attention-deficit/hyperactivity disorder in terms of both outward characteristics and genetic influences. They concluded, "It is possible, therefore, that some of the genetic causal pathways leading to each of these conditions are common to both" (p. 540).

Also using a sample obtained from a general population, Edelson and Saudino (2009) evaluated 313 pairs of 2-year-old same-sex twins who participated in the Boston University Twin Project. These researchers examined the extent to which genetic and environmental factors influenced behaviors that are typical of ASDs such as impaired social interaction, communication problems, repetitive behaviors, and limited interests. Parents of the toddlers in this study completed the pervasive developmental problems subscale from an instrument called the Child Behavior Checklist for Ages 1½ to 5 (Achenbach & Rescorla, 2000). To corroborate parental reports, raters performed observations of the child participants in a laboratory setting and completed the orientation/engagement subscale of the Behavior Rating Scale, which is a component in the second edition of the Bayley Scales of Infant Development (Bayley, 1993). The researchers used these data to perform correlational and model-fitting analyses.

As anticipated, children whose parents described them as having a higher number of ASD behaviors generally received lower scores from raters with regard to the youngsters' level of social engagement. Correlational data which compared identical versus fraternal twins implied that genetic factors contributed to ASD behaviors, although both shared and nonshared environmental factors also were involved. According to the findings of model-fitting analyses, ASD behaviors and level of social engagement both were found to be heritable, yet each of these characteristics included significant effects of shared environment as well as nonshared environmental effects. Edelson and Saudino (2009) expressed bewilderment about finding that shared environment contributed to both ASD behaviors and level of social engagement. They recommended that their study should be replicated, and suggested that future research should continue to investigate relationships between various ASD characteristics in order to examine whether all of them have a common underlying cause.

Early environmental influences on ASDs were the focus of a brief article by Bohm and Stewart (2009), in which they commented that identical (i.e., monozygotic) twins may not always share a completely identical prenatal environment. These authors noted that during the gestational period, some identical twins develop within a single chorionic membrane (albeit in separate amniotic sacks), while other identical twins develop within two separate chorionic membranes. Bohm and Stewart reported that the membranes surrounding amniotic sacks may allow the exchange of amniotic fluid; however, because chorionic membranes are thicker, amniotic fluid exchange between two separate chorionic membranes is less likely. As a consequence, the prenatal environment of monochorionic identical twins will be more similar than that of dichorionic identical twins, especially during the first trimester of pregnancy. According to Bohm and Stewart, monochorionic identical twins may yield ASD concordance rates of more than 95% whereas dichorionic identical twins may have ASD concordance rates that are more similar to those of fraternal twins or any other two siblings. These authors also observed that monochorionic identical twins occur twice as often as dichorionic identical twins, which would account for the ASD concordance rates of approximately 60% to 70% that have usually been reported in the literature for identical twins. Unfortunately, twin studies of the past have not differentiated between monochorionic and dichorionic identical twin pairs; however, Bohm and Stewart (2009) cautioned that this distinction should be considered when conducting any future twin studies.

In yet another population-based twin study (Dworzynski, Happé, Bolton, & Ronald, 2009), the research team identified social deficits, impaired communication, and behavioral rigidity as core features of ASDs and sought to determine whether these three kinds of symptoms share the same genetic causal factors. They obtained participants from 326 families who were enrolled in the Twins Early Development Study, previously described in this section. When these youngsters were between 10 to 12 years of age, their parents completed the Development and Wellbeing Assessment (Goodman, Ford, Richards, Gatward, & Meltzer, 2000), an instrument that identifies psychiatric diagnoses in children and adolescents. Parents provided Development and Wellbeing Assessment responses for both twins in each pair, whether or not the twin was thought to be at risk for an ASD.

Using what they termed a "bottom-up approach" (p. 1198), Dworzynski et al. (2009) conducted an exploratory factor analysis of Development and Wellbeing Assessment data to examine whether ASD traits were a single entity or a combination of separate features. Their results indicated that ASD features could be subdivided into five different subcategories: social functioning, communication, repetitive behavior, language ability, and the need for sameness. This study also included a "top-down" aspect (p. 1198) in which the researchers used correlational and multiple regression analyses to examine the relative roles of genetics versus environment as causes of ASD symptoms. They reported that language abilities seem to be genetically related to social and communication deficits but genetically unrelated to repetitious behaviors and rigid interests.

Restricted interests and repetitive behaviors also served as the topic of inquiry in a 2009 study by Smith et al. Nearly 250 individuals with ASDs who ranged in age from 5 to 22 years old participated in this investigation. Participants were evaluated by a rater who was experienced in the use of the Autism Diagnostic Interview-Revised (Lord, Rutter, & LeCouteur, 1994), a semistructured standardized tool for gathering information about behaviors associated with ASDs. The researchers also interviewed a subset of participants' parents using a measure called the Modified Personality Assessment Scale-Revised, which was derived from another instrument called the Personality Assessment Schedule (Tyrer, 1988). The Modified Personality Assessment Scale-Revised was administered to examine whether parents might have the so-called *broader autism phenotype*, a personality type that includes the traits of aloofness, anxiety, rigidity, and hypersensitivity (Smith et al., 2009). Autism Diagnostic Interview-Revised items underwent factor analysis, producing the following latent factors: insistence on sameness, repetitive simple motor behaviors, repetitive complex motor behaviors, and intense preoccupations. Correlational analyses revealed that two of these factors, insistence on sameness and intense preoccupations, tended to aggregate in multiplex families. When examining the relationship between these factors and the broader autism phenotype, significant correlations were observed only for the intense preoccupations factor, which was related to both aloofness and rigidity in fathers. According to Smith and colleagues (2009), their study suggests that intense preoccupations may be an ASD trait whose genetic underpinnings are related to the behavioral qualities of rigidity and aloofness that are found in the broader autism phenotype.

Researchers affiliated with Washington University (Virkud, Todd, Abbacchi, Zhang, & Constantino, 2009) compared patterns of inheritance among simplex families (in which only one member has an ASD) against inheritance patterns in multiplex families containing more than one person with an ASD. Virkud and colleagues (2009) located 80 simplex families and 210 multiplex families. Next, they asked parents and teachers to complete the child/adolescent version of a measure called the Social Responsiveness scale (SRS; Constantino & Gruber, 2005) with regard to each male child in the simplex families and all ASD children in the multiplex families. The SRS is a 65-item questionnaire that provides a quantitative measure about the severity of social deficits associated with ASDs. Spouses also completed an adult version of the SRS concerning each other.

Upon analyzing the questionnaire data, Virkud et al. (2009) noticed differences in the patterns of SRS scores when comparing simplex versus multiplex families. They interpreted these differences to signify that the genetic mechanisms leading to ASDs in simplex families are not the same as the genetic factors leading to ASDs in multiplex families. Virkud et al. speculated that interactions between several genetic loci may contribute to multiple cases of ASD within a family. Within this sample of families, the authors also noted evidence of assortative mating among the parents in both simplex and multiplex families.

Most recently, a team of 16 researchers led by Joachim Hallmayer at Stanford University (Hallmayer et al., 2011) conducted "the largest population-based twin study of autism that used contemporary standards for the diagnosis of autism" (p. E7). These investigators recruited 192 twin pairs, born between the years 1987 through 2004, in which at least one twin per pair had an ASD. Using data from the Autism Diagnostic Interview-Revised (described earlier) and the Autism Diagnostic Observation Schedule (Lord et al., 2000), they compared rates of concordance for 54 identical twin pairs and 138 fraternal twin pairs. When the researchers used a strict definition of autism, they found rates of concordance for identical twins in the range of 58% to 60%, and concordance rates for fraternal twins ranging anywhere from 3.7% to 50%. When adopting a broader definition of ASDs, concordance rates for identical twins were 50% to 77%, as compared to fraternal twin concordance rates that ranged from 5.3% to 50%. Surprisingly, Hallmayer et al. (2011) discovered that rates of concordance for fraternal twins were higher than what had typically been reported in earlier twin studies.

Next, these investigators performed model-fitting analyses to evaluate the relative contributions of genetic and environmental factors in their results. On the basis of their data, they reported that genetic factors accounted for 37% of narrowly defined autism and 38% for ASDs. In contrast, shared environmental factors accounted for more of the variance in the data: 55% for strict autism and 58% for ASD. As Hallmayer et al. (2011) wrote, "Although genetic factors also play an important role, they are of substantially lower magnitude than estimates from prior twin studies of autism" (p. E7). These authors pointed out that concordance rates for fraternal twins seem to have been markedly underestimated in the past, and they observed that shared prenatal environmental factors such as parental age, maternal infections during the gestational period, and multiple births should be paid greater attention in future studies. It is possible that environmental factors may interact with genetic makeup to either increase or decrease a child's likelihood of developing an ASD.

Studies of twins reared apart, as well as adoption studies, are other research methods that can be used to separate the relative influences of genetics and environment on the etiology of a condition. However, these types of studies have not been conducted in relation to ASDs because there are too few of these living arrangements to perform these kinds of studies (Freitag, 2007).

GENETIC SYNDROMES LINKED WITH ASDS

Research studies (see Aitken, 2010; Cohen et al., 2005) have identified a wide array of genetically caused clinical syndromes that are known to be associated with ASDs. For example, Aitken (2010) discussed 80 different genetic conditions that have been linked with ASDs. Due to space limitations, this chapter will focus on 10 conditions which have been found among individuals with ASDs. These can be subdivided into chromosomal disorders and single gene disorders (Cohen et al., 2005).

To facilitate the study of specific genetic locations that give rise to these kinds of disorders, biologists have developed terminology to identify chromosomes and describe various locations within them. Human cells contain 23 pairs of chromosomes; a chromosome is a strand of tightly coiled material that contains genes, which are the molecular codes for building the various components of the human body (Aitken, 2010; Roth, 2010). There are approximately 25,000 genes in the human genetic code (Joober & Boksa, 2009; Overbye, 2011).

Twenty-two of the chromosome pairs are called autosomal chromosomes; these are not sex-linked. There is also one pair of sex chromosomes, labeled X and Y, which determine whether a person is biologically male or female (Halgin & Whitbourne, 2010). Each person inherits one set of 22 autosomal chromosomes from his or her mother, and another set from his or her father (Halgin & Whitbourne, 2010). Numbers from 1 through 22 are used to identify each autosomal chromosome; these identification numbers were assigned according to descending length, with chromosome 1 being the longest and chromosome 22 the shortest (Aitken, 2010). The sex chromosomes X and Y differ in size and shape. The Y chromosome can be transmitted only from father to son, while an X chromosome may come from either parent (Roth, 2010). Embedded within each chromosome is a structure called a centromere that divides the chromosome into two pieces, one longer and one shorter. To distinguish these two segments, the letter "q" refers to the long arm and the letter "p" indicates the short arm of the chromosome. Numbers that follow the letter p or q denote the distance of a chromosomal region from the centromere, with a higher number signifying a greater distance from the centromere (Aitken, 2010).

One of the chromosomal conditions associated with ASDs is Angelman syndrome (Cohen et al., 2005), a disorder whose physical features include below-average head circumference, a broad head shape that appears flattened toward the back of the head, a protruding jaw, a narrow upper lip, and deep-set eyes. In many cases, these individuals also have pale skin and pale blue eye color. Behavioral characteristics of Angelman syndrome involve sleep difficulties, excessive interest in sensory stimuli, dietary fixations, a stiff gait, hyperactivity, and frequent laughter. Seizure disorders, gastrointestinal difficulties, and scoliosis are medical problems that are common among persons with Angelman syndrome (Aitken, 2010; Caglayan, 2010). Cognitively, many of these individuals are nonverbal or have an extremely small vocabulary. They also suffer from severe intellectual deficits and significantly impaired concentration (Aitken, 2010; Caglayan, 2010; Cohen et al., 2005).

Angelman syndrome accounts for 1% to 2% of cases of ASDs (Abrahams & Geschwind, 2008; Cohen et al., 2005; Moss & Howlin, 2009), and anywhere from 40% to 80% or more of persons with Angelman syndrome will meet criteria for an ASD (Abrahams & Geschwind, 2008; Cohen et al., 2005). Repetitive behaviors, insistence on sameness, and temper tantrums are symptoms that are common to both Angelman syndrome and ASDs (Cohen et al., 2005). However, Moss and Howlin (2009) reported that typical ASD behaviors such as lining up or spinning of objects, finger- or hand-flicking, and lack of affection are rarely seen in persons with Angelman syndrome.

At least 70% of cases of Angelman syndrome occur due to deletions on maternal chromosome 15, specifically in the region called 15q11-q13 (Aitken, 2010; Cohen et al., 2005; Moss & Howlin, 2009). This region of chromosome 15 typically contains a gene called *UBE3A*, or the "A ubiquitin-protein ligase" gene (Cohen et al., 2005, p. 106). Most cases of Angelman syndrome arise due to so-called *de novo* 15q11-q13 deletions; these are random, isolated occurrences with a low likelihood of recurrence risk (Aitken, 2010). Another genetic cause of Angelman syndrome, occurring in about 2% to 5% of cases, is paternal isodisomy of the same chromosome region. In other words, the affected individual inherits two copies of 15q11-q13 from his or her father (Aitken, 2010; Moss & Howlin, 2009). Still another 2% to 4% of cases arise from other kinds of genetic causes (Aitken, 2010; Moss & Howlin, 2009), yet in as many as 15% of cases, no genetic abnormalities can be detected (Cohen et al., 2005).

Down syndrome, also known as trisomy 21, is another chromosomal disorder that may be linked with ASDs (Aitken, 2010; Cohen et al., 2005; Molloy et al., 2009; Moss & Howlin, 2009). Nincty-five percent of cases of Down syndrome occur as a result of having been born with three copies of chromosome 21, rather than two copies (Aitken, 2010; Wicks-Nelson & Israel, 2009). Physical characteristics of this disorder include short height, tiny skin folds that cover the inner corners of the eyes, a flattened bridge of the nose, a receding chin, an enlarged tongue, and small hands (Aitken, 2010). A variety of health problems may accompany Down syndrome, such as hearing loss, celiac disease, cardiac and gastrointestinal defects, and hypothyroidism, among others (Aitken, 2010; Molloy et al., 2008). Cognitive impairment may range from mild to severe, and delays in language acquisition are common (Wicks-Nelson & Israel, 2009). The most typically reported risk factor for Down syndrome is maternal age; the risk of having a child with this condition escalates from 1 in 1,000 at 30 years of age to 1 in 110 at age 40 (Aitken, 2010).

It was once thought that Down syndrome might confer some protection against ASD symptoms (Moss & Howlin, 2009). However, more recently there have been reports of cases in which both Down syndrome and an ASD coexist. Molloy et al. (2009) stated that "autism occurs 10 times more often in children with Down syndrome than in the general population" (p. 143). Among persons with Down syndrome, it is estimated that from 5% to as many as 39% also meet criteria for having an ASD (Moss & Howlin, 2009). Most children who are comorbid for both Down syndrome and ASDs are male (Caglayan, 2010). Children who have both conditions tend to have markedly greater impairments in cognitive, language, and adaptive behavior abilities in comparison to children with Down syndrome alone. Those who have both disorders also demonstrate key features of ASDs (e.g., communication problems, social deficits, and repetitive behaviors) that cannot be explained solely on the basis of poor intellectual functioning (Molloy et al., 2009).

Smith-Magenis syndrome is yet another chromosomal disorder that has been studied in connection with ASDs (Aitken, 2010; Cohen et al., 2005; Laje et al., 2010). The cause of this condition is a microdeletion of a portion of chromosome 17, located at 17p11.2, that contains a gene called *RA11* (Aitken, 2010; Cohen et al., 2005; Laje et al., 2010). At present the mechanism by which this deletion leads to developmental anomalies is unknown (Laje et al., 2010). Individuals with Smith-Magenis syndrome manifest with short height, reduced muscle tone, a head shape that is short from front to back relative to the width of the skull, flattened facial planes, a broadened bridge of the nose, and a bow-shaped mouth. Associated health problems may include abnormalities of the eyes and ears, cleft lip or palate, peripheral neuropathy, reduced muscle tone, scoliosis, and other health concerns. Mild to moderate intellectual deficits may be present, and significantly impaired speech is frequently observed (Cohen et al. 2005). Smith-Magenis syndrome is noteworthy for the symptoms of self-injurious and self-hugging behaviors (Aitken, 2010). Both of these symptoms are similar to what might be seen with ASDs; repetitive self-hugging can be considered a form of stereotyped behavior (Cohen et al., 2005). Laje et al. (2010) studied 11 boys and 15 girls who had confirmed cases of Smith-Magenis syndrome by asking their parents or caregivers to complete the Social Responsiveness Scale (SRS, described earlier in this chapter) and found that 90% of the children in their sample obtained SRS scores that indicated the presence of an ASD.

Among the single gene disorders, fragile X syndrome can be found among almost 5% of persons with ASDs (Cohen et al., 2005), and from 21% to 50% of those with fragile X syndrome display ASD characteristics (Moss & Howlin, 2009). Because the condition is sex-linked, it is much more common among males than females, occurring in roughly 1 in 2500 males but in only 1 in 8,000 females (Caglayan, 2010). The etiology of this disorder is an expansion of the FMR1 gene, located at Xq27.3; in that region of the X chromosome, there are excessive repetitions of the cytosine-guanine-guanine nucleotide triplet sequence (Aitken, 2010; Cohen et al., 2005). Physical features associated with fragile X syndrome include tall height, a large head, an elongated facial shape, large ears, double-jointed thumbs, and flat feet (Aitken, 2010). Cognitive functioning for these individuals tends to be mildly to moderately impaired, and attention problems also are evident (Aitken, 2010; Cohen et al., 2005). Common behavioral features of fragile X syndrome involve hyperactivity, hand-flapping, hand-biting, head-banging, lack of eye contact, and impaired social functioning (Aitken, 2010; Caglayan, 2010). Heightened anxiety and oversensitivity to visual, auditory, and tactile stimuli also may be found, in addition to communications problems such as echolalia or repetitive speech (Caglayan, 2010; Cohen et al., 2005). Many of the symptoms of fragile X syndrome can be found among persons with ASDs as well (Cohen et al., 2005).

Tuberous sclerosis (sometimes referred to as tuberous sclerosis complex) has been reported in from 1% to 4% of ASD cases (Caglayan, 2010; Cohen et al., 2005), and ASD traits may be evident in from 24% to 60% of persons with this condition (Caglayan, 2010; Moss & Howlin, 2009). Most individuals who are born with tuberous sclerosis have leaf-shaped, de-pigmented skin lesions which sometimes may be visible only under ultraviolet light (Aitken, 2010; Cohen et al., 2005). Affected persons also are likely to suffer from seizures, kidney problems, and pitted tooth enamel (Aitken, 2010; Cohen et al., 2005). About 40% of tuberous sclerosis patients exhibit significant cognitive deficits as well (Cohen et al., 2005). Tuberous sclerosis is more likely to be comorbid with an ASD in persons who have seizures and significant intellectual impairment (Caglayan, 2010; Cohen et al., 2005). In at least 50% of cases, deletions of two genes are observed: the *TSC1* gene, located at chromosome 9q34, and the *TSC2* gene, found at chromosome 16p13 (Cohen et al., 2005).

In the developmental disorder known as CHARGE syndrome, the acronym in its name stands for "Coloboma of the eye, Heart defects, Atresia of the choanae, Retardation of growth and/or development, Genital and/or urinary abnormalities, and Ear abnormalities and deafness" (Moss & Howlin, 2009, p. 862). The term *coloboma* refers to "a hole in any of the primary structures of the eye" (Aitken, 2010, p. 418); this eye disorder may eventually lead to either glaucoma or retinal detachment and needs ongoing monitoring (Aitken, 2010). *Atresia of the choanae* involves "blockage of the nasal passages due to an overgrowth of bone or tissue" (Aitken, 2010, p. 156). Other health problems may be found in connection with CHARGE syndrome, such as recurrent middle-ear infections, or neural defects leading to facial palsy, problems with swallowing, or olfactory difficulties. The physical characteristics of an affected individual might include malformed outer ears, underdeveloped genitalia, and/or cleft lip or palate. Behavioral traits that could be observed in this condition might include sleep disturbances, delays in learning to walk, tic disorders, compulsions, and hyperactivity (Aitken, 2010; Moss & Howlin, 2009). Approximately 60% of cases of CHARGE syndrome are due to a mutation in the *CHD7* gene, found at chromosome 8q12.1. A smaller percentage of cases may be due to the translocation of the *SEMA3E* gene from its place on chromosome 7 (7q21.1) to a new site on chromosome 2 (Aitken, 2010). Estimates indicate that from 15% to 50% of individuals with CHARGE syndrome also have an ASD (Moss & Howlin, 2009). ASDs are believed to be more likely in CHARGE patients who are nonverbal and whose intellectual functioning is in the range of severe to profound mental retardation. Also, it does not appear that ASD traits in comorbid individuals can be explained solely on the basis of visual or auditory deficits that accompany CHARGE syndrome (Moss & Howlin, 2009).

Phenylketonuria (PKU) is a metabolic disorder of genetic origin that prevents the breakdown of phenylalanine, an amino acid that is a component of some proteins (Aitken, 2010; Cohen et al., 2005; Manzi, Loizzo, Giana, & Curatolo, 2008; Moss & Howlin, 2009). It occurs as a result of a defect or mutation in an autosomal recessive gene located at chromosome 12q24.1 (Aitken, 2010). Thus, the condition will manifest only when two copies of the defective gene are inherited, one from each parent (PubMed Health, 2009). In PKU, a buildup of phenylalanine in the body leads to the loss of brain cells and other neurons, fewer connections between nerve cells, reduced levels of neural chemical messengers such as dopamine and serotonin, and lesser amounts of myelin in the nervous system (Manzi et al., 2008). Intellectual impairment, seizures, and other health problems can be the end result (Moss & Howlin, 2009). Abnormalities in stance, gait, and sitting posture, as well as eczema and the emitting of an unpleasant odor due to the excretion of phenylacetic acid are external features that have been found among individuals with PKU (Aitken, 2010).

If detected early, adverse effects of PKU can be prevented by adhering to a diet that is free of proteins containing phenylalanine. With the advent of a screening test in the 1960s, routine screening of neonates for PKU has become common practice in North America and western Europe. Although PKU is now rare in these areas, it can still be found in eastern Europe and other developing regions of the world where newborn screening for this condition is not performed regularly (Aitken, 2010; Cohen et al., 2005; Manzi et al., 2008). Similarities between ASDs and PKU include cognitive impairment, seizures, hyperactivity, tantrums, and self-injury (Cohen et al., 2005). Since the 1990s, however, the prevalence rate of ASDs among persons with PKU has declined from 20% to less than 6% as a result of early screening and detection (Manzi et al., 2008).

Similar to PKU, Smith-Lemli-Opitz syndrome (SLOS) is the result of an autosomal recessive gene. In this condition, the gene *DHCR7* appears at chromosome 11q12-q13 and alters the production of an enzyme called 7-dehydrocholesterol reductase, thereby leading to abnormally low levels of cholesterol in the blood and body tissues (Aitken, 2010; Caglayan, 2010; Manzi et al., 2008).

Physical manifestations of SLOS are short stature, smaller-than-usual head size, drooping upper eyelids, small skin folds across the inner corners of the eyes, a short nose with nostrils that tilt forward, an arched and narrow palate or cleft palate, extra digits on the hands or feet, webbing between the second and third toes, and structural abnormalities of the genitalia (Aitken, 2010; Cohen et al., 2005; Manzi et al., 2008). Deformities also may occur in internal organs such as the heart, lungs, gastrointestinal tract, or brain (Manzi et al., 2008). In addition, impaired language development and cognitive functioning accompany this disorder (Aitken, 2010; Cohen et al., 2005; Manzi et al., 2008). Behavioral features of SLOS may involve problems in infancy such as difficulties in sucking or failure to thrive (Aitken, 2010). Other behavioral symptoms include irritability, disturbed sleep, and self-injury (Aitken, 2010; Cohen et al., 2005; Manzi et al., 2008). Some individuals with SLOS may engage in two stereotyped movements that are particular to this disorder. Approximately half of them will repeatedly throw their upper body backward, and roughly one-third will perform a repetitive stretching motion of the upper body during which they also flick their hands (Cohen et al., 2005). From 50% to 86% of SLOS patients meet diagnostic criteria for an ASD (Caglayan, 2010; Cohen et al., 2005; Manzi et al., 2008). The severity of SLOS varies considerably, depending on the affected person's intake of cholesterol; cholesterol supplementation in the diet can lead to symptom improvement (Aitken, 2010; Cohen et al., 2005; Manzi et al., 2008).

Rett's disorder is one of the categories currently listed in the revised fourth edition of the *Diagnostic and Statistical Manual of Mental Disorders* (*DSM-IV-TR*; American Psychiatric Association, 2000) as a pervasive developmental disorder. Although it traditionally has been considered an ASD, Cohen et al. (2005) identify Rett's disorder as a progressive form of dementia. Over 85% of Rett's disorder cases result from mutations in the gene *MECP2*, located at chromosome Xq28 (Aitken, 2010; Cohen et al., 2005; Moss & Howlin, 2009). A different gene, *FOXG1*, has been implicated in some cases; this gene appears at chromosome 14q13. Symptoms of Rett's disorder due to *FOXG1* mutations are much the same as those caused by *MECP2* mutations (Aitken, 2010).

Most Rett's disorder patients are female, although some cases have been found among males (Aitken, 2010). Slowed head growth is a physical trait found among these individuals (Aitken, 2010); other physical features may include sunken eyes, arched eyebrows, and an abnormally protruding jaw (Cohen et al., 2005). Abnormalities in the functioning of the heart, autonomic nervous system, and immune system are health problems associated with Rett's disorder. Gradual paralysis of the lower extremities may begin in midadolescence, and seizures may ensue in early adulthood. Behavioral features of Rett's disorder include hand-biting and repetitive hand-wringing or hand-washing motions (Aitken, 2010).

Persons with Rett's disorder may appear to develop normally for the first 6 to 18 months of life, after which they exhibit significant growth regression and other symptoms (Moss & Howlin, 2009). According to Moss and Howlin (2009), up to 18% of Rett's disorder patients first will be identified as having an ASD before receiving the correct diagnosis.

Among those with Rett's disorder, anywhere from 25% to 40% or more might meet criteria for having an ASD; for those whose speech abilities are preserved, as many as 97% might meet criteria for an ASD. However, the social interaction skills of these individuals may be better than what is typically found among persons with ASDs (Moss & Howlin, 2009). In fact, the work group that is responsible for the forthcoming revision of *DSM-IV-TR* has proposed that Rett's disorder should be removed from the *DSM-5*, claiming that ASD symptoms are evident in Rett's disorder patients "for only a brief period during early childhood" (Hebebrand & Buitelaar, 2011, p. 58).

San Filippo syndrome constitutes yet another autosomal recessive condition. There are four different versions of this syndrome, labeled A, B, C, and D, with type A as the most serious form of the condition (PubMed Health, 2009; Trefz, 2010). Each of the four variants is associated with a different gene locus. San Filippo type A involves a gene found at chromosome 17q25.3, and the gene for type B is located at 17q21. Both chromosome 8 and 14 are implicated in type C, and the locus for type D appears at 12q14 (Trefz, 2010). Each of these gene loci is associated with an enzyme that is supposed to degrade long chains of sugar molecules known as mucopolysaccharides (Cohen et al., 2005; Manzi et al., 2008; PubMed Health, 2009).

Symptoms of San Filippo syndrome begin to appear between 2 to 6 years of age; prior to that time, the child's development appears normal (Cohen et al., 2005; Manzi et al., 2008; PubMed Health, 2009). In type A, a mucopolysaccharide called heparan sulphate accumulates in the brain and other bodily tissues of patients with San Filippo syndrome (Caglayan, 2010; PubMed Health, 2009). As a consequence, affected individuals experience stunted growth, an enlarged head, coarse eyebrows and hair, and thicker-than-usual skin, tongue, and gums (Alliance Sanfilippo, n.d.). Associated health concerns may include enlargement of the liver and spleen, chronic ear and nasal infections, blindness, seizures, and bone disorders that cause joint stiffness and progressively hinder physical movement (Alliance Sanfilippo, n.d.; PubMed Health, 2009). Persons with San Filippo syndrome suffer from severe cognitive deficiency and loss of language ability over time (Alliance Sanfilippo, n.d.; PubMed Health, 2009). Behavioral manifestations of this condition include sleep difficulties, hyperactivity, aggressiveness, inappropriate affect, repetitive motions, and social withdrawal (Cohen et al., 2005; Manzi et al., 2008). As many as 1% of ASD patients may have San Filippo syndrome, which is akin to the formal diagnostic category of childhood disintegrative disorder (Cohen et al., 2005).

MOLECULAR STUDIES OF ASD GENETICS

The information presented in the preceding section demonstrates that some cases of ASDs can be linked with genetically caused medical syndromes (Aitken, 2010; Caglayan, 2010; Cohen et al., 2005; Moss & Howlin, 2009). However, even with 80 or more identified genetic syndromes that have been associated with ASDs (Aitken, 2010), these examples still comprise a minority. According to Schiff et al. (2011), "Currently, genetic causes (chromosomal abnormalities or genetic alterations) of ASD can be identified in about 10-20% of cases" (p. e21932). Thus, more than 80% of ASD cases can be classified as nonsyndromic, meaning that they do not present with a recognizable medical condition whose etiology has already been determined (Caglayan, 2010; Schiff et al., 2011). Some authors (e.g., Dissanayake, Bui, Bulhak-Paterson, Huggins, & Loesch, 2009; Freitag, 2007; Roth, 2010) may refer to nonsyndromic conditions as idiopathic ASDs. The term *idiopathic* signifies that the cause of a disorder is unknown (Roth, 2010).

In the quest to identify the genetic causes of ASDs, scientists are searching for answers to the following mysteries: (1) whether human genome sequences associated with ASDs are rare or common within the general population; (2) the number of genes that may be involved, in a single person and/or in the ASD population as a group; (3) whether genetic alterations must take place within only one gene, or whether changes in various genes must occur simultaneously; (4) the degree of risk associated with particular genetic sequences; and (5) whether genetic mutations alone give rise to ASDs, or whether these must somehow interact with environmental factors in order to cause these disorders (El-Fishawy & State, 2010). To learn about these issues, researchers have conducted molecular genetics studies involving several different approaches such as genome screens and linkage analysis (e.g., Duvall et al., 2007; Risch et al., 1999), genome-wide association studies, cytogenetic studies of copy number variation, and candidate gene studies (El-Fishawy & State, 2010).

A 1999 study by Risch et al. provides an example of a genome screen to find genetic loci that contribute to the development of ASDs. Based on the findings of past research, this team of 31 investigators knew from the start that "autism does not follow a simple mode of inheritance" (Risch et al., 1999, p. 494). They began with a sample of 90 multiplex families, including 97 pairs of ASD siblings, 51 unaffected sibling pairs, and their parents. This entire group of participants was dubbed "family set 1 (FS1)" (Risch et al., 1999, p. 495). Risch and colleagues also conducted a second set of analyses on another group of 49 multiplex families; family set 2 (FS2) consisted of 99 siblings with ASDs, 15 unaffected sibs, and their parents.

Blood samples were drawn from all of these participants, and genetic material (i.e., deoxyribonucleic acid, or DNA; Halgin & Whitbourne, 2010) was extracted from their blood cells. Genetic sequences for each participant were derived in two different laboratories, using two different sequencing procedures. These gene sequences were then compared against a set of 362 genetic markers that were previously identified as part of the human genome. After examining the initial data set from FS1, the research team identified another 157 genetic markers, which they added to the initial set for a total of 519 possible markers (Risch et al., 1999). The follow-up analysis located 149 genetic markers in the FS2 gene sequencing data. This study generated over 160,000 genotypes (Risch et al., 1999).

Using a statistical method called linkage analysis, Risch and colleagues (1999) compared ASD sibling pairs to unaffected pairs and found a higher percentage of shared alleles among the ASD pairs. An *allele* is "one of two different variations of a gene" (Halgin & Whitbourne, 2010, p. G-1). The authors of this study determined that possibly 15 or more genetic loci might be responsible for their results. They specifically remarked that their findings contradicted those obtained by Pickles et al. (1995), described earlier in this chapter. Instead, the findings of Risch et al. (1999) "clearly exclude a model with as few as 3 loci and are also inconsistent with a model with as few as 10 loci" (p. 504). Risch and colleagues further determined that genetic loci on chromosome 1p and possibly on chromosome 17p might pertain to ASDs. Despite this, however, they wrote that "our genomic screen results are largely negative, in that we did not identify a chromosomal region with significant linkage evidence" (Risch et al., 1999, p. 505).

Using a different approach called quantitative trait locus analysis, Duvall et al. (2007) sought to identify possible gene loci for ASDs by examining a genome-wide scan in connection with data from the SRS, a questionnaire that was described earlier in this chapter. These authors cited the failure of previous genome screens to identify gene loci for ASDs that were replicated in subsequent research. Therefore, they decided to use the SRS as a quantitative measure of social traits because "as with autism, Social Responsiveness Scale scores are highly heritable" (Duvall et al., 2007, p. 657). In other words, Duvall et al. employed SRS data as an endophenotype for the trait of sociability. According to Gottesman and Gould (2003), *endophenotypes* are "measurable components unseen by the unaided eye along the pathway between disease and distal genotype" that "represent simpler clues to genetic underpinnings than the disease syndrome itself" (p. 636).

Duvall and colleagues (2007) obtained a sample of 99 families for which teacher-reported SRS scores were available. They also had access to phenotype data for these families from a public website. In addition, parents and all children in these families, whether affected by ASDs or not, were genotyped for 408 gene markers. After these data underwent quantitative linkage analysis, Duvall et al. identified two potential genetic loci, one on chromosome 11 and another on chromosome 17. When they repeated the analysis using data from only male participants, chromosomes 11 and 17 once again emerged as possible sites of relevant gene loci. However, three other potential loci also were suggested by the latter analysis; these involved portions of chromosomes 4, 8, and 10. Duvall and associates (2007) concluded that "while highly heritable, the observed phenotype of autism may not be specific enough to the underlying genetic risk, which is multifactorial and heterogeneous" (p. 661). For this reason, they recommended that future studies should use the SRS as a quantitative endophenotype for the trait of sociability, because it might facilitate the identification of ASD gene loci more readily than by using qualitative data, such as might be gathered via the Autism Diagnostic Interview-Revised.

In 2007, Ma and colleagues conducted a genome screen on 26 extended families in which two to four members had ASDs. They found possible sites of interest on chromosomes 1q, 2q, 5q, 6p, 11q, 12q, and 14q. Of these, only chromosome 12q yielded significant results, which appeared to be particularly relevant for males with ASDs.

Another investigation (Kumar et al., 2008) concerned a whole-genome study of 180 persons with ASDs and a control group of 372 participants. Their initial analysis discovered "a recurrent 16p11.2 microdeletion" (Kumar et al., 2008, p. 628) in two of the ASD participants but none of the controls. This research team followed with another screen involving 532 people with ASDs and 465 control participants. They again observed the same microdeletion region containing 25 genes in two ASD participants but in none of the control individuals. However, Kumar and associates (2008) also found that persons with the 16p11.2 deletion could not be distinguished as a separate subtype of ASD on the basis of behavioral features.

Allen-Brady et al. (2009) also conducted a genome screen of seven male members of an extended family to search for ASD-related genes, but identified different chromosomal regions than what had been reported by Ma et al. (2007) and Kumar et al. (2008). In the study by Allen-Brady et al. (2009), the following five regions were suspected of being involved in ASDs: 3q13.2-q13.31, 3q26.31-q27.3, 7p14.1-p11.22, 9p24.3, and 20q11.21-q13.12.

Yet another chromosome region emerged as noteworthy in a genome-wide association study by Wang et al. (2009). Here, a team of 56 researchers collaborated to study 780 families who had children with ASDs, followed by another sample containing over 1200 individuals with ASDs and nearly 6500 control participants. All participants were of European descent, and all were genotyped for more than 550,000 genetic markers. Because these samples did not yield significant results when each sample was analyzed separately, the researchers combined the two data sets and analyzed them as if conducting a meta-analysis. One gene locus, found at 5p14.1, was significant. Wang et al. replicated their findings using two more samples and again "established that common genetic variants on 5p14.1 confer susceptibility to ASDs" (Wang et al., 2009, p. 529). This portion of the human genome contains genes called *CDH9* and *CDH10*, which are implicated in the production of neural cell adhesion molecules. Wang et al. (2009) drew parallels between their genetic findings and the results of neuroimaging and neuroanatomical studies which show that people with ASDs exhibit "cortical underconnectivity" (p. 532). As a result, these scientists concluded that "ASDs may represent a neuronal disconnection syndrome" (Wang et al., 2009, p. 532).

A different approach for studying the genetics of ASDs, involving the identification of chromosomal regions called copy number variations (CNVs), constitutes a "new genetic frontier" for researchers (Copy number variation, 2008, p. 6). This way of examining the genetic causes of psychiatric and developmental disorders has become so popular that one article referred to this "new wave" of genetic research as a "tsunami" (Joober & Boksa, 2009, p. 55).

In traditional genetics studies, scientists look for miniscule changes in gene sequences; these minute changes are called single nucleotide polymorphisms. A SNP involves an alteration in a single nucleotide of a sequence in the human genome. DNA is composed of four building blocks, or nucleotides, called adenine, thymine, guanine, and cytosine. These four nucleotides are the building blocks of the "blueprints for life" (Roth, 2010, p. 148), in much the same way that the 26 letters of the alphabet enable the formation of myriad words. The human genome contains three billion of these building blocks (Overbye, 2011). A SNP occurs when, for example, thymine appears in the place where cytosine should be in the gene code (U.S. Department of Energy, 2008). An example of a SNP that has been connected to ASDs is a variant called rs4307059 which is found at 5p14.1, between genes named *CHD9* and *CHD10*. This SNP has been shown to be related to poor conversational and pragmatic language skills (St. Pourcain et al., 2010).

A widely held assumption is that single nucleotide polymorphisms might explain the risks of inheriting a genetically based disorder. More recently, however, the focus of inquiry has somewhat shifted away from single nucleotide polymorphisms in favor of searching for other kinds of structural changes in genetic material that are known as CNVs; these can be found even in healthy individuals. In some instances the changes are due to the deletion of genetic information. Other kinds of CNVs may involve overduplication of genes, or the insertion of genes into the wrong location within the genome (Copy number variation, 2008). Researchers are hoping to differentiate CNVs that are causally linked with disorders from those that are benign or unimportant (Joober & Boksa, 2009; U.S. Department of Energy, 2008).

According to Cook and Scherer (2008), "Evidence is accumulating that multiple rare *de novo* (and some inherited) CNVs contribute to the genetic component of vulnerability to ASD" (p. 920). Sebat et al. (2007) performed a groundbreaking investigation into this issue. They obtained DNA from 118 youngsters with ASDs and their parents, as well as DNA from 196 neurotypical children and their parents. The researchers examined the genomes of both groups of children to detect CNVs that were not found in their parents, that is, *de novo* CNVs. Sebat et al. (2007) discovered that 10% of the children with ASDs had *de novo* CNVs, while the same could be said for only 1% of the children in the control group. They reported that the affected chromosomal regions contained a variety of single-gene mutations, and concluded, "These findings establish *de novo* germline mutation as a more significant risk factor for ASD than previously recognized" (p. 445).

Several other recent studies have looked at the role of CNVs in the development of ASDs. Two such studies (Marshall et al., 2008; Sykes et al., 2009) have suggested that CNVs in a gene called *SHANK3* may be involved in the etiology of ASDs. The *SHANK3* gene codes for the building of proteins that serve as "molecular scaffolds," allowing cells to build larger complexes of interactive proteins (Sykes et al., 2009, p. 1348). *SHANK3* exerts its effects in the brain within the areas of the hippocampus, cerebellum, and cortex. It can be found at chromosome 22q13.3, and past studies have shown that deletions in this chromosome region are associated with extreme cognitive impairment, severe delays in expressive language, and autism (Sykes et al., 2009).

In addition to implicating *SHANK3* in the development of ASDs, Marshall et al. (2008) also discovered two other genes, *NLGN4* and *NRXN1-PSD*, which appear to be involved in the etiology of ASDs. These authors further noted that CNVs on the maternal X chromosome were being transmitted to male offspring, and posited that this mechanism might help to explain the higher prevalence rate of ASDs among males in comparison to females.

Also in 2008, Christian and associates conducted a copy number variation study of DNA from nearly 400 persons with ASDs. They identified 51 CNVs among 46 ASD participants. Seven of the CNVs were *de novo* mutations and 44 were inherited. In this study, the affected regions of the genome included maternal duplications of 15q11-q13 (discussed earlier in this chapter). Christian et al. (2008) additionally uncovered other duplications as well as microdeletions. They calculated that these CNVs were associated with 272 genes, some of which might be pertinent to the development of ASDs.

A copy number variation study performed by Glessner et al. (2009) had some findings that replicated those of other researchers. By comparing the genomes of almost 860 children with ASDs to those of over 1400 neurotypical children, this research team cited the genes *NRXN1* and *UBEA3* as two genes associated with ASDs. (Both of these genes were mentioned earlier in the chapter.) Additional genes identified in this study included *CNTN4*, *NLGN1*, *ASTN2*, *PARK2*, *RFWD2*, and *FBXO40*; it is possible that errors in any of these genes might increase a person's risk of developing an ASD (Glessner et al., 2009).

Again in 2009, Ozgen et al. examined CNVs in four patients with ASDs, two male and two female, all of whom were found to have abnormalities in the microcephalin 1 gene (*MCPH1*). This gene is located at 8p23.1 and "is expressed in the developing cerebral cortex of the foetal brain where it serves as a specific regulator of brain size" (Ozgen et al., 2009, p. 354). However, these authors noted that in some instances the *MCPH1* gene may be linked with ASDs even in the absence of any obvious effect on brain size.

As illustrated by the studies described above, one of the goals of copy number variation studies is to identify so-called candidate genes for ASDs. A *candidate gene* is a gene that is believed to be involved in the development of a disease (U.S. Department of Energy Office of Science, 2010). Several of these, such as *MECP2* (Lintas & Persico, 2009; Loat et al., 2008; Tabares-Seisdedos & Rubenstein, 2009) and *SHANK3* (Lintas & Persico, 2009; Moessner et al., 2007) have already been discussed. However, many other ASD susceptibility genes have been suggested. These include: *TRIP8* and *REEP3*, found at 10q21.3 (Castermans et al., 2007); the G22A variant of the *ADA* gene, found at 20q13.1 (Hettinger, Liu, & Holden, 2008); *CSMD3*, located at 8q23 (Floris et al., 2008); *MET*, found at 7q31.2 (Campbell et al., 2009; Sousa et al., 2009); and *DLX1* and *DLX2*, located at 2q32 (Liu et al., 2009).

A newly identified candidate gene called retinoic acid-related orphan receptor-alpha (*RORA*), located on chromosome 15, may be helpful in furthering knowledge about the gender disparities that are observed in relation to ASDs (Sarachana, Xu, Wu, & Hu, 2011). Among individuals with ASDs, the ratio of males to females is roughly 4 to 1; however, the reason for this gender difference is unknown. Sarachana et al. (2011) demonstrated that the expression of the *RORA* gene is regulated by the sex hormones testosterone and estrogen in opposing directions. Testosterone tends to suppress *RORA*'s expression, thereby leading to reduced levels of *RORA* protein in the brain. Sarachana et al (2011) believe that a reduction of *RORA* protein in the human brain has effects that may be similar to what has been observed in a strain of mice called staggerer mice. These mice, whose brains have *RORA* protein deficiencies, engage in activities that resemble ASD symptoms in humans, such as repetitive behaviors, fixations on objects, and impaired spatial learning. The authors of this study pointed out that not everyone with an ASD will have low brain levels of *RORA* protein, and they also mentioned that low levels of *RORA* protein have been found in both males and females with ASDs. However, they noted that higher levels of estrogen in females may confer protection against the development of ASDs by allowing greater expression of the *RORA* gene.

THEORIES OF AUTISM TRANSMISSION

Information shared in the preceding section illustrates that ASDs may derive from a variety of genetic factors, some of which may be affected by interactions with features of the environment. In an effort to organize so many pieces of seemingly disparate information, members of the scientific community have proposed several theories that might explain the genetics of ASDs.

One theory that has been considered in relation to ASDs is the so-called "common disease-common variant (CDCV) hypothesis" (El-Fishawy & State, 2010). A common disease is defined as a condition that affects at least 1% of the population. This theory begins with the supposition that the entire world population originated from an ancestral group in Africa comprised of approximately 10,000 individuals. The original population could not have survived and expanded, had their genomes contained a large number of pathogenic genes. Therefore, if a disease was common in the original ancestral population, then its genes would have been common among them. By the same token, genes for rare diseases would have been infrequent in the genetic endowments of this original group. As this founding population expanded, genes for both common and rare diseases would become more widespread throughout the group; however, genes for rare diseases would not be as widespread in the general population as genes for more common disorders (El-Fishawy & State, 2010).

Another aspect of the CDCV hypothesis concerns the fact that new mutations occur in the genome, thereby diluting out both common and rare disease alleles. The rate of increase for these mutations is much slower than the proliferation of disease alleles that took place with the rapid burst of growth in the size of the initial ancestral population. Therefore, scientists expected that most complex disease conditions could be explained on the basis of commonly occurring alleles (El-Fishawy & State, 2010).

However, questions have arisen concerning the ability of the CDCV hypothesis to explain the genetics of ASDs. For one thing, this theory assumes that the entire world population began in Africa. If this assumption is inaccurate, then the explanation deriving from it about the way that disease genes spread throughout the human population also would change significantly. Of greater importance, the CDCV hypothesis assumes that common diseases in the ancestral population did not adversely impact reproductive fitness; if those diseases had a negative effect on reproductive ability, then the number of disease alleles eventually would lessen in the population as a whole. However, impaired social communication is a feature of ASDs that might decrease the likelihood that affected individuals would reproduce, which would result in lowering the number of ASD genes in a general population. For these reasons, the CDCV hypothesis may not be the best theory to explain the transmission of ASD genes. Instead, it may be the case that a large number of rare genes are responsible for ASDs (El-Fishawy & State, 2010). "ASD might well reflect a collection of rare disorders resulting from hundreds of different genetic defects but leading to a shared phenotype, similar to the case of mental retardation" (El-Fishawy & State, 2010, p. 88).

Other authors have offered alternative theories about the genetic transmission of ASDs. According to Levitt and Campbell (2009), ASDs arise from two different genetic mechanisms. In some cases, they are caused by a rare mutation in a single gene; in others, they are the result of "inherited, common functional variants of a combination of genes, each having a small to moderate effect in increasing ASD risk" (Levitt & Campbell, 2009, p. 747).

Zhao et al. (2007) also proposed that ASDs are caused by two different mechanisms. They believe that *de novo* mutations account for ASDs in simplex families; these constitute most cases of ASDs. However, according to these authors, it appears that ASDs are inherited in multiplex families. When more than one member of a family has an ASD, Zhao et al. (2007) suspect that the mother may have a new mutation which does not affect her but is transmitted to her offspring, such that approximately 50% of her male children will have an ASD. However, Zhao and associates stipulated that they could not exclude prenatal environmental factors (e.g., parental age, or complications during pregnancy) as contributors to the development of ASDs, nor could they eliminate the possibility of other, more complex modes of inheritance. These researchers further noted that as yet unidentified modifier genes might affect the symptoms that are present in a person with ASD, as well as the severity of the condition (Zhao et al., 2007).

IMPLICATIONS FOR GENETIC COUNSELING

Based on the research described in this chapter, it is abundantly clear that "there is not a single gene or genetic test that definitely diagnoses autism" (El-Fishawy & State, 2010, p. 97). Despite this current reality, genetic testing sometimes might serve as an aid to diagnosis. In addition, it may be important for family planning purposes (El-Fishawy & State, 2010).

Genetic screening for ASDs may not be appropriate or necessary for all families who have a member with ASD. A referral for genetic screening is warranted when a person's clinical presentation or family history indicates reason for concern. Examples of warning signs that would suggest a need for genetic screening include significant intellectual impairment in a person, or a family history or such impairment, as well as the presence of abnormal physical characteristics (El-Fishawy & State, 2010).

Lintas and Persico (2009) pointed out that "the genetic or genomic anomalies responsible for ASD are not detectable using current prenatal screening methods" (p. 5). They offered guidelines to genetic counselors working with families of children with ASDs. First, parents should be informed that if their child has a nonsyndromic form of ASD, then there is a 5% to 6% probability that a second child also will have an ASD (Lintas & Persico, 2009). In families that already have two children with ASDs, the recurrence risk increases above 8% and may go as high as 25%. Parents should be made aware of these risks so that they can consider them in regard to future family planning (Johnson, Myers, & The Council on Children with Disabilities, 2007).

Next, a *karyotype* should be obtained for the affected person (Lintas & Persico, 2009); this is a photograph showing all of the individual's chromosomes, arranged in numerical order. By inspecting a karyotype, a geneticist can look for chromosomal abnormalities that are known to be associated with syndromic medical conditions (U.S. Department of Energy Office of Science, 2007).

Even if a karyotype appears normal, however, chromosomal rearrangements still might have occurred, especially among patients with neurological symptoms and unusual physical characteristics. For these patients, it might be advisable to conduct testing with the use of either the bacterial artificial chromosome technique or comparative genome hybridization; these tests help to identify genetic deletions or duplications that are associated with abnormal physical features (Lintas & Persico, 2009).

Other tests also may be helpful. For example, testing for fragile X syndrome is routinely recommended for individuals who appear to have a nonsyndromic ASD (Lintas & Persico, 2009; Schaefer & Mendelsohn, 2008; Volker & Lopata, 2008). Specific testing for the *SHANK3* gene might be useful in cases where the affected person has extreme deficits in language and social abilities. Testing for the *MECP2* gene should be required for all girls who are comorbid for an ASD and intellectual disability, to check for the possible presence of Rett's disorder (Lintas & Persico, 2009). Volker and Lopata (2008) recommended screening for 15q11-q13 duplications and 22q13 deletions in cases of ASD that are accompanied by moderate to severe cognitive impairment. Also, Schaefer and Mendelsohn (2008) indicated that screening for anomalies in a gene known as *PTEN* should be conducted in cases of nonsyndromic ASDs in which the affected individual has a head circumference that is significantly larger than average.

Jordan and Tsai (2010) raised ethical concerns about the widespread use of commercialized genetic testing for ASDs. These authors believe that certain conditions must be met in order for genetic testing to be useful. First, replicable and scientifically validated evidence must establish a definite connection between a gene and a disorder. Second, there must be reason to believe that the gene in question will have a significant effect on the affected person. Third, the results of genetic testing should have some clinical usefulness, in terms of either selecting an appropriate treatment to improve outcome, or modifying one's lifestyle and goals in light of the information obtained from the test. Because ASDs may be the product of multiple genes, it is possible that either false positive or false negative results could complicate the use of commercialized genetic tests for these conditions (Jordan & Tsai, 2010).

CONCLUDING REMARKS

With the advent of new technologies and methods, there has been considerable progress in the past decade regarding knowledge about the genetic causes of ASDs. However, a fully developed understanding about the genetic factors that contribute to these conditions is still a long way off, and the genetic discoveries that have been made thus far have raised additional questions. For example, do genetic factors for ASDs influence the development of these conditions solely on the basis of gene sequences, or do epigenetic factors also play a role? According to Rutter (2011),"epigenetics refers to neuro-chemical changes that influence gene expression" (p. 400). These kinds of factors appear to affect gene expression in ways that are specific to both tissue type and phase of development, but at this time the role of epigenetics in the etiology of ASDs is unclear and requires further study (Rutter, 2011).

A limitation in the study of ASD genetics which needs to be remedied is the routine exclusion of African American families from ASD genetic research. Hilton et al. (2010) used data from the Centers for Disease Control regarding attempts to recruit and enroll African American children with ASDs and their relatives in genetic research investigations. They discovered that 67% of all families who were willing to participate were not included in ASD genetic research studies on the basis of their family structure. If one or both parents were unavailable to the scientific team, or if the youngster with an ASD had no siblings or no full siblings, then researchers often decided not to enroll such a family in a genetic study. Hilton et al. (2010) acknowledged that ASD genetics studies are somewhat easier to perform and interpret in situations when all parents and siblings in a family are available. However, they also pointed out that technological advancements and newer research methods have now made it possible to study ASD susceptibility genes even in situations where siblings and both parents are unavailable. Therefore, they urged future investigators to aim for better representation of racial and ethnic minority group members in ASD genetic research.

Volkmar, State, and Klin (2009) cited another limitation of current research into ASD genetics, namely, the finding that a mutation may be outwardly expressed in a variety of ways. For example, "a single mutation in a germ line may increase the risk for autism, mental retardation without social disability, Asperger's syndrome or [pervasive developmental disorder not otherwise specified]" (Volkmar et al., 2009, p. 110). Similar to Rutter (2011), these authors spoke about the need to consider not only genetic factors, but also how these may interact with nongenetic influences, and how these interactions may differ depending on an affected person's stage of development.

When considering the present state of knowledge concerning the genetics of ASDs, the popular representation of ASD awareness as a collection of jigsaw puzzle pieces (Autism Society, n.d.) seems particularly appropriate. Scientists are beginning to fit the puzzle pieces together, but it will take considerably more time and effort before the complete picture of ASD genetics emerges.

REFERENCES

Abrahams, B. S., & Geschwind, D. H. (2008). Advances in autism genetics: On the threshold of a new neurobiology. *Nature Reviews: Genetics*, *9*(5), 341-355. Retrieved from http://web.ebscohost.com

Achenbach, T. M., & Rescorla, L. A. (2000). *Manual for the ASEBA preschool forms and profiles*. Burlington, VT: University of Vermont Research Center for Children, Youth, & Families.

Aitken, K. J. (2010). *An A-Z of genetic factors in autism: A handbook for parents and carers*. Philadelphia, PA: Jessica Kingsley.

Allen-Brady, K., Miller, J., Matsunami, N., Stevens, J., Block, H., Farley, M., … Coon, H. (2009). A high-density SNP genome-wide linkage scan in a large autism extended pedigree. *Molecular Psychiatry, 14*, 590-600. doi:10.1038/mp.2008.14

Alliance Sanfilippo. (n.d.). *Sanfilippo syndrome: What are the symptoms?* Retrieved from http://www.sanfilippo-syndrome.org

American Psychiatric Association. (2000). *Diagnostic and statistical manual of mental disorders* (4th ed., text rev.). Arlington, VA: Author.

Autism Society. (n.d.) *National autism awareness month*. Retrieved from http://www.autism-society.org/about-us/national-autism-awareness-month/

Bailey, A., Le Couteur, A., Gottesman, I., Bolton, P., Simonoff, E., Yuzda, E., & Rutter, M. (1995). Autism as a strongly genetic disorder: Evidence from a British twin study. *Psychological Medicine, 25*(1), 63-77. doi:10.1017/S0033291700028099

Baron-Cohen, S., Wheelwright, S., Skinner, R., Martin, J., & Clubley, E. (2001). The Autism-spectrum Quotient (AQ): Evidence from Asperger syndrome/high-functioning autism, males and females, scientists and mathematicians. *Journal of Autism and Developmental Disorders, 31*(1), 5-17. doi:10.1023/A:1005653411471

Bayley, N. (1993). *Bayley scales of infant development* (2nd ed.). San Antonio, TX: The Psychological Corporation.

Bohm, H. V., & Stewart, M. G. (2009). Brief report: On the concordance percentages for autism spectrum disorder of twins. *Journal of Autism and Developmental Disorders, 39*(5), 806-808. doi:10.1007/s10803-008-0683-2

Bolton, P., Macdonald, H., Pickles, A., Rios, P., Goode, S., Crowson, M., … Rutter, M. (1994). A case-control family history study of autism. *Journal of Child Psychology and Psychiatry, 35*(5), 877-900. doi:10.1111/j.1469-7610.1994.tb02300.x

Bumiller, K. (2009). The geneticization of autism: From new reproductive technologies to the conception of genetic normalcy. *Signs: Journal of Women in Culture and Society, 34*(4), 875-899. doi:10.1086/597130

Caglayan, A. O. (2010). Genetic causes of syndromic and non-syndromic autism. *Developmental Medicine & Child Neurology*, 52(2), 130-138. doi:10.1111/j.1469-8749.2009.03523.x

Campbell, D. B., Buie, T. M., Winter, H., Bauman, M., Sutcliffe, J. S., Perrin, J. M., & Levitt, P. (2009). Distinct genetic risk based on association of MET in families with co-occurring autism and gastrointestinal conditions. *Pediatrics, 123*, 1018-1024. doi:10.1542/peds.2008-0819

Castermans, D., Vermeesch, J. R., Fryns, J.P., Steyaert, J. G., Van de Ven, W. J. M., Creemers, J. W. M., & Devriendt, K. (2007). Identification and characterization of the TRIP8 and REEP3 genes on chromosome 10q21.3 as novel candidate genes for autism. *European Journal of Human Genetics, 15*, 422-431. doi:10.1038/sj.ejhg.5201785

Christian, S. L., Brune, C. W., Sudi, J., Kumar, R. A., Liu, S., Karamohamed, S., ... Cook, E. H., Jr. (2008). Novel submicroscopic chromosomal abnormalities detected in autism spectrum disorder. *Biological Psychiatry, 63*, 1111-1117. doi:10.1016/j.biopsych.2008.01.009

Cook, E. H., Jr., & Scherer, S. W. (2008). Copy-number variations associated with neuropsychiatric conditions. *Nature, 455*(7215), 919-923. doi:10.1038/nature07458

Cohen, D., Pichard, N., Tordjman, S., Baumann, C., Burglen, L., Excoffier, E., ... Heron, D. (2005). Specific genetic disorders and autism: Clinical contribution towards their identification. *Journal of Autism and Developmental Disorders, 35*(1), 103-116. doi:10.1007/s10803-004-1038-2

Conners, C. K., Sitarenios, G., Parker, J. D., & Epstein, J. N. (1998). The revised Conners' Parent Rating Scale (CPRS-R): Factor structure, reliability, and criterion validity. *Journal of Abnormal Child Psychology, 26*(4), 257-268. doi:10.1023/A:1022602400621

Constantino, J. N., & Gruber, C. P. (2005). *The Social Responsiveness Scale manual.* Torrance, CA: Western Psychological Services.

Copy number variation: The new genetic frontier. (2008). *Harvard Mental Health Letter, 25*(4), 6-7. Retrieved from http://web.ebscohost.com

Deisinger, J. A. (2011). History of autism spectrum disorders. In A. F. Rotatori, F. E. Obiakor, & J. P. Bakken (Eds.), *History of special education* (pp. 237-267). Bingley, UK: Emerald.

DeLong, G. R., & Dwyer, J. T. (1988). Correlation of family history with specific autistic subgroups: Asperger's syndrome and bipolar affective disease. *Journal of Autism and Developmental Disorders, 18*(4), 593-600. doi:10.1007/BF02211877

Dissanayake, C., Bui, Q., Bulhak-Paterson, D., Huggins, R., & Loesch, D. Z. (2009). Behavioural and cognitive phenotypes in idiopathic autism versus autism associated with fragile X syndrome. *Journal of Child Psychology and Psychiatry, 50*(3), 290-299. doi:10.1111/j.1469-7610.2008.01988.x

Duvall, J. A., Lu, A., Cantor, R. M., Todd, R. D., Constantino, J. N., & Geschwind, D. H. (2007). A quantitative trait locus analysis of social responsiveness in multiplex autism families. *American Journal of Psychiatry, 164*(4), 656-662. doi:10.1176/appi.ajp.164.4.656

Dworzynski, K., Happé, F., Bolton, P., & Ronald, A. (2009). Relationship between symptom domains in autism spectrum disorders: A population based twin study. *Journal of Autism and Developmental Disorders, 39*(8), 1197-1210. doi:10.1007/s10803-009-0736-1

El-Fishawy, P., & State, M. W. (2010). The genetics of autism: Key issues, recent findings, and clinical implications. *Psychiatric Clinics of North America, 33*, 83-105. doi:10.1016/j.psc.2009.12.002

Edelson, L. R., & Saudino, K. J. (2009). Genetic and environmental influences on autistic-like behaviors in 2-year-old twins. *Behavior Genetics, 39*, 255-264. doi:10.1007/s10519-009-9270-3

Floris, C., Rassu, S., Boccone, L., Gasperini, D., Cao, A., & Crisponi, L. (2008). Two patients with balanced translocations and autistic disorder: CSMD3 as a candidate gene for autism found in their common 8q23 breakpoint area. *European Journal of Human Genetics, 16*, 696-704. doi:10.1038/ejhg.2008.7

Folstein, S., & Rutter, M. (1977a). Genetic influences and infantile autism. *Nature, 265*(5596), 726-728. doi:10.1038/265726a0

Folstein, S., & Rutter, M. (1977b). Infantile autism: A genetic study of 21 twin pairs. *Journal of Child Psychology and Psychiatry, 18*(4), 297-321. doi:10.1111/j.1469-7610.1977.tb00443.x

Freitag, C. M. (2007). The genetics of autistic disorders and its clinical relevance: A review of the literature. *Molecular Psychiatry, 12*, 2-22. doi:10.1038/sj.mp.4001896

Glessner, J. T., Wang, K., Cai, G., Korvatska, O., Kim, C. E., Wood, S., … Hakonarson, H. (2009). Autism genome-wide copy number variation reveals ubiquitin and neuronal genes. *Nature, 459*, 569-573. doi:10.1038/nature07953

Goodman, R. (2001). Psychometric properties of the Strengths and Difficulties Questionnaire. *Journal of the American Academy of Child and Adolescent Psychiatry, 40*(11), 1337-1345. doi:10.1097/00004583-200111000-00015

Goodman, R., Ford, T., Richards, H., Gatward, R., & Meltzer, H. (2000). The development and well-being assessment: Description and initial validation of an integrated assessment of child and adolescent psychopthology. *Journal of Child Psychology and Psychiatry and Allied Disciplines, 41*, 645-655. doi:10.1111/j.1469-7610.2000.tb02345.x

Gottesman, I. I., & Gould, T. D. (2003). The endophenotype concept in psychiatry: Etymology and strategic intentions. *American Journal of Psychiatry, 160*(4), 636-645. Retrieved from http://ajp.psychiatryonline.org/cgi/content/full/160/4/636

Halgin, R. P., & Whitbourne, S. K. (2010). *Abnormal psychology: Clinical perspectives on psychological disorders* (6th ed.). New York, NY: McGraw-Hill.

Hallmayer, J., Cleveland, S., Torres, A., Phillips, J., Cohen, B., Torigoe, T., …Risch, N. (2011,July 4). Genetic heritability and shared environment factors among twin pairs with autism. *Archives of General Psychiatry*, Online First, E1-E8. doi:10.1001/archgenpsychiatry.2011.76

Hanson, D. R., & Gottesman, I. I. (1976). The genetics, if any, of infantile autism and childhood schizophrenia. *Journal of Autism and Developmental Disorders, 6*(3), 209-234. doi:10.1007/BF01543463

Hebebrand, J., & Buitelaar, J. K. (2011). On the way to DSM-V. *European Child and Adolescent Psychiatry, 20*(2), 57-60. doi:10.1007/s00787-010-0157-x

Hettinger, J. A., Liu, X., & Holden, J. J. A. (2008). The G22A polymorphism of the ADA gene and susceptibility to autism spectrum disorders. *Journal of Autism and Developmental Disorders, 38*, 14-19. doi:10.1007/s10803-006-0354-0

Hilton, C. L., Fitzgerald, R. T., Jackson, K. M., Maxim, R. A., Bosworth, C. C., Shattuck, P. T., … Constantino, J. N. (2010). Brief report: Under-representation of African-Americans in autism genetic research: A rationale for inclusion of subjects representing diverse family structures. *Journal of Autism and Developmental Disorders, 40*(5), 633-639. doi:10.1007/s10803-009-0905-2

Hoekstra, R. A., Bartels, M., Hudziak, J. J., Van Beijsterveldt, T. C. E. M., & Boomsma, D. I. (2007a). Genetic and environmental covariation between autistic traits and behavioral problems. *Twin Research and Human Genetics, 10*(6), 853-860. doi:10.1375/twin.10.6.853

Hoekstra, R. A., Bartels, M., Verweij, C. J. H., & Boomsma, D. J. (2007b). Heritability of autistic traits in the general population. *Archives of Pediatric and Adolescent Medicine, 161*(4), 372-377. doi:10.1001/archpedi.161.4.372

Hopper, J. L., Bishop, D. T., & Easton, D. F. (2005). Genetic epidemiology 6: Population-based family studies in genetic epidemiology. *Lancet, 366*(9494), 1397-1406. doi:10.1016/S0140-6736(05)67570-8

Johnson, C. P., Myers, S. M., & Council on Children with Disabilities. (2007). Identification and evaluation of children with autism spectrum disorders. *Pediatrics, 120*(5), 1183-1215. doi:10.1542/peds.2007-2361

Joober, R., & Boksa, P. (2009). A new wave in the genetics of psychiatric disorders: The copy number variant tsunami. *Journal of Psychiatry & Neuroscience, 34*(1), 55-59. Retrieved from http://web.ebscohost.com

Jordan, B. R., & Tsai, D. F. C. (2010). Whole-genome association studies for multigenic diseases: Ethical dilemmas arising from commercialization—The case of genetic testing for autism. *Journal of Medical Ethics, 36*, 440-444. doi:10.1136/jme.2009.031385

Kumar, R. A., Karamohamed, S., Sudi, J., Conrad, D. F., Brune, C., Badner, J. A., … Christian, S. L. (2008). Recurrent 16p11.2 microdeletions in autism. *Human Molecular Genetics, 17*(4), 628-638. doi:10.1093/hmg/ddm376

Laje, G., Morse, R., Richter, W., Ball, J., Pao, M., & Smith, A. C. (2010). Autism spectrum features in Smith-Magenis syndrome. *American Journal of Medical Genetics, Part C: Seminars in Medical Genetics, 154C*(4), 456-462. doi:10.1002/ajmg.c.30275

Le Couteur, A., Rutter, M., Lord, C., Rios, P., Robertson, S., Hodlgrafer, M., & McLennan, J. (1989). Autism Diagnostic Interview: A standardized investigator-based instrument. *Journal of Autism and Developmental Disorders, 19*(3), 363-387. doi:10.1007/BF02212936

Levitt, P., & Campbell, D. B. (2009). The genetic and neurobiologic compass points toward common signaling dysfunctions in autism spectrum disorders. *The Journal of Clinical Investigation, 119*(4), 747-754. doi:10.1172/JCI37934

Lintas, C., & Persico, A. M. (2009). Autistic phenotypes and genetic testing: State-of-the-art for the clinical geneticist. *Journal of Medical Genetics, 46*(1), 1-8. doi:10.1136/jmg.2008.060871

Liu, X., Novosedlik, N., Wang, A., Hudson, M. L., Cohen, I. L., Chudley, A., E., … Holden, J. J. A. (2009). The DLX1 and DLX2 genes and susceptibility to autism spectrum disorders. *European Journal of Human Genetics, 17*, 228-235. doi:10.1038/ejhg.2008.148

Loat, C. S., Curran, S., Lewis, C. M., Duvall, J., Geschwind, D., Bolton, P., & Craig, I. W. (2008). Methyl-CpG-binding protein 2 polymorphisms and vulnerability to autism. *Genes, Brain and Behavior, 7*, 754-760. doi:10.1111/j.1601-183X.2008.00414.x

Lord, C., Risi, S., Lamprecht, L., Cook, E. H., Jr., Leventhal, B. L. DiLavore, P. C., … Rutter, M. (2000). The Autism Diagnostic Observation Schedule-Generic:

A standard measure of social and communication deficits associated with the spectrum of autism. *Journal of Autism and Developmental Disorders, 30*(3), 205-223. doi:10.1023/A:1005592401947

Lord, C., Rutter, M., & Le Couteur, A. (1994). Autism Diagnostic Interview-Revised: A revised version of a diagnostic interview for caregivers of individuals with possible pervasive developmental disorders. *Journal of Autism and Developmental Disorders, 24*(5), 659-685. doi:10.1007/BF02172145

Ma, D. Q., Cuccaro, M. L., Jaworski, J. M., Haynes, C. S., Stephan, D. A., Parod, J., ... Pericak-Vance, M. A. (2007). Dissecting the locus heterogeneity of autism: Significant linkage to chromosome 12q14. *Molecular Psychiatry, 12*, 376-384. doi:10.1038/sj.mp.4001927

MacLean, J. E., Szatmari, P., Jones, M. B., Bryson, S. E., Mahoney, W., Bartolucci, G., & Tuff, L. (1999). Familial factors influence level of functioning in pervasive developmental disorder. *Journal of the Academy of Child and Adolescent Psychiatry, 38*(6), 746-753. Retrieved from http://sxu.illiad.oclc.org.ezp.sxu.edu

Manzi, B., Loizzo, A. L., Giana, G., & Curatolo, P. (2008). Autism and metabolic diseases. *Journal of Child Neurology, 23*(3), 307-314. doi:10.1177/0883073807308698

Marshall, C. R., Noor, A., Vincent, J. B., Lionel, A. C., Feuk, L., Skaug, J., ... Scherer, S. W. (2008). Structural variation of chromosomes in autism spectrum disorder. *American Journal of Human Genetics, 82*, 477-488. doi:10.1016/j.ajhg.2007.12.009

Merriam-Webster. (2011). *Heritability*. Retrieved from http://www.m-w.com

Moessner, R., Marshall, C. R., Sutcliffe, J. S., Skaug, J., Pinto, D., Vincent, J., ... Scherer, S. W. (2007). Contribution of SHANK3 mutations to autism spectrum disorders. *American Journal of Human Genetics, 81*, 1289-1297. doi:10.1086/522590

Molloy, C. A., Murray, D. S., Kinsman, A., Castillo, H., Mitchell, T., Hickey, F. J., & Patterson, B. (2009). Differences in the clinical presentation of trisomy 21 with and without autism. *Journal of Intellectual Disability Research, 53*(2), 143-151. doi:10.1111/j.1365-2788.2008.01138.x

Moss. J., & Howlin, P. (2009). Autism spectrum disorders in genetic syndromes: Implications for diagnosis, intervention and understanding the wider autism spectrum disorder population. *Journal of Intellectual Disability Research, 53*(10), 852-873. doi:10.1111/j.1365-2788.2009.01197.x

Overbye, D. (2011, July 27). 'It's alive! It's alive!' Maybe right here on Earth. *The New York Times*. Retrieved from http://www.nytimes.com/2011/07/28/science/28life.html?_r=1&emc=eta1

Ozgen, H. M., van Daalen, E., Bolton, P. F., Maloney, V. K., Huang, S., Cresswell, L., ... Poot, M. (2009). Copy number changes of the microcephalin 1 gene (MCPH1) in patients with autism spectrum disorders. *Clinical Genetics, 76*, 348-356. doi:10.1111/j.1399-0004.2009.01254.x

Pickles, A., Bolton, P., Macdonald, H., Bailey, A., Le Couteur, A., Sim, C. -H., & Rutter, M. (1995). Latent-class analysis of recurrence risks for complex phenotypes with selection and measurement error: A twin and family history study of autism. *American Journal of Human Genetics, 57*(3), 717-726. Retrieved from http://www.ncbi.nlm.nih.gov/pmc/articles/PMC1801262/pdf/ajhg00035-0200.pdf

PubMed Health. (2009, May 11). *Sanfilippo syndrome*. Retrieved from http://www.ncbi.nlm.nih.gov/pubmedhealth/PMH0002190/

Risch, N., Spiker, D., Lotspeich, L., Nassim, N., Hinds, D., Hallmayer, J., ... Myers, R. M. (1999). A genomic screen of autism: Evidence for a multilocus etiology. *American Journal of Human Genetics, 65*, 493-507. doi:10.1086/302497

Ritvo, E. R., Freeman, B. J., Mason-Brothers, A., Mo, A., & Ritvo, A. M. (1985). Concordance for the syndrome of autism in 40 pairs of afflicted twins. *American Journal of Psychiatry, 142*, 74-77. Retrieved from http://ajp.psychiatryonline.org/cgi/content/abstract/142/1/74

Ronald, A., Simonoff, E., Kuntsi, J., Asherson, P., & Plomin, R. (2008). Evidence for overlapping genetic influences on autistic and ADHD behaviours in a community twin sample. *Journal of Child Psychology and Psychiatry, 49*(5), 535-542. doi:10.1111/j.1469-7610.2007.01857.x

Roth, I. (2010). *The autism spectrum in the 21st century: Exploring psychology, biology, and practice*. Philadelphia, PA: Jessica Kingsley.

Rutter, M. (2000). Genetic studies of autism: From the 1970s into the millennium. *Journal of Abnormal Child Psychology, 28*(1), 3-14. doi:10.1023/A:1005113900068

Rutter, M. (2005). Genetic influences and autism. In F. R. Volkmar, R. Paul, A. Klin, & D. Cohen (Eds.), *Handbook of autism and pervasive developmental disorders* (3rd ed., Vol. 1, pp. 453-472). Hoboken, NJ: Wiley.

Rutter, M. L. (2011). Progress in understanding autism: 2007-2010. *Journal of Autism and Developmental Disorders, 41*(4), 395-404. doi:10.1007/s10803-011-1184-2

Sarachana, T., Xu, M., Wu, R.C., & Hu, V. W. (2011, February 16). Sex hormones in autism: Androgens and estrogens differentially and reciprocally regulate RORA, a novel candidate gene for autism. *PLoS ONE, 6*(2), e17116. doi:10.1371/journal.pone.0017116

Schaefer, G. B., & Mendelsohn, N. J. (2008). Genetics evaluation for the etiologic diagnosis of autism spectrum disorders. *Genetics in Medicine, 10*(1), 4-12. doi:10.1097/GIM.0b013e31815efdd7

Schiff, M., Benoist, J. -F., Aissaoui, S., Boepsflug-Tanguy, O., Mouren, M.-C., de Baulny, H. O., & Delorme, R. (2011). Should metabolic diseases be systematically screened in nonsyndromic autism spectrum disorders? *PLoS ONE, 6*(7), e21932. doi:10.1371/journal.pone.0021932

Scott, F. J., Baron-Cohen, S., Bolton, P., & Brayne, C. (2002). The CAST (Childhood Asperger Syndrome Test): Preliminary development of a UK screen for mainstream primary-school-age children. *Autism, 6*(1), 9-31. doi:10.1177/1362361302006001003

Sebat, J., Lakshmi, B., Malhotra, D., Troge, J., Lese-Martin, C. Walsh, T., ... Wigler, M. (2007). Strong association of de novo copy number mutations in autism. *Science, 316*(5823), 445-449. doi:10.1126/science.1138659

Smith, C. J., Lang, C. M., Kryzak, L., Reichenberg, A., Hollander, E., & Silverman, J. M. (2009). Familial associations of intense preoccupations, an empirical factor of the restricted, repetitive behaviors and interests domain of autism.

Journal of Child Psychology and Psychiatry, 50(8), 982-990. doi:10.1111/j.1469-7610.2009.02060.x

Sousa, I., Clark, T. G., Toma, C., Kobayashi, K., Choma, M., Holt, R., ... International Molecular Genetic Study of Autism Consortium. (2009). MET and autism susceptibility: Family and case-control studies. *European Journal of Human Genetics, 17*, 749-758. doi:10.1038/ejhg.2008.215

Spiker, D., Lotspeich, L., Kraemer, H. C., Hallmayer, J., McMahon, W., Petersen, P. B., ... Ciaranello, R. D. (1994). Genetics of autism: Characteristics of affected and unaffected children from 37 multiplex families. *American Journal of Medical Genetics, 54*, 27-35. Retrieved from http://sxu.illiad.oclc.org.ezp.sxu.edu

Steffenburg, S., Gillberg, C., Hellgren, L., Andersson, L., Gillberg. I. C., Jakobsson, G., & Bohman, M. (1989). A twin study of autism in Denmark, Finland, Iceland, Norway, and Sweden. *Journal of Child Psychology and Psychiatry, 30*(3), 405-416. doi:10.1111/j.1469-7610.1989.tb00254.x

St. Pourcain, B., Wang, K., Glessner, J. T., Golding, J., Steer, C., Ring, S. M., ... Smith, G. D. (2010). Association between a high-risk autism locus on 5p14 and social communication spectrum phenotypes in the general population. *American Journal of Psychiatry, 167*(11), 1364-1372. doi:10.1176/appi.ajp.2010.09121789

Sykes, N. H., Toma, C., Wilson, N., Volpi, E. V., Sousa, I., Pagnamenta, A. T., ... International Molecular Genetic Study of Autism Consortium. (2009). Copy number variation and association analysis of SHANK3 as a candidate gene for autism in the IMGSAC collection. *European Journal of Human Genetics, 17*, 1347-1353. doi:10.1038/ejhg.2009.47

Tabares-Seisdedos, R., & Rubenstein, J. L. R. (2009). Chromosome 8p as a potential hub for developmental neuropsychiatric disorders: Implications for schizophrenia, autism, and cancer. *Molecular Psychiatry, 14*, 563-589. doi:10.1038/mp.2009.2

Trefz, F. (2010, Oct. 17). *Mucopolysaccharidosis III, San Filippo syndrome*. Retrieved from http://www.metagene.de

Tyrer, P. (1988). Personality Assessment Schedule. In P. Tyrer (Ed.), *Personality disorders: Diagnosis, management, and course* (pp. 43-62). Kent, England: Wright/Butterworth Scientific.

U.S. Department of Energy Office of Science. (2007). Karyotype. *Human Genome Project information: Genome glossary.* Retrieved from http://www.ornl.gov/sci/techresources/Human_Genome/glossary/glossary_k.shtml

U.S. Department of Energy Office of Science. (2008). *Human Genome Project information: SNP fact sheet*. Retrieved from http://www.ornl.gov/sci/techresources/Human_Genome/faq/snps.shtml

U.S. Department of Energy Office of Science. (2010). Candidate gene. *Human Genome Project information: Genome glossary.* Retrieved from http://www.ornl.gov/sci/techresources/Human_Genome/glossary/glossary_c.shtml

Verhulst, F. C., Van der Ende, J., & Koot, H. M. (1997). *Handleiding voor de Youth Self Report (YSR)* [Dutch manual for the YSR]. Rotterdam, The Netherlands: Academic Medica l Centre Rotterdam/Erasmus University, Sophia Children's Hospital, Department of Child Psychiatry.

Virkud, Y. V., Todd, R. D., Abbacchi, A. M., Zhang, Y., & Constantino, J. N. (2009). Familiar aggregation of quantitative autistic traits in multiplex versus simplex autism. *American Journal of Medical Genetics: Part B, Neuropsychiatric Genetics, 150B*(3), 328-334. doi:10.1002/ajmg.b.30810

Volker, M. A., & Lopata, C. (2008). Autism: A review of biological bases, assessment, and intervention. *School Psychology Quarterly, 23*(2), 258-270. doi:10.1037/1045-3830.23.2.258

Volkmar, F. R., State, M., & Klin, A. (2009). Autism and autism spectrum disorders: Diagnostic issues for the coming decade. *Journal of Child Psychology and Psychiatry, 50*(1-2), 108-115. doi:10.1111/j.1469-7610.2008.02010.x

Wang, K., Zhang, H., Ma, D., Bucan, M., Glessner, J. T., Abrahams, B. S., ... Hakonarson, H. (2009). Common genetic variants on 5p14.1 associate with autism spectrum disorders. *Nature, 459*, 528-533. doi:10.1038/nature07999

Wicks-Nelson, R., & Israel, A. C. (2009). *Abnormal child and adolescent psychology* (7th ed.). Upper Saddle River, NJ: Pearson/Prentice Hall.

Zhao, X., Leotta, A., Kustanovich, V., Lajonchere, C., Geschwind, D. H., Law, K., ... Wigler, M. (2007). A unified genetic theory for sporadic and inherited autism. *Proceedings of the National Academy of Sciences, 104*(31), 12831-12836. doi:10.1073/pnas.0705803104

CHAPTER 5

RECENT FINDINGS ABOUT SIBLINGS OF PEOPLE WITH AUTISM SPECTRUM DISORDERS

Julie A. Deisinger

Autism spectrum disorders (ASDs) are pervasive developmental conditions in which genetic factors play a major causative role (Gamliel, Yirmiya, Jaffe, Manor, & Sigman, 2009; Regehr & Feldman, 2009; Yoder, Stone, Walden, & Malesa, 2009). As a result, siblings of individuals with ASDs comprise a population that is at increased risk for developing an ASD (Constantino, Zhang, Frazier, Abbacchi, & Law, 2010; Deisinger, 2008; Nadig et al., 2007; Yoder et al., 2009; Zwaigenbaum et al., 2007). However, even if they themselves are unimpaired, they still may experience heightened stress and coping difficulties due to having a brother or sister who has been diagnosed with an ASD (Smith & Elder, 2010).

This chapter will summarize the findings of recent investigations about siblings of people with ASDs. Studies involving siblings as a high-risk population will be reported. Current information about adjustment to living with a brother or sister who has an ASD also will be described, including the perspectives of neurotypical adolescent and adult siblings. Finally, recommendations will be offered concerning future research.

Autism Spectrum Disorders: Inclusive Community for the Twenty-First Century, pp. 113–138

INFANT SIBLINGS AS AN AT-RISK POPULATION

Early diagnosis of ASDs typically leads to earlier intervention, which in turn may yield better outcomes for affected individuals (Elder, Dawson, Toth, Fein, & Munson, 2008; Nadig et al., 2007; Zwaigenbaum et al., 2007). For this reason, researchers have been attempting to identify warning signs of ASDs by conducting prospective studies of infants who have siblings already diagnosed with an ASD. Prior investigations have shown that these infants are at increased risk for ASDs (Rogers, 2009; Zwaigenbaum et al., 2007). From 3% to 10% of children who have a brother or sister with an ASD also will develop an ASD (Elder et al., 2008; Rogers, 2009; Noland, Reznick, Stone, Walden, & Sheridan, 2009; Zwaigenbaum et al., 2007). These rates are approximately 20 times greater than the rates of ASD that are found among the general public (Constantino et al., 2010; Zwaigenbaum et al., 2007). In fact, some investigators are reporting that the current rates may under-estimate the recurrence risks for ASDs because they are based on studies using diagnostic criteria from more than 20 years ago (Constantino et al., 2010; Zwaigenbaum et al., 2007).

During a prospective study, researchers locate infants who have siblings diagnosed with an ASD and then observe the infants' ongoing development, often focusing on a physical or behavioral characteristic that is suspected of being an early marker for ASDs. This method offers advantages in comparison to retrospective studies, which look backward in an effort to detect signs of ASDs in children who already have been diagnosed (Zwaigenbaum et al., 2007). A common problem with retrospective studies is that parents may be unfamiliar with subtle indicators of ASDs and therefore may not recall them accurately. Prospective studies eliminate such recall errors; additionally, they make it possible to examine how a delay in one area of development might affect later development in a different domain (Zwaigenbaum et al., 2007).

A study by Nadig and colleagues (2007) considered whether an infant's lack of response to his or her own name might signal the presence of an ASD. In this investigation, infants who had older siblings diagnosed with ASDs served as the experimental group and infants with neurotypical older siblings were the control group. Participants were videotaped at 6 months and 12 months of age while undergoing the following procedure. The researcher gave a small toy to the seated child. Next, the investigator moved to a position behind the infant, clearly said the child's name, and observed whether the child turned and made eye contact in response. If the baby did not respond the first time, this procedure was repeated after three seconds and was repeated a third time if necessary. The infants' videotaped responses were coded by a rater who was not told whether the babies being observed were in the at-risk or control group. Results of this study found that by 12 months of age, 100% of the control infants responded to the first or second calling of their name; in comparison, only 86% of at-risk infants responded in this fashion. By age 24 months, three fourths of the babies who failed the response-to-name test were found to have developmental difficulties. Nadig et al. stated that although a lack of response to one's name by 12 months of age may not identify all children who are at risk for later development of ASDs, failures of this sort suggest the strong possibility of developmental problems that should be further evaluated. According to these authors, a procedure similar to the one used in this research would be easy to include during routine pediatric check-ups for 1-year-olds as a way to screen for developmental delays (Nadig et al., 2007).

An investigation by Elder et al. (2008) evaluated the possibility that changes in the growth rate of infants' head circumference might predict the presence of ASDs. They studied 18- to 24-month-old infants who had older siblings diagnosed with ASDs, using medical records obtained from well-baby check-ups to track changes in head circumference during the first 2 years of life. Analyses determined that ASDs are linked with accelerated growth in head circumference from ages 6 to12 months followed by slowed head circumference growth from 12 to 24 months. Given these findings, Elder et al. recommended that pediatricians should monitor head circumference growth patterns in at-risk infants and perform additional screening if atypical patterns of growth are discovered.

In 2009, Garon and associates examined how variations in temperament might differentiate between infants who will later develop ASDs and those whose development will proceed as expected. These authors defined temperament as "constitutionally based individual differences in reactivity and regulation" (Garon et al., 2009, p. 60). They chose to investigate three components of temperament that they referred to as extraversion, negative affect, and effortful control. Extraversion is related to sociability and includes positive expressions of emotion such as smiling and laughing. These behaviors can be observed in neurotypical infants beginning around 2 months of age. Negative affect refers to distressing emotions such as fear and anger, which start to manifest in babies around 4 to 8 months of age. Effortful control involves the regulation of attention, emotion, and behavior to reach goals, and is not evident until around 1 year of age (Garon et al., 2009).

The 2009 study by Garon et al. included three groups of infants. Participants in the first group were 138 full-term babies who had older siblings already diagnosed with an ASD. The second group contained 34 infants who had siblings with ASDs, and who themselves eventually were diagnosed with an ASD by the time they reached 36 months of age. The control group was comprised of 73 full-term infants who had no close relatives with an ASD. When the infants in these three groups were 24 months old, their parents completed an instrument called the Toddler Behavior Assessment Questionnaire-Revised. On the basis of the questionnaire responses, Garon and colleagues discovered that an infant temperament characterized by high levels of activity, low levels of attention-shifting, and low excitement in response to cues about forthcoming rewards was linked with receiving an ASD diagnosis at age 36 months. They also determined that an infant temperament comprised of low positive affect, problems with attention, and difficulties in regulating negative emotions could distinguish the control group from the two other groups in this study. Furthermore, their analyses uncovered that infant temperament yielded additional predictive information about the likelihood of being diagnosed with an ASD at 36 months of age, above and beyond other factors such as intelligence level and the presence of ASD symptoms at 24 months of age. They concluded that at-risk infants who later receive an ASD diagnosis can be differentiated from controls at age 24 months because they possess temperaments involving fewer displays of positive emotions, more frequent negative emotions, and a lesser capacity to regulate their behavior and attention (Garon et al., 2009).

Using groups that were somewhat similar to those in the study just described, Christensen et al. (2010) sought to find whether observable differences in play behavior might be early signs of ASDs. This research team chose to examine play behavior as a potential marker for ASDs due to its associations with language, relationship skills, and imaginative ability, all of which may be problematic among children with ASDs. Participants in this investigation fell into one of four groups: (1) infant siblings of children with ASDs who themselves had an ASD; (2) infant siblings who did not meet criteria for an ASD but who manifested delays in language, cognition, or sociability; (3) infant siblings of children with ASDs who themselves showed no developmental delays; and (4) a control group of infants who neither had an ASD themselves nor had a sibling with an ASD.

When they were 18 months old, the infants in the Christensen et al. (2010) study were videotaped during a 4-minute assessment in which they were presented with a standardized set of toys that included such things as blocks, dolls, pretend food, play cookware, and pretend dishware and utensils. The babies' videotaped play activities were classified as examples of either functional play, symbolic play, or repeated play. These researchers defined functional play to mean activities associated with the functional properties of the toys, such as using a brush on a doll's hair. Symbolic play was defined as either imaginary play, such as making noises to simulate the sounds of food cooking, or substitution play, such as when a child might put a toy plate on its head to pretend that the plate was a hat. As suggested by its name, repeated play involved actions that the infant performed repetitively. This category was further divided to separately examine functional repeated play (such as holding a spoon to a doll's mouth over and over again to simulate spoon-feeding) and nonfunctional repeated play, during which the toys were repetitively manipulated in ways that were neither functional nor symbolic (such as repetitiously placing objects into a toy pot and then removing them).

Christenson and colleagues (2010) found that as they had predicted, infant siblings who themselves were diagnosed with ASDs engaged less often in functional play and more often in nonfunctional repeated play in comparison to neurotypical infants in the control group. Similarly, when compared to the controls, the other two groups of at-risk infants also displayed significantly more examples of nonfunctional repeated play. The authors of this study suggested that unusual play behavior in infancy may be a marker of risk for an ASD and may be an indicator of the broader autism phenotype, "in which autistic-like characteristics exist at subclinical levels in relatives of individuals with autism" (Christenson et al., 2010, p. 948).

The aforementioned studies prospectively examined skill deficits in at-risk infants. In contrast, research conducted by Noland et al. (2009) identified a cognitive ability in which at-risk infants' performance was better than that of neurotypical infants. These scientists investigated infant siblings of children with ASDs regarding their working memory ability, which they defined as an information-processing ability during which an infant creates and updates transitory mental representations of objects. They chose to study working memory in at-risk infants because some studies of children with ASDs and their parents had identified their working memory abilities as poor. Based on these earlier findings, Noland and colleagues speculated that a global deficit in working memory might be a characteristic of families affected by ASDs. Alternatively, they surmised that ASD-related deficits in working memory might depend on whether the information held in working memory was social or nonsocial.

Participants in the Noland et al. (2009) study included infant siblings of children with ASDs and infants who had neurotypical siblings. For the experiment, these infants were videotaped while seated in front of a screen behind which an examiner was hidden from the child's view. Each infant participated in a variation of "peek-a-boo," during which either a social target (the examiner) or a nonsocial target (a colorful toy with moving parts) would appear from behind the screen. Either the examiner or the toy was presented from behind the left, top, or right sides of the screen; 17 trials were conducted for each condition (i.e., social versus nonsocial target). After each trial, a distractor consisting of lights shining on six suspended jingle bells appeared to redirect the infant's gaze toward the center of the screen. Then the baby's gaze was monitored for three seconds when no target was present. The infant was coded as having a correct response if he or she looked toward the location where the target had appeared during the preceding trial. The results of this experiment yielded no significant between-group differences for the social condition. However, there was a significant interaction between infant group and type of target, with at-risk infants obtaining significantly higher working memory scores for the nonsocial condition in comparison to the typically developing infants. The authors of this study stated that they did not know if this advantage might disappear with increasing age, but they suspected that a preference for nonsocial targets might be linked to social communication differences in siblings of children with ASDs.

Elsabbagh et al. (2009) also explored at-risk infants' visual attention as a possible marker for ASDs. These researchers measured the efficiency of the infants' ability to shift their gaze from a central visual stimulus to a peripheral stimulus, as well as their ability to create expectations about where visual stimuli might next appear. Their experimental group consisted of infants who had older siblings with ASDs; controls were age-matched infants with no first- or second-degree relatives who had an ASD. Participants were videotaped while shown a cartoon in the center of a monitor; the peripheral visual stimulus was a moving image of a green balloon that was randomly shown either to the right or left of center. The infants' reactions times were measured concerning how long they took to shift gaze from the central cartoon toward the balloon presented peripherally. During some trials, the presentation of the balloon image overlapped in time with the presentation of the cartoon. This phase was referred to as the disengagement condition because infants had to disengage from looking at the cartoon in order to look at the balloon in the periphery. In other trials, there was a momentary time gap between the disappearance of the central image and the appearance of the peripheral image. This was called the facilitation condition, so called because the time gap could serve as a visual cue to facilitate looking for a new stimulus. This study revealed that in comparison to the control infants, infants who had older siblings with ASDs took longer to shift their gaze from the central to the peripheral stimulus and showed less facilitation than controls. Its authors suggested that early differences in visual orienting ability might be a feature of the broader autism phenotype (Elsabbagh et al., 2009).

A study by Yoder et al. (2009) incorporated visual orienting in order to consider how well at-risk infants respond to joint attention, defined as the ability to shift attention in response to cues from another person. In addition, this research examined a construct known as weighted triadic communication, which "involves the child's use of a combination of gestures, vocalizations, gaze shifts, and sometimes symbolic means to communicate a message about an object or event to another person" (Yoder et al., 2009, p. 1383). In this study, communication was weighted because points were assigned based on the number of words accompanying a communicative effort. Multiword communications were given more weight (i.e., assigned more points) than single-word communications, which in turn were weighted more heavily than nonverbal communication (Yoder et al., 2009). This investigation sought to find out whether response to joint attention and weighted triadic communication could be used to predict an eventual ASD diagnosis in infant siblings of children already identified as having ASDs.

Participants in the study by Yoder et al. (2009) were 12- to 23-month-old infants, some of whom had older siblings on the autism spectrum and others who had neurotypical siblings. These infants were videotaped during a response to joint attention task, during which an experimenter gave verbal and physical cues (such as pointing, or shifts in head position) to redirect the infants' gaze toward novel stimuli in the room. Observers who were unaware of each participant's group membership coded the infants' responses. This protocol was administered on four occasions, each separated by a time increment of about 4 months, to look for improved accuracy over time. Results found that the infants' initial ability (or lack thereof) for response to joint attention, in combination with the growth rate of their weighted triadic communication over time, predicted whether the child would eventually receive an ASD diagnosis (Yoder et al., 2009).

Eminent autism researcher Sally Rogers (2009) performed a review of prospective studies on at-risk infants and identified several major findings. First, research has not yet been able to pinpoint any behavioral markers of ASD in 6-month-olds. According to Rogers, early behavioral differences are hard to notice; as a result, biological rather than behavioral markers may be needed to detect ASDs in early infancy. Second, studies to date reveal tremendous variety concerning when ASD symptoms first appear and what course they may follow. In some cases, differences in motor development, activity level, or sensory sensitivity are noticeable even before the emergence of problems in social interaction. This finding implies that ASDs are not merely disorders of social communication but instead are conditions that simultaneously affect other domains of development as well. A third noteworthy observation from the prospective studies of at-risk infants is that ASD symptom severity can be extremely variable, ranging from mild to severe. As a consequence, pediatric screening for ASDs needs to be done repeatedly before 3 years of age, using screening tools that have the ability to identify children with milder symptoms. Rogers also noted that current studies of at-risk infants do not tell us whether at-risk infants without full-blown ASDs, yet who do manifest some anomalous developmental differences, will go on to show characteristics of the broad autism phenotype when they are older. Larger longitudinal studies are needed to elucidate that issue.

Because at-risk infants by definition have older siblings already diagnosed with an ASD, parents may be likely to closely scrutinize these infants and initiate treatments for them if they appear to have symptoms suggestive of ASD. Regehr and Feldman (2009) surveyed parents and learned that on average, they used one to two interventions for their at-risk infants. Unfortunately, however, most of the interventions chosen by parents were not evidence-based treatments. Regehr and Feldman recommended that parents of at-risk infants should be educated about treatment options so that they can make better-informed decisions for their children.

STUDIES INVOLVING OLDER SIBLINGS

Three recent studies examined aspects of biological structure and function in children, adolescents, and young adults with siblings on the autism spectrum. Sarasella et al. (2009) discussed the concept of an "autism endophenotype," which they defined as "simple biological aspects of a disease that can be observed in unaffected relatives at a higher rate than in the general population" (p. 978). Based on their usage of the term, the autism endophenotype appears to be related to (or perhaps even synonymous with) the broader autism phenotype that was discussed earlier in this chapter.

Some studies have found impaired immune system functioning in children with autism. For this reason, Sarasella and colleagues (2009) wondered whether differences in the functioning of the immune system might be a manifestation of an autism endophenotype. For their study, they recruited three groups of participants whose ages ranged from 5 to 17 years old. The first group included 20 children and adolescents with a diagnosis of autism. The second group contained 15 siblings of the first group, who themselves did not have an ASD diagnosis. Participants in the third group were 20 neurotypical controls. Blood samples were obtained from the members of each group and were analyzed to examine various aspects of immune function. Result indicated that both the participants diagnosed with autism and their nonautistic siblings demonstrated immune system dysregulation in the form of increased production of an antiinflammatory protein called interleukin-10. Increased production of this substance was not found in the control group. Sarasella et al. described their findings as "novel and unexpected" (p. 982), and concluded that ASDs can be observed not only on the basis of delays in language and cognitive development, but also in the form of immune system dysfunction.

Dalton, Nacewicz, Alexander, and Davidson (2007) also investigated the broad autism phenotype, employing a face-processing task to study brain structure and function in siblings of persons with ASDs. Similar to the study described above, Dalton et al. (2007) examined three groups of participants: an autism group, a group who had siblings with ASDs, and a group of healthy controls. The ages of these individuals ranged from 8 to 25 years old. Prior to actual data collection, all participants were allowed to become accustomed to being in a magnetic resonance imaging (MRI) scanner and were given instructions about a face recognition task that they would perform while undergoing an MRI scan. During the scan, participants were shown photographs of family members and friends, as well as photographs of unfamiliar faces that were matched to the first set of pictures with regard to age, gender, and facial expression. Participants were instructed to push a button each time that they were shown a familiar face. While they looked at photographs, their eye movements were recorded and both structural and functional MRI scans were obtained.

Past studies of brain activation have identified the fusiform gyrus as a part of the brain that is strongly activated during facial processing in the brains of neurotypical individuals (Dalton et al., 2007). However, brain scans from the Dalton et al. (2007) study indicated that in comparison to the controls, participants in both the autism group and the sibling group showed less activation in the right fusiform gyrus in response to looking at facial photographs. This research team also discovered that when compared to controls, participants from both the autism group and the sibling group spent significantly less time looking at the eyes of the people whose photographs they were shown. In addition, the volume of an interior brain structure called the amygdala was significantly decreased in both the autism group and in the sibling group when compared to the amygdala volume of control participants. This area of the brain is involved in processing emotionally laden information (Halgin & Whitbourne, 2010). Based on their results, Dalton et al. suggested that eye fixation might serve as a behavioral marker for the kinds of social deficits that are associated with ASDs.

In 2010 Barnea-Goraly, Lotspeich, and Reiss conducted a study that utilized children with autism, siblings who did not exhibit the broader autism phenotype, and healthy control participants to examine the structure of white matter in their brains. These authors cited prior research that found white matter structural abnormalities in the brains of persons with autism. This discovery was noteworthy because white matter is involved in connecting brain cells and allowing them to communicate

(Barnea-Goraly et al., 2010). The study by Barnea-Goraly et al. was the first investigation of white matter structure in the siblings of children with autism. Its authors hypothesized that brain scans of siblings would reveal differences in their white matter structure, and that these differences would be intermediate between the structural differences found in children with autism and the white matter structure of healthy unaffected children.

Barnea-Goraly and colleagues (2010) used a type of MRI scan called diffusion tensor imaging to acquire white matter images from their participants, whose ages ranged from 6 to 13 years old. All of them were first trained in a mock scanner prior to the actual scanning procedure. Analyses of the data obtained from the brain images revealed no significant differences between children with autism and their unaffected siblings with regard to white matter structure; however, both of these groups showed significant differences in white matter structure when compared with controls. These differences were observed in many regions of the brain, including areas that are known to be important for face processing, theory of mind, and social cognition. Structural differences in white matter also were seen in brain pathways that relate to sensory, motor, and other mental functions. Barnea-Goraly et al. pointed out that the structural differences in white matter which they found were not due to differences in intellectual level, because unaffected siblings in their study were similar to the control participants in terms of intelligence. They recommended further studies to obtain a better understanding about how structural differences in white matter of the brain are related to ASDs.

Rather than looking at brain structure, a team of researchers in Japan examined brain function by studying the cognitive organizing abilities of adults who have siblings with ASDs (Sumiyoshi, Kawakubo, Suga, Sumiyoshi, & Kasai, 2011). To do this, Sumiyoshi and colleagues administered a computerized version of the Wisconsin Card Sort, a test that measures the ability to detect the properties that are being used to sort stimulus cards. They also gave participants a Japanese version of the Verbal Learning Task, which evaluates how well a test-taker makes mental associations based on implicit categories in word lists. This investigation revealed that while the neurotypical siblings performed adequately on both tests, they made errors on the Wisconsin Card Sort that were similar to those of individuals with ASDs. Also, the siblings of persons with ASDs failed to produce a linear increase in scores on the Verbal Learning Task. Sumiyoshi et al. (2011) interpreted their results to suggest that difficulties in cognitive organizational ability may be an endophenotype for ASDs.

A longitudinal investigation by Gamliel et al. (2009) followed the development of children who had older siblings with ASDs and compared them to a closely matched group of children with typically developing siblings. The study began when its participants were 4 months old, after which they were evaluated periodically until they reached 7 years of age. Gamliel and associates used standardized, norm-referenced instruments to measure the participants' level of intellectual functioning, academic achievement, and language development. Participants' parents also were interviewed to gather information about the participants' developmental histories. Data from formal testing and parental interviews were analyzed using a technique called growth curve analysis; a growth curve was generated for each group to examine its developmental pattern from 4 to 54 months of age. Gamliel et al. found that by the time the children had reached 7 years of age, 40% of those who had siblings with ASDs demonstrated problems in language, cognition, or academic performance. They also discovered that language scores, but not cognitive scores, from ages 14 to 54 months of age were significantly lower in siblings of children with ASDs, whether or not they eventually manifested the characteristics of the broad autism phenotype. Therefore, Gamliel and colleagues (2009) suggested that early problems in the language development of youngsters who have siblings with ASDs may signify that such children should obtain early intervention.

A recent article examined the ratio of males to females among siblings of children with ASDs as a way to investigate causal theories of autism. Mouridsen, Rich, and Isager (2010) studied siblings of 326 children and adolescents with ASDs, of whom approximately 75% were males. These authors reviewed previous epidemiological studies and found that on average, the ratio of males to females with ASDs was 4 to 1. Mouridsen and colleagues wondered whether siblings of individuals with ASDs also might be predominantly male. They found that among the 513 siblings of these individuals, males comprised 58.5% of the sibling group. Mouridsen et al. noted that throughout industrialized nations the proportion of male children that are born tends to be around 50.5% to 52%. Thus, the percentage of male siblings in their study differed significantly from the percentage of males in the general population. These authors interpreted their data as supportive of the so-called androgen theory of autism, which claims that "individuals with ASD were exposed to relatively high levels of testosterone in utero" (Mouridsen et al., 2010, p. 291).

INVESTIGATIONS OF SIBLINGS' ADJUSTMENT

This section will examine recent investigations of sibling adjustment, which is an important focus of research because in comparison to other disorders of childhood, ASDs tend to impose greater stress on family members (Benson & Karlof, 2008; Petalas, Hastings, Nash, Dowey, &

Reilly, 2009; Quintero & McIntyre, 2010; Rao & Beidel, 2009). Reduced parental attention, heightened parental expectations, the need to sometimes assume roles that may exceed one's developmental level, little or no participation in extra-curricular activities due to helping at home, and the difficulty of trying to play with a child who has an ASD all may contribute to the stress of having a brother or sister on the autism spectrum (Aronson, 2009; Barak-Levy, Goldstein, & Weinstock, 2010; Ivey & Ward, 2010; Quintero & McIntyre, 2010). In response, some youngsters who have siblings with ASDs may experience a variety of unpleasant emotions such as sadness, anger, embarrassment, and/or guilt (Aronson, 2009; Deisinger, 2008; Ivey & Ward, 2010.) In this segment, the impact of parent and family characteristics on siblings' functioning will be described; in addition, cultural factors that may affect siblings' outcomes will be discussed.

As previously mentioned, siblings of persons diagnosed with ASDs may themselves be at risk for developmental differences due to genetic factors. Articles by Benson and Karlof (2008) and by Meadan, Halle, and Ebata (2010) cited genetic vulnerability as an issue that might explain the conflicting scientific literature to date regarding the adjustment of individuals who have siblings with ASDs. Some prior studies have suggested that siblings display adjustment problems such as depression, maladaptive behavior, or loneliness; in contrast, other studies have reported either good adjustment or at least the absence of negative outcomes (Meadan et al., 2010). Meadan and associates recommended that future studies need to consider the role of genetic risk factors on the adjustment of people who have siblings with ASDs. They also mentioned several demographic factors that may be associated with poorer outcomes for siblings of individuals with ASDs. These include low socioeconomic status, having only one sibling, being older than the child with ASD, having an ASD sibling with challenging behaviors, and the presence of marital conflict in the family (Meadan et al., 2010).

Macks and Reeve (2007) also highlighted the role of demographic factors in their study of children and teens who had siblings with ASDs. They gathered data from 51 families in which there was both a child with autism and a neurotypical sibling who was from 7 to 17 years old. This study employed a comparison group containing 35 youngsters, also 7 to 17 years of age, who had nondisabled siblings. Child and adolescent participants in this investigation completed a standardized depression scale and a self-concept scale. Mothers from both groups completed a demographic questionnaire as well as a rating scale evaluating the neurotypical children's behavior.

According to Macks and Reeve (2007), participants who had siblings with ASDs had more favorable self-concepts than the participants with neurotypical siblings, as shown by their responses on the self-concept questionnaire. Surprisingly, however, the mothers of children with ASDs rated the nondisabled siblings' adjustment less positively than did the mothers of children in the comparison group (i.e., those who had no children with ASDs). The authors of this study provided three possible explanations for this result. They speculated that perhaps mothers of children with ASDs have to spend so much time caring for a child with an ASD that they have developed an inaccurate view about the adjustment of the nondisabled child. Alternatively, parents of children with ASDs may mistakenly assume that because the parents themselves are under a great deal of stress, then their nondisabled child must be similarly distressed. A third possibility identified by Macks and Reeve was that parents might unconsciously project frustrations about the child with ASD onto the nondisabled sibling. In light of their findings, these authors suggested that studies of youngsters who have siblings with ASDs should seek information from multiple informants, rather than relying solely on parental reports.

A more noteworthy finding reported by Macks and Reeve (2007) concerns the relationship between demographic risk factors and the adjustment of children who have siblings with ASDs. These investigators looked at such factors as being older than the child with an ASD, having only one sibling, having low socioeconomic status, and being male. Based on their findings, they concluded that when few demographic risk factors exist, the emotional and social development of children who have siblings with ASDs may be enhanced. However, the likelihood of poor psychological adjustment for siblings of children with ASDs increases in the presence of multiple risk factors (Macks & Reeve, 2007).

Benson and Karlof (2008) considered a variety of factors that might influence the adjustment of children who have siblings with ASDs. They recruited 72 families which contained at least one child with autism and at least one other child. Some of these siblings themselves had an ASD or some other clinical condition, most commonly attention-deficit/hyperactivity disorder; others were nondisabled. Parents of these families underwent interviews and completed questionnaires to provide information about their child with ASD, their other child, the presence of life stressors, the quality of emotional life within the family, and the nature and intensity of any parental involvement in delivering educational or therapeutic services to the child with ASD. Data analyses revealed that in general, siblings of children with ASDs who themselves did not have a clinical diagnosis were not at greater risk for adjustment problems. The severity of a brother's or sister's ASD symptoms, and the presence of stressful life events, both were predictive of adjustment problems for siblings, but the extent of parental involvement in psychoeducational service delivery to the child with ASD was not associated with negative effects for other nondiagnosed children in a family. Finally, a family climate that included low marital conflict and high family cohesion predicted positive outcomes for siblings of children with ASDs (Benson & Karlof, 2008).

As mentioned earlier in this section, parents sometimes may harbor differing rules and expectations for their nondisabled children. Rivers and Stoneman (2008) explored this issue, as well as the role of child temperament, in a study of 50 families that contained a child with ASD and a neurotypical sibling. These authors cited previous research indicating that parents may treat their children differently in response to their children's differing temperaments. However, past studies have found that differential parenting may lead to increased competition and conflict among siblings. Rivers and Stoneman also reported about prior studies showing that sibling relationships likewise can be affected by differences in child temperament; siblings whose temperaments are more similar tend to have more positive relationships with each other.

Drawing upon these two lines of inquiry, Rivers and Stoneman (2008) recruited families who had a young child with an ASD as well as a neurotypical older sibling. In each of these families, one parent (most typically the mother) and the nondisabled sibling each completed questionnaires to assess the quality of the sibling relationship, as well as items concerning differential parenting. Parents also completed measures to rate the temperaments of both their child with ASD and their neurotypical child. When considering the influence of temperament, the characteristic of persistence was linked with the quality of the relationship between the child with ASD and the neurotypical sibling, If both children were low in persistence, then the parents and the neurotypical siblings rated the sibling relationship less positively. Rivers and Stoneman (2008) also identified the phenomenon of "temperament buffering" (p. 1747). In other words, the potential negative effects of a difficult temperament in one child may be offset by a more positive temperament in the other child. The authors observed that neurotypical children who are high in persistence may be more successful at fostering a positive relationship with a brother or sister who has an ASD because they are more likely to make repeated attempts at social interactions with their ASD siblings. Finally, as predicted by these investigators, sibling relationships were rated more negatively when the neurotypical sibling was dissatisfied with differential parenting (Rivers & Stoneman, 2008).

Knowing that parents of children with ASDs experience more stress than other parents, Quintero and McIntyre (2010) evaluated the effects of maternal well-being on the adjustment of school-aged children who had younger siblings with ASDs. These researchers studied families that included one preschooler and one elementary-school-aged child. In half the families, the younger child had an ASD; in the other families, both children were neurotypical. Parents completed questionnaires to rate their own levels of stress and depression, as well as questionnaires examining their school-aged child's adjustment. The older children's teachers also filled out questionnaires rating the older siblings' adjustment. Results of this study yielded significant correlations between mothers' self-reported stress and parental reports of behavioral problems in school-aged siblings of preschoolers with ASDs. Similarly, among families in which mothers reported more depression and stress, teachers rated the older siblings as manifesting more problem behaviors than their same-aged peers. Quintero and McIntyre highlighted the need for both parents and siblings of persons with ASDs to obtain support across the lifespan, to assist them in caring for an ASD family member.

In addition to family composition, ethnicity also may influence how well children adjust to having a brother or sister with an ASD. Sage and Jegatheesan (2010) explored this issue by comparing the perceptions of a typically developing European American boy and a neurotypical Vietnamese American boy, both of whom have a younger brother with autism. Each of the two participants was interviewed using a method called the draw-and-tell technique, which allowed them to respond to interview questions either verbally or in the form of a drawing. The parents of both boys also were interviewed.

Results of this study suggested that ethnicity may impact the quality of the sibling relationship. The two families differed in their understanding about the cause of autism; the European American parents viewed genetics as a causal factor in their son's autism, while the Vietnamese parents believed that their son's autism was karma's punishment upon them for past wrongdoing. Such a view is consistent with Vietnamese culture, which stigmatizes developmental disabilities and considers them a source of shame for a family (Sage & Jegatheesan, 2010). These worldviews apparently influenced the sibling relationship in each family. The relationship between the neurotypical European American sibling and his brother was described as close and affectionate, while the relationship between the Vietnamese siblings was said to be conflictual. The neurotypical sibling in the Asian American family explained his feelings toward his brother with autism by saying, "I have a smile outside but feel angry inside" (Sage & Jagetheesen, 2010, p. 103).

It is not possible to draw generalizeable conclusions on the basis of only two families. However, two other investigations studied the effects of Asian cultures on siblings of children with autism. The first of these (Hwang & Charnley, 2010), conducted in Korea, discussed a widespread Korean belief that disability is considered to be "the result of inauspicious sites for graves and houses, punishment for sins committed in a previous life, the responsibility of ancestors or wicked ghosts" (p. 581). Hwang and Charnley (2010) wrote that when one member of a Korean family is impaired or disabled, the entire family experiences feelings of shame. To examine such issues, these investigators recruited five boys and four girls in Korea who had siblings with autism. The participants, ranging in age from 7 to 15 years old, made videotaped diaries of their daily lives in which they revealed their thoughts and feelings about their siblings with autism. According to the authors of this study, all nine participants often experienced negative attitudes when in public settings with their sibling with autism. Also, none of the participants reportedly talked with friends about their sibling with autism, out of a desire to avoid being pitied. Nevertheless, these young people did engage in social activities and their lives were not completely defined by the presence of autism in their families (Hwang & Charnley, 2010).

Using a considerably larger sample, Gau et al. (2010) sought to learn about Taiwanese children who had siblings with autism. In this study, 134 families had a child with autism and at least one typically developing sibling; 131 families with neurotypical children served as controls. Parents of these children completed the Chinese version of the Child Behavior Checklist, which is a questionnaire used to rate 10 different types of behavioral problems that children might be experiencing. Gau et al. discovered that the neurotypical siblings of children with autism were rated as having more depressive and anxious symptoms, more social withdrawal, more thought problems, and more externalizing behavioral problems than the children in the comparison group.

The Child Behavior Checklist also served as a data collection instrument in a study by Ross and Cuskelly (2006). These researchers wished to study the adjustment of youngsters in Australia who had a brother or sister with autism. In particular, they wished to ascertain how coping skills and knowledge about ASDs might affect the adjustment of 25 neurotypical children and teens who have siblings with ASDs. Participants whose ages ranged from 8 to 15 years old completed questionnaires designed to measure their knowledge about ASDs and to determine the kinds of coping strategies they used in response to problem behaviors demonstrated by a sibling with ASD. Their mothers completed the Child Behavior Checklist to indicate whether the typically developing children exhibited problems like depression, anxiety, or aggression.

Results of this study found that the participants had a fairly good understanding about ASDs. Despite this, 40% of them suffered from a clinically significant adjustment problem, most commonly in the form of internalizing problems such as depression or anxiety. These youngsters also reported experiencing problematic interactions with their ASD sibling; 84% of them identified the aggressive behavior of their ASD sibling as a frequent stressor. Participants' other complaints involved being disturbed by the ASD sibling, or having property destroyed by the brother or sister with ASD. When the participants were victims of aggressive behavior from siblings, they most often used the coping strategies of emotion regulation and wishful thinking. Although this study did not uncover a significant relationship between coping strategies and adjustment, Ross and Cuskelly (2006) surmised that this finding could have been due to their small sample size. They also speculated that other variables not measured in their study, such as parenting style or level of parental distress, might be more relevant to the adjustment of children who have siblings with ASDs.

Several other recent studies outside the United States also have sought to learn more about the adjustment of children and teens who have siblings with ASDs. The Eurasian nation of Turkey was the site of an investigation by Aksoy and Bercin Yildirim (2008); they recruited preteen and adolescent participants who had siblings with a variety of disabilities, including Down syndrome, cerebral palsy, mental retardation, learning disability, and autism. Participants responded to questionnaires that assessed their attitudes toward their disabled sibling as well as their attitudes toward people with other disabilities. Findings indicated that in comparison to youngsters who had siblings with learning disabilities, those who had siblings with autism had more negative attitudes toward the ASD sibling. In addition, participants who had siblings with autism reported more loneliness and more concerns about the future of the ASD sibling. The authors of this study pointed out that having a sibling on the autism spectrum may be especially challenging due to the lack of outward indicators of disability, coupled with the severity of this form of disability. They recommended that siblings need to be educated about the nature of a disability in order to cope with it effectively.

Participants in a 2007 study by Benderix and Sivberg echoed concerns similar to those expressed in the investigations described above. This research involved interviews with 14 neurotypical siblings from five families in Sweden, each of which included a child diagnosed with both autism and cognitive impairment. For each participant, the interview took place shortly before the ASD sibling was relocated to a group home. A qualitative analysis of the interview data identified the following themes: feelings of obligation, pity, and empathy for the sibling with autism, exposure to the abnormal behaviors of the ASD sibling (e.g., kicking, screaming, or smearing feces), feelings of anxiety triggered by the ASD sibling's unusual behaviors, negative effects on friendships as a result of having a sibling with ASD, and hope that the ASD sibling's move to a group home would result in family relief and more parental attention (Benderix & Sivberg, 2007). In the closing segment of this article, the authors noted that the participants in this study sometimes were afraid to disclose their own needs to their parents due to a fear of placing an additional burden to their already overburdened parents. Benderix and Sivberg (2007) emphasized the need for family education and early intervention as ways to reduce the stress of typically developing children who have brothers or sisters with autism.

Also using interviews and qualitative analytic methods, Petalas, Hastings, Nash, Dowey et al. (2009) asked about the experiences and thoughts of neurotypical youngsters, ages 8 to 17 years, who had a brother with an ASD. Five themes emerged from the interview data. The first theme involved the negative impact of having a brother with ASD due to disruptions in daily life, the need to make concessions in response to the brother's challenging behaviors, and the care-giving duties that had to be assumed. The second theme concerned having to deal with negative attitudes from friends and strangers, which triggered emotions of anger, anxiety, and embarrassment. In the third theme, a dichotomy emerged between accepting the ASD brother's condition and longing for change. The fourth theme found in this study was that of positive feelings and experiences connected to having a brother with ASD. The fifth theme identified in this research had to do with sources of formal or informal support for the neurotypical siblings.

Based on their findings, Petalas, Hastings, Nash, Dowey et al. (2009) proposed several implications of their study. These authors suggested that siblings of children with ASDs would benefit from training aimed at enhancing their interactions with brothers who have ASDs. Petalas and colleagues also observed that sibling support groups need to consider the developmental level of members in such groups and tailor their activities accordingly. They further recommended that supporting families of children with ASDs may be accomplished in part by educating communities about ASDs (Petalas, Hastings, Nash, Dowey et al., 2009).

In a separate study, Petalas, Hastings, Nash, Lloyd, and Dowey (2009) wondered whether the struggles experienced by neurotypical siblings of children with autism were due to the disabled sibling's autism, or instead due to the sibling's intellectual deficits. To tease apart these issues, the authors located a group of typically developing children and adolescents who had siblings with autism and intellectual impairment, and compared them with another group of neurotypical youngsters who had siblings with only intellectual impairment. Participants' mothers filled out an instrument called the Strengths and Difficulties Questionnaire to examine their children's socioemotional adjustment. In comparison to children whose siblings had only intellectual disabilities, the children whose siblings had both autism and intellectual deficits were more likely to be rated as having emotional and behavioral problems. Factors associated with having emotional or behavioral problems included having a brother rather than a sister with ASD, being younger than the child with ASD, and being from a lower socioeconomic bracket. Similar to what has been reported by other investigators, Petalas, Hastings, Nash, Lloyd et al. pointed out that their findings could be due in part to an autism phenotype in these families. Also, they reiterated that when evaluating neurotypical siblings, multiple informants in addition to mothers would help to eliminate possible biases in the descriptions of the children's behavior.

RESEARCH FOCUSING ON ADOLESCENT AND ADULT SIBLINGS

According to Petalas et al. (2009a), "the sibling viewpoint is conspicuously absent in the literature and the siblings themselves are seldom given the opportunity to provide first-hand information" (p. 396). This section will present research studies about teens and adults who have siblings on the autism spectrum, as well as descriptions of their views about having a brother or sister who has ASD.

Orsmond and Seltzer (2009) performed an investigation to test the hypothesis that a diathesis-stress model might explain disparate findings about the adjustment and functioning of individuals who have a sibling with an ASD. According to such a model, the diathesis is a vulnerability (e.g., genetic makeup) that predisposes a person toward experiencing psychological distress. However, this model also claims that psychological distress will become evident only when the preexisting susceptibility interacts with stressors in the person's environment.

Participants in the Orsmond and Seltzer (2009) study were 57 adolescents who had siblings with ASDs. Most of them were younger than the sibling with ASD and 74% of them lived with the affected sibling. Participants completed interviews and questionnaires designed to measure their anxiety levels and identify stressful life experiences. Their mothers, who also were interviewed, completed inventories to assess maternal depression, identify broader autism phenotype (BAP) features in themselves and in the participants, and report problem behaviors exhibited by their son or daughter with ASD.

Orsmond and Seltzer (2009) defined the diathesis as characteristics of an adolescent participant that would be considered part of the BAP. Three types of stressors were examined: behavioral problems manifested by a sibling with an ASD, depressive symptoms in the participant's mother, and stressful events in the participant's own life. When analyzing their results, these authors discovered that adolescent female participants reported increased levels of depression and anxiety but male participants did not. Orsmond and Seltzer provided two possible interpretations of these findings. On the one hand, the observed gender difference might reflect the fact that in general, adolescent girls are more at risk for depression than are adolescent boys. However, it also might be true that sisters in this study could be affected differently than brothers by having a sibling with an ASD, due to a greater likelihood that sisters might be expected to assume caregiving duties. These researchers also stated that their results offered some support for the diathesis-stress model as an explanatory framework for understanding the well-being of individuals who have siblings with ASDs. They noted, "Siblings who had a higher number of BAP characteristics and who experienced a greater number of stressful life events in the past year reported elevated depressive and anxiety symptoms" (Orsmond & Seltzer, p. 1061). In other words, BAP features may be markers for an underlying genetic makeup that places siblings at risk for emotional distress when subjected to unpleasant life events. Thus, siblings who have BAP traits may need help in accessing resources that could enable them to better cope with the stress of having a brother or sister on the autism spectrum (Orsmond & Seltzer).

Another study by Orsmond, Kuo, and Seltzer (2009) examined differences between adolescents and adults who have a sibling with an ASD. Their study looked at the following issues that might differ from adolescents to adults who have siblings with ASDs: (1) possible differences in positive emotions and shared activities; (2) differences in coping strategies and social support; (3) gender differences and how these might affect relationships with ASD siblings; and (4) whether the ASD siblings' behavioral problems predict the likelihood of positive feelings and shared activities with neurotypical sibs. Fifty-seven teenagers (ages 12 to18 years) and 142 adults (from 19 to 55 years old), all of whom had a sibling with an ASD, served as participants in this study. Data collection took place by means of questionnaires for adults; adolescent participants were interviewed by telephone in addition to filling out brief questionnaires.

Orsmond et al. (2009) learned that adults did not differ from adolescents in terms of the amount of positive affect in their relationship with their ASD sibling. This finding was somewhat surprising because neurotypical individuals tend to become less emotionally close to siblings during adolescence, while increasing in closeness during middle and late adulthood. Not surprisingly, however, the authors found that teen participants in their study utilized more emotion-focused coping and less problem-focused coping than the adult participants. Adolescent participants reported obtaining more social support from their parents and friends than did adult participants. Gender differences also were apparent in adulthood; adult sisters of sisters with ASD were most engaged with their ASD sibling, whereas adult brothers were least engaged if the sibling was a sister with ASD. In addition, behavioral problems manifested by the sibling with ASD tended to have a negative impact on relationships with neurotypical siblings. Orsmond et al. (2009) also reported that other characteristics, such as family size and whether the ASD sibling is older or younger than a neurotypical sibling, also will influence the sibling relationship. They underscored the need for parents and siblings of persons with ASDs to obtain support in order to cope effectively with the stress of caring for a family member on the autism spectrum.

Two studies compared the impact of Down syndrome versus ASD on the lives of adult siblings. The first one (Orsmond & Seltzer, 2007) recruited 77 adults who had a sibling with Down syndrome and a similar group of 77 adults who had a sibling with ASD. The ages of participants in both groups ranged between 21 to 56 years old, and more than 50% of each group were female. Participants in both groups completed questionnaires that asked about the frequency of contact with the developmentally disabled sibling, the quality of the emotional relationship between the siblings, and the functional abilities of the disabled sibling. This investigation revealed that adults who had a sibling with an ASD had less frequent contact with the sibling than did the siblings of individuals with Down syndrome. Adults of ASD siblings also reported less positive feelings toward the sibling and had more pessimistic expectations about the future of the affected sibling. Orsmond and Seltzer (2007) warned that adult siblings of persons with ASDs may experience difficulties when their parents are no longer able to serve as primary caregivers for the sibling with an ASD. This difficulty sometimes might be the product of broader autism phenotype characteristics in the adult siblings, which could play a factor in the reduced level of closeness between siblings. Orsmond and Seltzer suggested that helping adults to use problem-focused coping strategies might improve their ability to cope with a sibling who has an ASD.

Hodapp and Urbano (2007) also performed a study comparing adults who had siblings with Down syndrome versus those who had siblings with ASDs. These researchers accessed a larger sample than the study just described, due to the use of a national Internet-based survey as their method of data collection. They obtained survey data from 284 adults who had a sibling with Down syndrome and 176 adults who had a sibling with autism. Hodapp and Urbano reported that in comparison to adult siblings of persons with Down syndrome, adults who had siblings with autism had slightly poorer health, fewer contacts and less emotional closeness with their sibling, and increased levels of depression. More frequent contacts and more positive emotions were likely to be found in situations where the sibling with autism had fewer behavioral problems. These authors advocated for the importance of providing information and support to adult siblings who are increasingly likely to assume caregiving responsibilities as they and their siblings age.

Because the experience of having a brother or sister with an ASD has been a neglected focus of inquiry to date, researchers at the Waisman Center affiliated with the University of Wisconsin-Madison have sought to address this dearth of information. In one study (Seltzer, Krauss, & Orsmond, 2009), 60 adolescent siblings were interviewed; in another (Krauss & Seltzer, 2009), interviews were conducted with more than 200 adult siblings. The purpose of both studies was to gather the interviewees' thoughts and feelings about having a sibling on the autism spectrum. The interviews covered a wide range of topics, including the participants' own childhood and family relationships, the issue of acceptance in the community, the effect of having a sibling with an ASD on the decision to have one's own children, concerns about the future, and the positive and negative aspects of having an ASD sibling.

Many of the adolescent interviewees expressed awareness and worry that they eventually would have to care for their sibling. However, they also spoke with pride in their siblings' accomplishments and mentioned feelings of greater closeness with their parents (Seltzer et al. 2009). Many adult interviewees expressed similar sentiments. When asked to give advice to adolescents who have siblings with ASDs, the adults suggested that the teens should learn about the condition and seek the support of peers or professionals. The adults also shared advice for parents of children with ASDs, including reminders to communicate openly and to set aside time for the children in the family who do not have an ASD (Krauss & Seltzer, 2009).

FUTURE DIRECTIONS

The research discussed in this chapter points toward future avenues of investigation. For example, Zwaigenbaum et al. (2007) highlighted the need to study at-risk infants during the crucial age bracket of 6 to 18 months, because behavioral markers for ASDs might become more evident at that age. These authors also recommended that research teams should collaborate as a way to obtain sufficiently large samples in their studies of individuals who have siblings with ASDs. They further mentioned the value of interdisciplinary work with investigators from the fields of neurobiology and genetics, to elucidate the characteristics of autism endophenotypes and their underlying genetic composition.

Rogers (2009) suggested that newly available methods such as eye tracking technology should be used in studies of high-risk infants, to explore the direction and duration of gazing behavior as a possible marker for developmental differences. Studies of at-risk infants also may yield additional information about the nature of the BAP (Rogers, 2009).

Finally, Smith and Elder (2010) recommended that a sibling survey should be created for the purpose of identifying interactions between risk factors that may affect siblings of persons with ASDs. Similar to other authors mentioned in this chapter, Smith and Elder wrote about the importance of reducing bias in the ratings of neurotypical siblings' behavior. They also cited a need for research to find effective interventions for individuals who must deal with aggressive or severely disabled siblings on the autism spectrum.

In conclusion, much has already been learned about siblings of individuals with ASDs. However, much remains to be learned. Studying this population may yield a deeper understanding about the nature of ASDs. In addition, future research may assist siblings by identifying the most effective methods that can be used across the lifespan to meet the challenge of having a brother or sister with an ASD.

REFERENCES

Aksoy, A. B., & Bercin Yildirim, G. (2008). A study of the relationships and acknowledgement of non-disabled children with disabled siblings. *Educational Sciences: Theory and Practice, 8*(3), 769-779. Retrieved from http://web.ebscohost.com

Aronson, S. (2009). Am I my brother's keeper? Challenges for the siblings of autistic children. *Journal of Infant, Child, and Adolescent Psychotherapy, 8*(1), 49-56. doi:10.1080/15289160802683450

Barak-Levy, Y., Goldstein, E., & Weinstock, M. (2010). Adjustment characteristics of healthy siblings of children with autism. *Journal of Family Studies, 16*(2), 155-164. doi:10.5172/jfs.16.2.155

Barnea-Goraly, N., Lotspeich, L. J., & Reiss, A. L. (2010). Similar white matter aberrations in children with autism and their unaffected siblings: A diffusion tensor imaging study using tract-based spatial statistics. *Archives of General Psychiatry, 67*(10), 1052-1060. doi:10.1001/archgenpsychiatry.2010.123

Benderix, Y., & Sivberg, B. (2007). Siblings' experiences of having a brother or sister with autism and mental retardation: A case study of 14 siblings from five families. *Journal of Pediatric Nursing, 22*(5), 410-418. doi:10.1016/j.pedn.2007.08.013

Benson, P. R., & Karlof, K. L. (2008). Child, parent, and family predictors of latter adjustment in siblings of children with autism. *Research in Autism Spectrum Disorders, 2*, 583-600. doi:10.1016/j.rasd.2007.12.002

Christensen, L., Hutman, T., Rozga, A., Young, G. S., Ozonoff, S., Rogers, S. J., … Sigman, M. (2010). Play and developmental outcomes in infant siblings of children with autism. *Journal of Autism and Developmental Disorders, 40*, 946-957. doi:10.1007/s10803-010-0941-y

Constantino, J. N., Zhang, Y., Frazier, T., Abbacchi, A. M., & Law, P. (2010). Sibling recurrence and the genetic epidemiology of autism. *American Journal of Psychiatry, 167*(11), 1349-1356. doi:10.1176/appi.ajp.2010.09101470

Dalton, K. M., Nacewicz, B. M., Alexander, A. L., & Davidson, R. J. (2007). Gaze-fixation, brain activation, and amygdale volume in unaffected siblings of individuals with autism. *Biological Psychiatry, 61*, 512-520. doi:10.1016/j.biopsych.2006.05.019

Deisinger, J. A. (2008). Issues pertaining to siblings of individuals with autism spectrum disorders. In A. F. Rotatori, F. E. Obiakor, & S. Burkhardt (Eds.), *Autism and developmental disabilities: Current practices and issues* (pp. 135-155). London, England: Emerald.

Elder, L. M., Dawson, G., Toth, K., Fein, D., & Munson, J. (2008). Head circumference as an early predictor of autism symptoms in younger siblings of children with autism spectrum disorder. *Journal of Autism and Developmental Disorders, 38*, 1104-1111. doi:10.1007/s10803-007-0495-9

Elsabbagh, M., Volein, A., Holmboe, K., Tucker, L., Csibra, G., Baron-Cohen, S., ... Johnson, M. H. (2009). Visual orienting in the early broader autism phenotype: Disengagement and facilitation. *Journal of Child Psychology and Psychiatry, 50*(5), 637-642. doi:10.1111/j.1469-7610.2008.02051.x

Gamliel, I., Yirmiya, N., Jaffe, D. H., Manor, O., & Sigman, M. (2009). Developmental trajectories in siblings of children with autism: Cognition and language from 4 months to 7 years. *Journal of Autism and Developmental Disorders, 39*, 1131-1144. doi:10.1007/s10803-009-0727-2

Garon, N., Bryson, S. E., Zwaigenbaum, L., Smith, I. M., Brian, J., Roberts, W., & Szatmari, P. (2009). Temperament and its relationship to autistic symptoms in a high-risk infant sib cohort. *Journal of Abnormal Child Psychology, 37*, 59-78. doi:10.1007/s10802-008-9258-0

Gau, S. S. -F., Chou, M. -C., Lee, J. -C., Wong, C. -C., Chou, W. -J., Chen, M. -F., ... Wu, Y. -Y. (2010). Behavioral problems and parenting style among Taiwanese children with autism and their siblings. *Psychiatry and Clinical Neurosciences, 64*, 70-78. doi:10.1111/j.1440-

Halgin, R. P., & Whitbourne, S. K. (2010). *Abnormal psychology: Clinical perspectives on psychological disorders* (6th ed.). New York, NY: McGraw-Hill.

Hodapp, R. M., & Urbano, R. C. (2007). Adult siblings of individuals with Down syndrome versus with autism: Findings from a large-scale US survey. *Journal of Intellectual Disability Research, 51*(12), 1018-1029. doi:10.1111/j.1365-2788.2007.00994.x

Hwang, S. K., & Charnley, H. (2010). Making the familiar strange and making the strange familiar: Understanding Korean children's experiences of living with an autistic sibling. *Disability & Society, 25*(5), 579-592. doi:10.1080/09687599.2010.489305

Ivey, J. K., & Ward, A. K. (2010). Dual familial roles: An Asperger's syndrome case story. *TEACHING Exceptional Children Plus, 6*(3), 3-10. Retrieved from http://web.ebscohost.com

Krauss, M. W., & Seltzer, M. M. (2009, July 8). *Reflections from adult siblings who have a brother or sister with an autism spectrum disorder.* Retrieved from http://www.waisman.wisc.edu/family/reports/autism/aaareport3.pdf

Macks, R. J., & Reeve, R. E. (2007). The adjustment of non-disabled siblings of children with autism. *Journal of Autism and Developmental Disorders, 37*, 1060-1067. doi:10.1007/s10803-006-0249-0

Meadan, H., Halle, J. W., & Ebata, A. T. (2010). Families with children who have autism spectrum disorders: Stress and support. *Exceptional Children, 77*(1), 7-36. Retrieved from http://web.ebscohost.com

Mouridsen, S. E., Rich, B., & Isager, T. (2010). Sibling sex ratio of individuals diagnosed with autism spectrum disorder as children. *Developmental Medicine & Child Neurology, 52*, 289-292. doi:10.1111/j.1469-8749.2009.03368.x

Nadig, A. S., Ozonoff, S., Young, G. S., Rozga, A., Sigman, M., & Rogers, S. J. (2007). A prospective study of response to name in infants at risk for autism. *Archives of Pediatrics and Adolescent Medicine, 161*, 378-383. Retrieved from http://scholar.google.com

Noland, J. S., Reznick, S., Stone, W. L., Walden, T., & Sheridan, E. H. (2010). Better working memory for non-social targets in infant siblings with autism spectrum disorder. *Developmental Science, 13*(1), 244-251. doi:10.1111/j.1467-7687.2009.00882.x

Orsmond, G. I., Kuo, H. -Y., & Seltzer, M. M. (2009). Siblings of individuals with an autism spectrum disorder: Sibling relationships and wellbeing in adolescence and adulthood. *Autism, 13*(1), 59-80. doi:10.1177/1362361308097119

Orsmond, G. I., & Seltzer, M. M. (2007). Siblings of individuals with autism or Down syndrome: Effects on adult lives. *Journal of Intellectual Disability Research, 51*(9), 682-696. doi:10.1111/j.1365-2788.2007.00954.x

Orsmond, G. I., & Seltzer, M. M. (2009). Adolescent siblings of individuals with an autism spectrum disorder: Testing a diathesis-stress model of sibling well-being. *Journal of Autism and Developmental Disorders, 39*, 1053-1065. doi:10.1007/s10803-009-0722-7

Petalas, M. A., Hastings, R. P., Nash, S., Dowey, A., & Reilly, D. (2009a). "I like that he always shows who he is": The perceptions and experiences of siblings with a brother with autism spectrum disorder. *International Journal of Disability, Development and Education, 56*(4), 381-399. doi:10.1080/10349120903306715

Petalas, M. A., Hastings, R. P., Nash, S., Lloyd, T., & Dowey, A. (2009b). Emotional and behavioral adjustment in siblings of children with intellectual impairment with and without autism. *Autism, 13*, 471-483. doi:10.1177/1362361309335721

Quintero, N., & McIntyre, L. L. (2010). Sibling adjustment and maternal well-being: An examination of families with and without a child with an autism spectrum disorder. *Focus on Autism and Other Developmental Disabilities, 25*(1), 37-46. doi:10.1177/1088357609350367

Rao, P. A., & Beidel, D. C. (2009). The impact of children with high-functioning autism on parental stress, sibling adjustment, and family functioning. *Behavior Modification, 33*(4), 437-451. doi:10.1177/0145445509336427

Regehr, K., & Feldman, M. (2009). Parent-selected interventions for infants at-risk for autism spectrum disorders and their affected siblings. *Behavioral Interventions, 24*, 237-248. doi:10.1002/bin.291

Rivers, J. W., & Stoneman, Z. (2008). Child temperaments, differential parenting, and the sibling relationships of children with autism spectrum disorder. *Journal of Autism and Developmental Disorders, 38*, 1740-1748. doi:10.1007/s10803-008-0560-z

Rogers, S. J. (2009). What are infant siblings teaching us about autism in infancy? *Autism Research, 2*(3), 125-137. doi:10.1002/aur.81

Ross, P., & Cuskelly, M. (2006). Adjustment, sibling problems and coping strategies of brothers and sisters of children with autism spectrum disorder. *Journal of Intellectual & Developmental Disability, 31*(2), 77-86. doi:10.1080/13668250600710864

Sage, K. D., & Jegatheesan, B. (2010). Perceptions of siblings with autism and relationships with them: European American and Asian American siblings draw and tell. *Journal of Intellectual & Developmental Disability, 35*(2), 92-103. doi:10.3109/13668251003712788

Sarasella, M., Marventano, I., Guerini, F. R., Mancuso, R., Ceresa, L., Zanzottera, M., ... Clerici, M. (2009). An autistic endophenotype results in complex immune dysfunction in healthy siblings of autistic children. *Biological Psychiatry, 66*, 978-984. doi:10.1016/j.biopsych.2009.6.020

Seltzer, M. M., Krauss, M. W., & Orsmond, G. (2009, July 8). *Reflections from adolescent siblings who have a brother or sister with an autism spectrum disorder.* Retrieved from http://www.waisman.wisc.edu/family/reports/autism/aaareport6.pdf

Smith, L. O., & Elder, J. H. (2010). Siblings and family environments of persons with autism spectrum disorder: A review of the literature. *Journal of Child and Adolescent Psychiatric Nursing, 23*(3), 189-195. doi:10.1111/j.1744-6171.2010.00240.x

Sumiyoshi, C., Kawakubo, Y., Suga, M., Sumiyoshi, T., & Kasai, K. (2011). Impaired ability to organize information in individuals with autism spectrum disorders and their siblings. *Neuroscience Research, 63*(3), 252-257. doi:10.1016/j.neures.2010.11.007

Yoder, P., Stone, W. L., Walden, T., & Malesa, E. (2009). Predicting social impairment and ASD diagnosis in younger siblings of children with autism spectrum disorder. *Journal of Autism and Developmental Disorders, 39*, 1381-1391. doi:10.1007/s10803-009-0753-0

Zwaigenbaum, L., Thurm, A., Stone, W., Baranek, G., Bryson, S., Iverson, J., ... Sigman, M. (2007). Studying the emergence of autism spectrum disorders in high-risk infants: Methodological and practical issues. *Journal of Autism and Developmental Disorders, 37*, 466-480. doi:10.1007/s10803-006-0179-x

CHAPTER 6

AN INNOVATIVE COMMUNITY-BASED CLINIC THAT SERVES INDIVIDUALS WITH AUTISM SPECTRUM DISORDERS

Anthony F. Rotatori, Julie A. Deisinger, Timothy J. Wahlberg, Sandra Burkhardt, and Festus E. Obiakor

There has been a noticeable increase in the prevalence and presence of individuals with autism spectrum disorders (ASD) in society and it has become the fastest growing disability (Autism Society of America, 2010). This increase is related to a number of factors such as: the provisions of the Individuals With Disabilities Education Act (1990) which added autism as a specific disability category that necessitates that public school districts provide students with ASD a school program that meets their individual education needs; the advances in and earlier diagnosing of individuals with ASD (see Deisinger, 2008a); a growing public awareness of ASD due to popular press and media coverage (Gargiulo, 2012); and the inclusive philosophy of educating, treating, and training of individuals with ASD in the community rather than institutional and residential centers (Rotatori, Obiakor, & Burkhardt, 2008). While this increase has lead to challenges in meeting the needs of individuals with ASD, it has

Autism Spectrum Disorders: Inclusive Community for the Twenty-First Century, pp. 139–161

also resulted in numerous advances in: diagnosing and identification; psychological functioning (sensory-perceptual, cognitive, sociocognitive parameters); genetics and brain functioning aspects; best practice treatment approaches; educational implications; implications of ASD through the life span; and the effect of ASD on family functioning (see Boutot & Myles, 2011; Deisinger, 2010; Deisinger 2011; Roth, 2010; Tantam, 2011). These advances were spearheaded by major medical and university clinic research programs. However, this growing increase of individuals with ASD has challenged the service capacity of these medical and university clinic research based providers to meet the needs of these individuals. What is critically needed today is the development of community-based services for individuals with ASD that are accessible, accountable, comprehensive, inclusive, family focused and utilize best practice and evidence based procedures. Thus, the purpose of this chapter is to describe a community based facility that is meeting this need.

THE PRAIRIE CLINIC

Vision and Mission

The Prairie Clinic (http://theprairieclinic.com/) is an innovative, comprehensive, community clinic that serves individuals with ASD. The clinic was founded on the vision of its clinic directors, namely, Timothy Wahlberg, PhD, and Angel Heredia, MD. Their vision stemmed from the desire to offer individuals with ASD and their families a broader continuum of services in both the medical and clinical aspects of treatment. Dr. Wahlberg is a licensed clinical psychologist and a certified school psychologist. He has clinical experience in the following settings: public school, university clinic, psychiatric facility, community mental health center and private practice. Dr. Wahlberg has published extensively on the subjects of autism and neurological impairments (see Arthur, Rotatori, & Wahlberg, 2001; Wahlberg, 2000; Wahlberg, 2001a, 2001b, 2001c, 2001d; Wahlberg, 2010; Wahlberg & Jordan, 2001; Wahlberg & Rotatori, 2001, Wahlberg, Rotatori, Deisinger, & Burkhardt, 2003). Dr. Heredia is board certified in child and adolescent psychiatrist as well as adult psychiatry by the American Board of Psychiatry and Neurology. He has expertise in evaluation and treatment in a wide spectrum of psychiatric problems including pervasive developmental disorders. In addition to Dr. Wahlberg and Dr. Heredia, the clinic is staffed by a variety of professionals with backgrounds in counseling, social work, clinical behavioral treatment, school psychology and educational intervention.

Clinic Services

The Prairie Clinic staff brings a broad array of services which is highly desirable in meeting the diverse needs of individuals with ASD who have significant social, affective and sensory motor difficulties. For example, the clinic offers the following services to individuals with ASD, their families, professionals and school districts: individual counseling, family counseling, staff training, school programming, in-services, and consultative services. The professional staff at the clinic emphasize the need for practitioners to employ evidence-based practice guidelines (American Psychological Association, 2005).

The clinic staff specializes in psychological evaluations of individuals with ASD that includes neurological, personality, achievement, neurosocial, and limited developmental testing. The staff administers a variety of diagnostic and screening devices. Over the past 10 years there has been an explosion of ASD diagnostic and screening devices (see Sapp, 2008). Psychological testing of individuals with ASD stresses the use of best practices that involve the administration of well established and researched devices. Some of the best devices on the market include the Autism Diagnostic Interview-Revised (Rutter, LeCouteur, & Lord, 2003) and the Autism Diagnostic Observation Schedule (Lord, Rutter, DiLavore, & Risi, 2001). Newer ASD screening devices include the Early Screening of Autistic Traits (Swinkels et al., 2006), the Early Developmental Questionnaire (Ozonoff, Williams, & Landa, 2005) and the Childhood Asperger Syndrome Test (Scott, Baron-Cohen, Bolton, & Brayne, 2002). According to Deisinger (2008a), the Childhood Asperger Syndrome Test may be a very useful screening device because it can be completed by parents to screen for the presence of Asperger's disorder and other ASDs in preschool to elementary aged children. Certain devices such as the Autism Diagnostic Observation Schedule require specialized training. The Prairie Clinic does have clinicians trained in the Autism Diagnostic Observation Schedule.

The clinic directors hold that early accurate diagnostic assessment is critical in identifying individuals with ASD due to the known delay that often occurs with individuals with ASD who do not have intellectual deficits (see Deisinger, 2008a). In addition to this factor, delays in diagnosing can result from clients "living in a rural community, near-poor family income status, impaired hearing, and oversensitivity to pain and having many pediatric health providers" (Deisinger, 2008a, p. 86). Also, there is some research that suggests a professional bias may be present in diagnosing African American children with ASD that leads to a later age of diagnosis (Theus, 2008). Sometimes, the delay in identifying African American children with ASD is due to barriers to help-seeking behaviors resulting from socioeconomic status, religion and cultural experiences (Theus, 2008). Another factor for delay of diagnosis results when children with mild ASD are first identified by mental health professionals as having oppositional defiant or attention-deficit hyperactivity disorder instead of ASD (Burkhardt & Rotatori, 2008).

Treatment of individuals with ASD at the Prairie Clinic involves the use of effective research based treatment approaches. These treatment approaches include the following: applied behavioral analysis (Boutot & Dukes, 2011), early intensive behavioral intervention (Foxx, 2008), discrete trial training (Granpeesheh, Tarbox, & Dixon, 2009), pivotal response training (Boutot & Dukes, 2011) and natural environmental training (Granspeesheh et al., 2009). According to Deisinger (2011), these effective treatments typically involve the observation of the individual with ASD in the environment and then the employment of positive reinforcement for identified appropriate behavior while not attending to undesirable consequences for the inappropriate behavior. Other best practices intervention approaches for individuals with ASD include: Learning Experiences which is an alternative program for preschoolers and parents (see Roth, 2010) and Treatment and Education of Autistic and related Communication-handicapped Children (TEACCH) (see Lord & Schopler, 1994).

Unfortunately, the increasing number of children with ASDs has resulted in a plethora of interventions (e.g., dietary, medication based, biomedical, and psychoeducational) that are not scientifically supported. Unsupported dietary interventions include the following: gluten-free/casein-free diet (see Elder, 2008; Romanczyk, Gillis, White, & Digennaro, 2008; Wallace, 2009), specific carbohydrate diet (see Levy & Hyman, 2005; Wallace, 2009), administration of vitamins such as A, C, and E (T. Smith & Wick, 2008), combination of vitamins such as vitamin B6 and the mineral magnesium (Schechtman, 2007), or nutritional supplements such as dimethylglycine (T. Smith & Wick, 2008). Unsupported medication intervention has centered on the hormone secretin which has been reported to increase expressive language and behavior in students with ASD (see Deisinger, 2010; T. Smith, 2008), however, no scientific evidence exists that it has any therapeutic value in treating children with ASDs (T. Smith, 2008; T. Smith & Wick, 2008). Also, the following medications have not been found to be scientifically effective interventions: antibiotic vancomycin (Schechtman, 2007), antiviral medication such as valacyclovir (Levy & Hyman, 2005; Schechtman, 2007), antifungal agents such as fluconazole, nystatin, or metronidazole (Levy & Hyman, 2005; T. Smith, 2008), and over the counter antacid famotidine (Pepcid) (Stephenson, 2002).

Other biomedical interventions for individuals with ASD such as magnet therapy have not been found to be scientifically effective in treating individuals with ASD (Ruscio, 2006, T. Smith, 2008). Another extremely controversial biomedical approach is nonvaccination (Fraleigh, 2009: Offit, 2008). According to this approach, the use of vaccinations such as the measles-mumps-rubella vaccine can cause an increase in the number of youngsters with ASD. This has resulted in the practice by some parents to refuse having their children vaccinated. Unfortunately, this issue arose over reported case study findings on vaccinations of individuals with ASD by a British researcher named Wakefield (M. J. Smith, Ellensberg, Bell, & Rubin, 2008). However, Deisinger (2010) stated that "Wakefield's findings have never been replicated (Fraleigh, 2009) and are now viewed by the scientific community as significantly flawed (M. J. Smith et al., 2008)" (p.224). Lastly, studies (see Curtis & Patel, 2008) have found that a component of vaccines, namely, Thimcrosal, does not have any risks related to the development of ASD.

Over the past 10 years, a number of psychoeducational interventions have been proposed to treat children with ASD that are not evidence based. These interventions include the following: options therapy (Son-Rise), facilitated communication, sensory integration therapy, auditory integration therapy, multisensory environment (Snoezelen environment), and animal therapy (horseback riding, dolphin-assisted therapy) (see Botts, Herschfedt, & Christensen-Sandfort, 2008; Herbert, Sharp, & Gaudiano, 2002; Romanczk, Arnstein, Soorya, & Gillis, 2003; Simpsom, 2008; T. Smith, 2008). According to Deisinger (2010), Son-Rise proposes that the behavior of residential children with ASD will improve when their caregivers express an attitude of acceptance and encouragement. According to Simpson (2008), proponents of facilitated communication state that children with impaired communication and ASD and apraxia can communicate with the assistance of a facilitator by typing on a keyboard. Sensory integration therapy users believe that deficit sensory and motor skills of children with ASD can be remediated by having the children engage in physical activities such as swinging on a swing or spinning in a chair (T. Smith, 2008). Auditory integration therapy interventionists stress that children with ASD who are overly sensitive to low or high sounds can learn to adapt to these sounds by having them "listen daily to music that has been filtered to eliminate these sound frequencies "(Deisinger, 2010, p. 226). The Snoezelen environment requires interventionists to gently stimulate the five basic senses which can result in improvement in areas such as coordination, mood, motivation, concentration, behavior and social relations (see Botts et al., 2008). Animal therapy treatment for individuals with ASD has received growing attention, however, studies (see Romanczyk et al., 2003; T. Smith, 2008) have not scientifically demonstrated the effectiveness of these approaches due to flawed experimental design and the lack of control for maturation (Romanczyk et al., 2003).

SOCIAL INTERVENTION FOCUS

A major treatment focus at the Prairie Clinic involves the development of social skill learning for individuals with ASD. The clinic staff has found that a group learning approach to social competence is an effective approach that has been supported in the literature (see Cotugno, 2009). Typically, clinic social groups are scheduled three times per year. The group sizes range from four to eight children which allows for personal interaction (e.g., peer to peer, peer to instructor). The social groups are continuous which allows group members to become comfortable with themselves and other individuals in always changing situations. Social groups are specifically designed to be a fun, interactive experience which creates the opportunity for individuals with ASD to become more aware of social cues and develop tools to effectively handle challenging emotional and social situations. In addition, the social groups allow members to become empowered to interact effectively with peers, teachers, and coaches and significant others while allowing the members to develop skills that are important for becoming an independent, respectful, successful adult. There are also special topics for older students that are discussed such as dating, finding a job, sexuality, being bullied, friendships, and succeeding in college. The social groups at the clinic are divided by age and school level (young children-ages 3 to 6 years, 6 to 8 years; young boys or girls-ages 8 to 11 years; middle school boys-ages 11 to 14 years; high school boys-ages 15 to 18 years; college students).

The value of learning effective and appropriate social skills is critical to the development of individuals with ASD due to the core deficits associated with this disorder which include qualitative impairment in social interactions and verbal and nonverbal communication; delays in the acquisition of expressive language; and restrictive interests. According to Burkhardt (2008), "teaching social competence by encouraging socialization has been an accepted intervention for students with ASD" (p. 4). Positively, educators of students with ASD have devised a number of effective programmatic socialization approaches such as: The Responsive Classroom (Brock, Nishida, Chiong, Grimm, & Rimm-Kaufman, 2008); Social Skills Training Project (Baker, 2003); Circle of Friends Program (Attwood, 2003); Special Friends Program (see Favazza, Phillipsen, & Kumar, 2000); the SCORE Skills Strategy Program (see Webb, Miller, Pierce, Strawser, & Jones, 2004); and Carol Gray's Social Stories Approach (Gray & White, 2002).

The teaching of social competence requires a diverse set of skills such as friendship and relationship development social behaviors (Burkhardt, 2008). For example, friendship development involves component skills such as tolerating criticism, responding to compliments, recognizing when and how to join in, resolving conflict, using body language to indicate interest and accepting the opinions of others (Burkhardt, 2008). Goals for relationship development may include the following: being more accepting, curious, creative, and flexible as well as being aware of personal and unique identity and thinking in terms of gray and not black and white (Burkhardt, 2008). In addition to establishing component skills and goals for social development, interventionists need to identify core supports of social competence for students with ASD (see Burkhardt, 2008). Stichter, Randolph, Gage, and Schmidt (2007) promote the following core supports: aptitude for social competence, social skills learning, interpersonal applications, and interpersonal effectiveness. However, evidence-based practices of social skill competence development for individuals with ASD may be impacted by barriers such as reliable and valid evaluation of social competence, limited generalization of social skills, accurate self-appraisal of one's social competence, and the influence of socialization demands as environmental stressors (Burkhardt, 2008).

Due to the above mentioned barriers, Burkhardt (2008) has proposed developing core social competence via a Hierarchy of Socialization Environment based upon three constituencies, namely, the students, parents and general educators, and special educations and researchers. According to Burkhardt, competitive socialization training would encompass three levels, namely, competitive, supportive and sheltered. Competitive socialization is demonstrated when an individual with ASD exhibits "sufficient interpersonal effectiveness to be judged socially competent by others" (Burkhardt, p. 18). Supportive socialization would be demonstrated when an individual with ASD is able to socialize with "familiars, those with whom a social relationship exists and from whom a degree of social competence can be anticipated" (Burkhardt, p. 18). Lastly, sheltered socialization entails an individual with ASD socializing with the aid of a skilled and accommodating person who structures and prompts the social interactions.

SUPPORTIVE OUTREACH TO FAMILIES MEMBERS

Another major service component of the community clinic treatment of individuals with ASD is clinical service and outreach to parents, spouses, and families. This service and outreach is critical according to Deisinger (2011), based upon the increasing research recognition to provide support for families of children with ASDs due to the high levels of family stress they encounter that often exceeds the stress associated with neurotypical children (see Symon & Boettcher, 2008). ASD community clinic outreach services include parent counseling, parent coaching and behavioral management training. For example, the Prairie Clinic is planning educational groups for parents of elementary or middle school-aged children who are more interested in acquiring effective tools to manage problem behaviors of their children as well as provide emotional support to them. Possible topics include the following: understanding the function of your child's behavior; learning effective strategies to change behavior in yourself and your child; learning techniques for applying positive reinforcement, praise, and rewards; understanding the difference between rewards and punishments for altering behavior; and identifying appropriate incentives to encourage positive behavior by your child. Parents of individuals with ASD can also be given a bibliography of related articles and books that assist parents in: advocating for their children's needs; initiating a dialogue between parents and school personnel; accessing community resources; helping them understand their child's ASD disorder and its effect on educational, social, behavioral, emotional and career aspects. (Readers interested in catalogs of excellent bestselling books on many of the above ASD topics are directed to the following publishers: Jessica Kingsley Publishers [http://www.jkp.com] and Autism Asperger Publishing Company [http://www.aapcpublishinh.net/-12k].) In addition, medical information related to understanding ASD and its management is provided. For example, parents are provided with a comprehensive biological and neurological overview of ASD and genetic disorders most commonly associated with autism such as immune dysfunction, gastrointestinal disturbances, and seizures (see Aitken, 2010).

Another unique social support group that can be helpful in serving individuals with ASD is a spouse support group. At times, spouses who have a partner with Asperger's disorder or high functioning autism may find themselves feeling frustrated or discouraged by their spouses: awkward social behavior, nonreciprocal emotional responses, unwillingness to show affection in public, refusal to sleep in the same bed, and difficulty holding a job (see Simone, 2009). While the initial diagnosis of a spouse with ASD may provide relief as there is a reason why he/she is behaving in such challenging ways, it may be a major disappointment to a spouse who realizes that the spouse's diagnosis will not change and the primary responsibility for the success of the relationship rests with the healthy spouse's capacity to: compensate for the husband/wife's inadequacies, be sensitive to their unique characteristics and work at overcoming the hurdles that are presented each day by their husband/wife (see Marshack, 2009). The Prairie Clinic staff is planning social support groups that will offer spouses a place to discuss the above marital problems, concerns, adjustments, compensations and issues. Examples of common issues that the clinic plans to discuss with spouses include the following: understanding Asperger's disorder; discussing questions and concerns related to your spouse's behavior; explaining the diagnosis to your children, family members and friends; ways to reduce stress and strain; seeing things from their spouses perspective; and balancing life and responsibilities within the family. Positively, there is an increasing literature base on this topic that can assist spouse's in managing their relationships (see Aston, 2002, 2003; Bentley, 2007; Marshack, 2009; Simone, 2009; Stanford, 2002). Also, there is a website, namely, Asperger Syndrome Partners and Individuals Resources, Encouragement and Support (http://www.Aspires-relationships.com) that is devoted to spouses and partners with Asperger Disorder that contains informative articles, survival tips and encouragement.

At times, professionals who work with parents of children with ASD recommend parent counseling due to issues specific to a child with ASD. According to Burkhardt (2001), parent counseling focuses on management of the child's disorder which may focus on treatment options and family accommodations to the child's special needs. While there is no cure for ASD, there are a variety of treatments options that parents need to consider (see Wilkinson, 2010). An early treatment consideration is whether to use home-based, clinic-based, school-based or group-based approaches (Deisinger, 2011). Typically, a home-based intensive behavioral programming such as Lovaas's applied behavioral analysis approach (see T. Smith, Wynn, & Lovaas, 1997) or Koegel, Koegel and McNerney's (2001) concept of pivotal areas for intervention is more effective for toddler/preschool children with ASD.

Throughout childhood, parents of children with ASD are exposed to a variety of stressors such as: obtaining an accurate diagnosis (Symon & Boettcher, 2008); uncertain progress (Symon & Boettcher, 2008); uncertainty about the child's uneven development; the occurrence of maladaptive behavior at home and in the public; the child's lack of emotional reciprocity, inflexibility, and communication difficulties; feelings of loss and isolation; and at times limited access to professional service providers (see Burkhardt, 2008; Deisinger, 2011; Marcus, Kunce, & Schopler, 2005; Theus, 2008). These stressors can augment to the point where they become risk factors for parents which necessitates counseling. If counseling is needed, Burkhardt (2001) recommends the following guidelines:

1. Help families engineer for success by understanding the role that expressed emotion, including negatively expressed emotion and

emotional overinvolvement, may play in the triggering, prolonging or escalating of dysfunctional interactions within the home.
2. Challenge to survive. Accepting or accommodating to deficit will not help the person with ASD to improve.
3. Accommodate to survive. Preserve parental resources through respite, planning, support and encouragement.
4. Create options for success for families of persons with ASD by defining a hierarchy of goals to be worked on.
5. Review the limitations in the development of social cognition that characterize ASD. Understand the difference between the inability of persons with ASD to identify and respond to social expectations and an insensitive refusal to be considerate of others. (p.230)

Another critical service that the Prairie Clinic is planning is the availability of a special sibling support group for siblings that have a brother or sister with ASD who has significant social, emotional or behavioral problems and concerns. This is especially important because growing up with a brother or sister with ASD can be challenging, annoying, tiring, frustrating, and lonely as well as rewarding (Johnson & Van Rensselaer, 2010). Sibling support groups can assist a sibling in understanding the nature of ASD and the perplexing behavioral and emotional responses of a brother or sister with ASD. One of the first group goals can be to explain the disorder and its characteristics so that misconceptions, fears and worries can be dealt with (Harris & Glasberg, 2003; Marcus et al., 2005). Another goal is to deal with negative emotions such as jealousy, resentment, guilt, sadness, loss of time and attention from parents and public embarrassment that is experienced due to the social awkwardness of the sibling with ASD in front of friends or at community gatherings (Bashe & Kirby, 2005; Bittner, 2006; Coyle, 2006; Feiges & Weiss, 2004; Orsmond & Seltzer, 2007; Papalia, Olds, & Feldman, 2006; Royko, 2007; Stillman, 2005). A third goal is to examine whether the sibling has experienced anger or feelings of abandonment because parents have overloaded the sibling with too much responsibility for the care of a brother or sister with ASD (Deisinger, 2008b; Siegel & Silverstein, 2001). A fourth goal is to discuss with the sibling ways to play and socialize with a brother or sister with ASD. Helpful play strategies would include establishing eye contact, prompting behavior, and rewarding the brother or sister with praise to increase the likelihood of appropriate interactive social and play behavior (Tsao & Odom, 2006). A fifth goal deals with issues that adults with ASD siblings may have such as fear of having a child with ASD, caring for a sibling when one's parents are unable to, assuming financial aid and/or legal guardianship, guilt feelings about moving away from a sibling with ASD due to career opportunities, and embarrassment or fear in establishing personal relationships (Feiges & Weiss, 2004; Harris & Glasberg, 2003; Strohm, 2005).

DISSEMINATION OF INFORMATION

Another unique service of the Prairie Clinic is its role in disseminating information on ASD to the community. The professional staff at the clinic, especially Dr. Wahlberg, is extremely active in outreach to the community in a variety of venues. For example, free parent seminars are scheduled throughout the year. Recent seminar topics included best practices for elementary and secondary students on the autistic spectrum; social skills development of autistic children in an academic environment; transitions for students with ASD; and legal aspects of managing ASDs at school. In addition, Dr. Wahlberg presents at state, regional, national and international conferences and conducts training seminars for local school districts. His recent topics have included the following: behavior and autism; autism: problem behaviors; and special education and autism. Information on ASD is also carried out by the publishing of an informational newsletter called "The Prairie News." The newsletter contains a variety of ASD information for families, teachers and therapists such as consumer news (e.g., understanding the new autism insurance law), short summaries of recent medication news (e.g., cognitive behavior therapy plus Zoloft is "Gold Standard" treatment for child anxiety), short summaries of published articles on ASD, upcoming conferences, training workshops and seminars and websites to obtain information on a variety of topics. Lastly, the newsletter has a special section entitled "Ask Dr. Tim" where parents, individuals with ASD, teachers and therapists can pose questions (e.g., what treatments are recommended for children with ASD?).

A unique information aspect is the availability of Dr. Wahlberg's (2010) book "*Finding the Grey: Understanding and Thinking in the Black and White World of Autism and Asperger's*. This book provides parents and professionals with useful information and clear strategies to cope with the behaviors and characteristics associated with ASD. Wahlberg writes with a conversational tone that invites readers in. Further, his ability to empathize and relate to parents and educators offers a respite for those who do not know where to turn for help related to meeting the needs of their child with ASD. The book can be purchased in soft cover or it can be downloaded for a small nominal price to clients and their families (http://www.findingthegray.com).

The advent of the internet has lead to numerous websites that provide bountiful information on ASD for clients, parents, families and professionals to access. Comprehensive and diverse information can be obtained by accessing national organizations, institutes and resource centers concerned with ASD (see Table 6.1). Community clinics serving individuals with ASD can post the websites' addresses and display free informational brochures from these organizations, institutes, and resource centers in the office waiting area. The following section describes the mission and services of the above organizations, institutes and resource centers.

The mission of the national organization Autism Society of America is to support families of individuals with ASD and to raise awareness about all aspects of living with, educating, treating and caring for a person with ASD. It publishes a magazine, *Autism Advocate*, four times a year which offers the latest information on research, legislation, and tips on living with ASD. Also, Autism Society of America sponsors the annual National Autism Conference where ASD professionals and families network and participate in workshops and presentations on ASD. Autism Society of America has a network of chapters in nearly every state. It also publishes 3 to 4 page brochures that include helpful information and recommended resources for a variety of topics (see Table 6.2). A unique component of the Autism Society of America has been their joint venture with AMC Entertainment to create sensory friendly films for children with ASD (see http://www.Autism.lovetoknow.com/Sensory_Friendly_Films).

Autism Network International is an international organization operated by and for individuals with ASD. The mission and founding principles advocate the anticure perspective which stresses that there should not be a goal to "cure" individuals with ASD. Each year Autism Network International hosts the conference "Autreat" for individuals with ASD. Autreat is specifically designed for individuals with ASD and offers an autistic-friendly environment, free of sensory bombardment. Conventioneers are under no obligation to interact socially. Each conventioneer wears a simple visual code in the form of a colored badge to indicate those who wish to interact with anyone and everyone, those who wish not to be approached by strangers, and those who wish not to be approached at all.

Autism Services Center was founded on the belief that each person with ASD has the capacity for growth and development. Also, Autism Services Center believes that each individual with ASD has a right to services that enhance well-being, quality of life, and opportunities to learn. Furthermore, individuals with ASD should have access to the most normal and least restrictive social and physical environments consistent with his or her needs. Autism Services Center stresses that even individuals who have the most challenging ASD behaviors can respond to dignified interaction in a structured, meaningful program with highly trained and supervised staff that work under an appropriate client/staff ratio. Lastly,

Table 6.1. National Organizations, Institutes, and Resource Centers Concerned With ASD

- Autism Network International
  P.O. Box 35448
  Syracuse, NY 13235
  http://www.autreat.com

- Autism Research Institute
  4182 Adams Avenue
  San Diego, CA 92116
  (866) 366-3361
  http://www.autismone.org/content/autism-research-institute-ari

- Autism Services Center
  929 4th Avenue
  Huntington, WA 25701
  http://www.autismservicescenter.org

- Autism Society of America
  4340 East-West Highway
  Suite 350
  Bethesda, MD 20814
  (800) 328-8476
  http://www.autism-society.org

- Autism Speaks
  2 Park Avenue
  11th Floor
  New York, NY 10016
  (212) 252-8584
  http://www.autismspeaks.org

- Indiana Resource Center for Autism (RICA)
  Indiana Institute on Disability and Community
  Indiana University
  2853 E. Tenth Street
  Bloomington, IN 47408
  (812) 855-6508
  http://www.iidc.indiana.edu/index.php?pageId=32

- Kennedy Krieger Institute
  707 N. Broadway
  Baltimore, MD 21205
  (888) 554-2080
  http://www.kennedykrieger.org

- Ohio Center for Autism and Low Incidence
  470 Glenmont, Avenue
  Columbus, OH 43214
  (866) 886-2254
  http://www.ocali.org

Table 6.2. Description of Informational Brochure Topics Available From ASA

- **Next step: A guide for families new to autism**. Provides readers with a general understanding of ASD. An overview of the various treatments options, and brief information about education and services that is helpful to children and adults with ASD.
- **Building our futures: Educating students on the autism spectrum**. Assists educators and school administrators in becoming familiar with the learning styles of students with ASD and the educational approaches designed to meet their unique needs.
- **Supporting appropriate behavior in students with Asperger's**. Points out that effective positive behavioral support requires highly individualized practices that address the primary areas of difficulty in social understanding and interactions, pragmatic communication, managing anxiety, preferences for sameness and rules, and ritualistic behaviors.
- **Moving from preschool to kindergarten**. Provides parents suggestions on ensuring a successful and less stressful transition of their child with ASD as they transition to kindergarten.
- **Going to middle school**. Provides suggestions for parents, educators and staff in preparing a successful and fluid transition plan for students with ASD as they transition to middle school.
- **Puberty and children on the Autism spectrum**. Provides parents with information, suggestions, and resources to assist their teenager with ASD as they navigate puberty.
- **Preparing to experience college living**. Provides parents with tips on preparing their senior high school student with ASD as they apply to and select colleges.
- **Growing up together**. Provides readers with information about people with ASD and how you can befriend them.
- **Siblings perspective: Guidelines for parents**. Provides parents with important information and practical suggestions for helping and supporting siblings who have a brother or sister with ASD.
- **Preparing for a lifetime.** Discusses critical life preparations for students graduating from high school as they enter the job market, find a place to live and establish long lasting relationships.
- **Autism information for social workers and counselors**. Provides information on characteristics of ASD as well as appropriate ways to communicate, respond and delivery of services for clients with ASD.
- **Autism information for paramedics and emergency room staff**. Provides comprehensive information on the characteristics of individuals with ASD and appropriate response/delivery of emergency services.

Autism Services Center encourages the use of best clinical practices and effective treatment for all.

Autism Speaks was founded in 2005 by Bob and Suzanne Wright, grandparents of a child with ASD. Presently, it is the nation's largest ASD science and advocacy organization that is dedicated to: funding research into the causes, prevention, treatments and cure for ASD; increasing awareness of ASD; and advocating for the needs of individuals with ASD and their families. It supports research in four domains: etiology-genetic and developmental aspects; biology-brain development; diagnosis; epidemiology and biomarkers; therapy-medication, behavioral, and psychological. Autism Speaks funds the Autism Genetic Resource Exchange (http://www.agre.org/) which is a DNA repository and family registry of genotypic and phenotypic data base that can be used by ASD researchers worldwide. It also funds the Autism Tissue Program (http://www.brainbank.org/) which is compromised of a network of ASD researchers that manage and distribute brain tissue for ASD research. Lastly, Autism Speaks supports the Clinical Trials Network, which focuses on the development of pharmacological interventions for individuals with ASD.

Autism Research Institute is a nonprofit organization that was established in 1967 by Bernard Rimland, who was an international recognized authority on ASD and the father of a son with ASD. Autism Research Institute is dedicated to conducting and disseminating research on the triggers of ASD and on methods of diagnosing and treating ASD. It provides research-based information to parents and professionals around the world. Autism Research Institute has the world's largest data base (presently, 40,000 detailed case histories of children with ASD from over 60 countries). It publishes Autism Research Review International, a quarterly newsletter, which covers biomedical and educational advances in ASD research.

In addition to the websites of the above organizations, institutes, and resource centers, there are numerous websites that provide clients, parent, families, and professionals diverse and unique information on ASD. One

Table 6.3. Websites Categories for Autism Resources Links

- Accounts of people with ASD (31 sites)
- Charities and foundations on ASD (9 sites)
- Information on Asperger syndrome (13 sites)
- Definitions of ASD (13 sites)
- Online discussions (27 sites)
- General information on ASD (18 sites)
- Specific issues on ASD (17 sites)
- Libraries with information on ASD (8 sites)
- Methods, treatments, and programs on ASD (98 sites)
- Organizations (124 sites)
- Academic resource programs (21 sites)
- Bibliography, books, and articles (37 sites)

Table 6.4. Assistive Technology Resource Websites for Educators and Parents of Students with ASD

- Ability Hub: Assistive Technology Solutions: http://www.abilityhub.com/index.html
- Alliance for Technology Access: http://www.ataccess.org/
- Center for Electronic Studying: http://www.ces.uoregon.edu/
- Closing The Gap: http://ww.closingthegap.cpm/
- Disability and Technology: A Resource Collection: http://www.home.nas.net/~galaambos/tech.htm
- DREAMS for Kids, Inc.: http://www.dreams.org
- EASI-Equal Access to Software and Information-K12 Connection: http://www.rit.edu/~easi/
- Family Village School-Assistive Technology for Students with Disabilities: http://www.familyvillage.wisc.edu/education/at.html
- Mac Access Passport: http://www.apple.com/education/k12/disability/map.html
- National Center to Improve Practice: http://www.edc.org/FSC/NCIP/
- National Center for Technology Innovation: http://www.nationaltechcenter.org/
- Special Education Technology British Columbia: http://www.setbc.org/lcindexer/
- Trace Research and Development Center: http://www.trace.wisc.edu/
- Wisconsin Assistive Technology AR Tools and Forms: http://www.dpi.state.wi.us/sped/at-wati-resources.html
- University of Toronto Assistive Technology Resource Center: http://www.utoronto.ca/atrc/reference/tech/techgloss.html
- Vendor Members of the Alliance for Technology Access: http://www.ataccess.org/member.Directory/atamembers.htm

is Autism Resources Links (http://www.autism-resources.com). This resource link provides web addresses for hundreds of ASD categories (see Table 6.3). Another interesting resource site is Autism Resources Network (http://www.autismshop.com) which is a one-of-a-kind book store that has compiled available merchandise and information for individuals with ASD and those who love, care and educate them (e.g. books, software, CDs, DVDs, games, cards, jewelry, and play things). For interventionists who are interested in free printables related to structured teaching there is Practical Autism Resources (http://www.practicalautismresources.com/printables)

Another valuable informational service that providers of ASD can undertake is making clients, families, care givers, and educators aware of the benefits of assistive technology (AT) (see Nkabinde, 2008; West, 2011). AT has become a critical component in the treatment and education of individuals with ASD after it was mandated as a "required consideration" in the development of individual education plans for students with disabilities by the Individuals With Disabilities Educational Improvement Act (2004) (see Parette & Peterson-Karlan, 2010). The utilization of AT for individuals with ASD increases their access and opportunity, independence and empowerment (Edyburn Higgins, & Boone, 2005). According to Bouck (2010)

> technology can provide a voice to those who may not otherwise have one per their disability (i.e., [augmentative and alternative communication devices]), read a text to a student who struggles with reading as a result of his/her disability (i.e., text-to-speech devices, screen readers, and reading pens), grant access to a computer and other electronic tools (i.e., switches and speech recognition), and offer low-tech devices such as pencil grips or lined paper to aid students in writing. (p. 92)

Deisinger (2011) indicates the successful utilization of AT for individuals with ASD necessitates making decisions about "the needs and skills of the student, the physical environment in which the AT will be implemented, the types of activities in which the AT will be employed, goals for their use, and the types of AT devices that would best serve the student (West, 2011)" (p. 256). Fortunately, there are more and more companies that are producing commercial AT devices with the intent to augment literacy and communication abilities, enhance interpersonal skills and promote increased independence (see Table 6.4 for AT resource websites for educators and parents of students with ASD).

REFERENCES

Aitken, K. J. (2010). *A-Z of genetic factors in autism*. Philadelphia, PA: Jessica Kingsley.

American Psychological Association. (2005). *Policy statement on evidence-based practice in psychology.* Retrieved from http://www.2apa.org/practice/ebpstatement.pdf

Arthur, M. R., Rotatori, A. F., & Wahlberg, T. (2001). Counseling techniques for individuals with autistic spectrum disorders. In T. Wahlberg, F. E. Obiakor, S. Burkhardt, & A. F. Rotatori (Eds.), *Autistic spectrum disorders: Educational and clinical interventions* (Vol. 14, pp. 235-254). Oxford, England: Elsevier Science.

Aston, M. (2002). *The other half of Asperger syndrome*. Shawnee Mission, KS: Autism Asperger.

Aston, M. (2003). *Aspergers in love: Couple relationship and family affairs*. Shawnee Mission, KS: Autism Asperger.

Attwood, T. (2003). Frameworks for behavioral interventions. *Childhood and Adolescent Psychiatric Clinics of North America, 12*(1), 65-86.

Autism Society of America. (2010). *About autism.* Retrieved from http://www.autism-society.org/site/PageServer?pagename=about_home

Baker, J. (2003). *Social skills training for children and adolescents with Asperger's syndrome and social communication problems.* Shawnee Mission, KS: Autism Asperger.

Bashe, P. R., & Kirby, B. L. (2005). *The OASIS guide to Asperger syndrome: Advice, support, insight, and inspiration* (Rev ed.). New York, NY: Crown.

Bentley, K. (2007). *Alone together: Making an Asperger marriage work.* Philadelphia, PA: Jessica Kingsley.

Bittner, K. M. (2006). An unexpected blessing. In C. N. Ariel & R. A. Naseef (Eds.), *Voices from the spectrum: Parents, grandparents, siblings, people with autism, and professionals share their wisdom* (pp. 141-144). Philadelphia, PA: Jessica Kingsley.

Botts, B. H., Herschfeldt, P. A., & Christensen-Sandfort, R. J. (2008). Snoezelen: Empirical review of product representation. *Focus on Autism and Other Developmental Disorders, 23*(3), 138-147.

Bouck, E. C. (2010). Technology and students with disabilities: Does it solve all the problems. In F. E. Obiakor, J. P. Bakken, & A. F. Rotatori (Eds.), *Current issues and trends in special education: Research, technology and teacher preparation* (Vol. 20, pp. 91-104). Bingley, England: Emerald.

Boutot, E. A. & Dukes, C. (2011). Evidence-based practices for educating students with autism spectrum disorders. In E. A. Boutot & B. S. Myles (Eds.), *Autism spectrum disorders: Foundations, characteristics, and effective strategies* (pp. 68-92). Upper Saddle River, NJ: Pearson.

Boutot, E. A. & Myles, B. S. (2011). *Autism spectrum disorders: Foundations, characteristics and effective strategies.* Upper Saddle River, NJ: Pearson.

Brock, L., Nishida, T., Chiong, V., Grimm, K., & Rimm-Kaufman, S. (2008). Children's perception of the classroom environment and social and academic performance: A longitudinal analysis of the contribution of the responsive classroom approach. *Journal of School Psychology, 46,* 129-149.

Burkhardt, S. (2001). Counseling issues for parents of children with autistic spectrum disorders. In T. Wahlberg, F. E. Obiakor, S. Burkhardt, & A. F. Rotatori (Eds.), *Autistic spectrum disorders: Educational and clinical interventions* (Vol. 14, pp. 211-223). Oxford, England: Elsevier Science.

Burkhardt, S. (2008).The challenge of social competence for students with autism spectrum disorders. In A. F. Rotatori, F. E. Obiakor, & S. Burkhardt (Eds.), *Autism and developmental disabilities: Current practices and issues* (Vol. 18, pp. 1-24). Bingley, England: Emerald.

Burkhardt, S., & Rotatori, A. F. (2008, May). *Autism spectrum disorders: Family and cultural considerations.* Paper presented at the Young Adult Institute, New York, NY.

Cotugno, A. J. (2009). *Group intervention for children with autism spectrum disorders: A focus on social competency and social skills.* Philadelphia, PA: Jessica Kingsley.

Coyle, S. (2006). Growing up with Bradley. In C. N. Ariel & R. A. Naseef (Eds.), *Voices from the spectrum: Parents, grandparents, siblings, people with autism and professionals share their wisdom* (pp. 145-148). Philadelphia, PA: Jessica Kingsley.

Curtis, L. T., & Patel, K. (2008). Nutritional and environmental approaches to preventing and treating autism and attention deficit hyperactivity disorder (ADHD): A review. *The Journal of Alternative and Complementary Medicine, 14(1),* 79-85.

Deisinger, J. A. (2008a). Recent developments in the diagnosis and assessment of autism spectrum disorders. In A. F. Rotatori, F. E. Obiakor, & S. Burkhardt (Eds.), *Autism and developmental disabilities: Current practices and issues* (Vol. 18, pp. 85-108). Bingley, England: Emerald.

Deisinger, J. A. (2008b). Issues pertaining to siblings of individuals with autism spectrum disorders. In A. F. Rotatori, F. E. Obiakor, & S. Burkhardt (Eds.), *Autism and developmental disabilities: Current practices and issues* (Vol. 18, pp. 135-155). Bingley, England: Emerald.

Deisinger, J. A. (2010). Scientifically unsupported treatments for students with special needs. In F. E. Obiakor, J. P. Bakken, & A. F. Rotatori (Eds.), *Current issues and trends in special education: Identification, assessment, and instruction* (Vol. 19, pp. 213-236). Bingley, England: Emerald.

Deisinger, J. A. (2011). History of autism spectrum disorders. In A. F. Rotatori, F. E. Obiakor, & J. P. Bakken (Eds.), *History of special education* (Vol. 21, pp. 237-267). Bingley, England: Emerald.

Edyburn, D. L., Higgins, K., & Boone, R. (2005). *Handbook of special education technology research and practice*. Whitefish Bay, WI: Knowledge by Design.

Elder, J. H. (2008). The gluten-free, casein-free diet in autism: An overview with clinical implications. *Nutrition in Clinical Practice, 23*(6), 583-588.

Favazza, P. C., Phillipsen, L., & Kumar, P. (2000). Measuring and promoting acceptance of young children with disabilities. *Exceptional Children, 66*(4), 491-508.

Feiges, L. S., & Weiss, M. J. (2004). *Siblings' stories: Reflections on life with a brother or sister on the autism spectrum.* Shewnee Mission, KS: Autism Asperger.

Foxx, R. M. (2008). Applied behavioral analysis treatment of autism: The state of the art. *Child and Adolescent Psychiatric Clinics of North America, 17*(4), 821-834.

Fraleigh, J. M. (2009). Vaccination: Compliance controversy. *RN, 72*(5), 36-40.

Gargiulo. R. M. (2012). *Special education in contemporary society: An introduction to exceptionality* (4th ed.). Los Angeles, CA: SAGE.

Granpeesheh, D., Tarbox, J., & Dixon, D. R. (2009). Applied behavioral analytic interventions for children with autism: A description and review of treatment research. *Annuals of Clinical Psychiatry, 21*(30), 162-173.

Gray, C., & White, A. L. (2002). *My social stories book.* Philadelphia, PA: Jessica Kingsley.

Harris, S. L., & Glasberg, B. A. (2003). *Siblings of children with autism: A guide for families* (2nd ed.). Bethesda, MD: Woodbine House.

Herbert, J. D., Sharp, I. R., & Gaudiano, B. A. (2002). Separating fact from fiction in the etiology and treatment of autism: A scientific review of the evidence. *Scientific Review of Mental Health Practice, 1*(1),4-19.

Johnson, J., & Van Rensselaer, A. (2010). *Siblings.* Philadelphia, PA: Jessica Kingsley.

Individuals with Disabilities Act. (2004). Washington, DC: U.S. Government Printing Office.

Koegel, R. L., Koegel, L. K., & McNerney, E. K. (2001). Pivotal areas in intervention for autism. *Journal of Clinical Child Psychology, 30*(1), 19-32.

Levy, S. E., & Hyman, S.L. (2005). Novel treatments for autism spectrum disorders. *Mental Retardation and Developmental Disabilities Research Reviews, 11*, 131-142.

Lord, C., Rutter, M., DiLavore, P., & Risi, S. (2001). *Autism diagnostic observation schedule*. Los Angeles, CA: Western Psychological Services.

Lord, C., & Schopler, E. (1994). TEACCH services for preschool children. In S. Harris & J. Handleman (Eds.), *Preschool education programs for children with autism* (pp. 102-126). Austin, TX: PRO-ED.

Marshack, K. (2009). *Life with a partner or spouse with Asperger syndrome: Going over the edge?* Shawnee Mission, KS: Autism Asperger.

Marcus, L. M., Kunce, L. J., & Schopler, E. (2005). Working with families. In F. R. Volkmar, R. Paul, A. Klin, & C. Cohen (Eds.), *Handbook of autism and pervasive developmental disorders* (Vol. 2, pp. 1161-1173). Hoboken, NJ: Wiley.

Nkabinde, Z. P. (2008). Using assistive technology to educate students with developmental disabilities and autism. In A. F. Rotatori, F. E. Obiakor, & S. Burkhardt (Eds.), *Autism and developmental disabilities: Current practices and issues* (Vol. 18, pp. 273-285). Bingley, England: Emerald.

Offit, P. A. (2008). *Autism's false prophets: Bad science, risky medicine, and the search for a cure*. New York, NY: Columbia University Press.

Orsmond, G. L.,& Selzter, M. M. (2007). Siblings of individuals with autism spectrum disorders across the life course. *Mental Retardation and Developmental Disabilities Research Reviews, 13*, 312-320.

Ozonoff, S., Williams, B.J., & Landa, R. (2005). Parental report of the early development of children with regressive autism: The delays-plus-regression phenotype. *Autism: The International Journal of Research and Practice, 9*(5), *461-486.*

Papalia, D. E., Olds, S. W., & Feldman, R. D. (2006). *A child's world: Infancy through adolescence* (10th ed.). Boston, MA: McGraw-Hill.

Parette, H. P., & Peterson-Karlan, G. R. (2010). Using assistive technology to support the instructional process of students with disabilities. In F. E. Obiakor, J. P. Bakken, & A. F. Rotatori (Eds.), *Current issues and trends in special education: Research, technology, and teacher preparation* (Vol. 20, pp. 73-89). Bingley, England: Emerald.

Romanczyk, R. G., Arnstein, L., Soorya, L. V., & Gillis, J. (2003). The myriad of controversial treatments for autism: A critical evaluation of efficacy. In S. O. Lilienfeld, S. J. Lynn, & J. M. Lohr (Eds.), *Science and pseudoscience in clinical psychology* (pp. 363-395). New York, NY: Guilford Press.

Romanczyk, R. G., Gillis, J. M., White, S., & Digennaro, F. (2008). Comprehensive treatment packages for ASD: Perceived vs. proven effectiveness. In J.L. Matson (Ed.), *Clinical assessment and intervention for autism spectrum disorders* (pp. 351-381). Burlington, MA: Academic Press.

Rotatori A. F., Obiakor, F. E., & Burkhardt, S. (2008). (Eds.). *Autism and developmental disabilities: Current practices and issues*. Bingley, England: Emerald.

Roth, I. (2010). *The autism spectrum in the 21st century: Exploring psychology, biology and practice*. Philadelphia, PA: Jessica Kingsley.

Royko, D. (2007, June 10). The chronicles of Ben. *Chicago Tribune Magazine*, pp. 10-15.

Ruscio, J. (2006). *Critical thinking in psychology: Separating sense from nonsense* (2nd ed.). Belmont, CA: Wadsworth Cengage Learning.

Rutter, M., LeCouteur, A., & Lord, C. (2003). *Autism diagnostic interview-revised-WPS (*WPS ed.). Los Angeles, CA: Western Psychological Services.

Sapp, M. (2008). Assessment of autism spectrum disorders. In A. F. Rotatori, F. E. Obiakor, & S. Burkhardt (Eds.), *Autism and developmental disabilities: Current practices and issues* (Vol. 18, pp. 59-83). Bingley, England: Emerald.

Schechtman, M. A. (2007). Scientifically unsupported therapies in the treatment of young children with autism spectrum disorders. *Pediatric Annals, 37(9),* 639-645.

Scott, F. J., Baron-Cohen, S., Bolton, P., & Brayne, C. (2002). The CAST (Childhood Asperger Syndrome Test): Preliminary development of a UK screen for mainstream primary-school-age children. *Autism: The International Journal of Research and Practice, 6(1),* 9-31.

Siegel, B., & Silverstein, S. (2001). *What about me? Growing up with a developmentally disabled sibling*. Cambridge, MA: Da Capo Press.

Simone, R. (2009). *Things a woman must know*. Philadelphia, PA: Jessica Kingsley.

Simpson, R. L. (2008). Children and youth with autism spectrum disorders: The search for effective methods. *Focus on Exceptional Children, 40*(7), 1-14.

Smith, M. J., Ellenberg, S. S., Bell, L. M., & Rubin, D. M. (2008). Media coverage of the measles-mumps-rubella vaccine and autism controversy and its relationship in the United States. *Pediatrics, 121*, e836-e843.

Smith, T. (2008). Empirically supported and unsupported treatments for autism spectrum disorders. *The Scientific Review of Mental Health Practices, 6*(1), 3-20.

Smith, T., & Wick, J. (2008). Controversial treatments. In K. Chawarska, A. Klin, & F. R. Volume (Eds.), *Autism spectrum disorders in infants and toddlers: Diagnosis, assessment, and treatment* (pp. 243-273). New York, NY: Guilford Press.

Smith, T., Wynn, J., & Lovaas, O.I. (1997, April). *Outcome in adulthood*. Paper presented at the Early Intervention Conference, Los Angeles, CA.

Stanford, A. (2002). *Asperger syndrome and long term relationships*. Philadelphia, PA: Jessica Kingsley.

Stephenson, J. (2002). Famotidine (Pepcid) and autistic spectrum disorders: A reason for optimism, or heartburn? *The Scientific Review of Mental Health Practice, 1*(2), 184-188.

Stichter, J., Randolph, J., Gage, N., & Schmidt, C. (2007). A review of recommended social competency programs for students with autism spectrum disorders. *Exceptionality, 15*, 219-232.

Stillman, W. (2005). *The everything parent's guide to children with Asperger's syndrome: Help, hope, and guidance*. Avon, MA: Adams Media.

Strohm, K. (2005). *Being the other one: Growing up with a brother or sister who have special needs*. Boston, MA: Shambhala Publications.

Swinkels, S. H. N., Dietz, C., van Daalen, E., Kerkhof, I.H., van Engeland, H., & Buitelaar, J. K. (2006). Screening for autism spectrum in children aged 14 to 15 months. 1. The development of the Early Screening of Autistic Traits

Questionnaire (ESAT) [Electronic version]. *Journal of Autism and Developmental Disorders, 36*, 723-732.

Symon, J. B. G., & Boettcher, M. A. (2008). Family participation and support. In J. K. Luiselli, D. C. Russo, W. P. Christian, & S. M. Wilczynski (Eds.), *Effective practices for children with autism: Educational and behavioral support interventions that work* (pp. 455-489). New York, NY: Oxford University Press.

Tantum, D. (2011). *Autism spectrum disorders through the lifespan*. Philadelphia, PA: Jessica Kingsley.

Theus, F. C. (2008). Asperger syndrome in the African American community: Barriers to diagnosis. In A. F. Rotatori, F. E. Obiakor, & S. Burkhardt (Eds.), *Autism and developmental disabilities: Current practices and issues* (Vol. 18, pp. 109-133). Bingley, England: Emerald.

Tsao, L., & Odom, S.L. (2006). Sibling minded social interaction intervention for young children with autism. *Topics in Early Childhood Special Education, 26*(2), 106-123.

Wahlberg, T. (2000). Intervention techniques for individuals with autism in inclusive settings. In F. E. Obiakor, S. A. Burkhardt, A. F. Rotatori, & T. Wahlberg (Eds.), *Intervention techniques for individuals with exceptionalities in inclusive settings* (Vol. 13, pp. 217-237). Stamford, CT: JAI Press.

Wahlberg, T. (2001a). Cognitive theories and symptomology of autism. In T. Wahlberg, F. E. Obiakor, S. Burkhardt, & A. F. Rotatori (Eds.), *Autistic spectrum disorders: Educational and clinical interventions* (Vol. 14, pp. 3-17). Oxford, England: Elsevier Science Ltd.

Wahlberg, T. (2001b). The control theory of autism. In T. Wahlberg, F. E. Obiakor, S. Burkhardt, & A. F. Rotatori (Eds.), *Autism spectrum disorders: Educational and clinical interventions* (Vol. 14, pp. 19-35). Oxford, England: Elsevier Science.

Wahlberg, T. (2001c). Autism: Neurological implications of autism and the aging process. In T. Wahlberg, F. E. Obiakor, S. Burkhardt, & A. F. Rotatori (Eds.), *Autistic spectrum disorders: Educational and clinical interventions* (Vol. 14, 37- 51). Oxford, England: Elsevier Science.

Wahlberg, T. (2001d). Language development and text comprehension in individuals with autism. In T. Wahlberg, F. E. Obiakor, S. Burkhardt, & A. F. Rotatori (Eds.), *Autistic spectrum disorders: Educational and clinical interventions* (Vol. 14, pp. 133-150). Oxford, England: Elsevier Science.

Wahlberg, T. (2010). *Finding the gray: Understanding and thriving in the black and white world of autism and Asperger's*. Geneva, IL: Wahlberg and Associates.

Wahlberg, T., & Jordan, S. (2001). A case study in the dynamics of autism. In T. Wahlberg, F. E. Obiakor, S. Burkhardt, & A. F. Rotatori (Eds.), *Autistic spectrum disorders: Educational and clinical interventions* (Vol. 14, pp. 5365). Oxford, England: Elsevier Science.

Wahlberg. T., & Rotatori, A. F. (2001). Interview with a high functioning adult with autism. In T. Wahlberg, F. E. Obiakor, S. Burkhardt, & A. F. Rotatori (Eds.), *Autistic spectrum disorders: Educational and clinical interventions* (Vol. 14, pp. 269-300). Oxford, England: Elsevier Science.

Wahlberg, T., Rotatori, A. F., Deisinger, J., & Burkhardt, S. (2003). Students with autism spectrum disorders. In F. E. Obiakor, C. A. Utley, & A. F. Rotatori

(Eds.), *Effective education for learners with exceptionalities* (Vol. 15, pp. 195-232). Oxford, England: Elsevier Science.

Wallace, L. S. (2009). What's the scoop on autism spectrum disorders and nutrition? *The Exceptional Parent, 39*(2), 28-30.

Webb, B. J., Miller, S. P., Pierce, T. B., Strawser, S., & Jones, W. P. (2004). Effects of social skills instruction for high functioning adolescents with autism spectrum disorders. *Focus on Autism and Other Developmental Disabilities, 19*(1), 53-62.

West, E. (2011). Assistive technology for students with autism. In E. A. Boutot & B. S. Myles (Eds.), *Autism spectrum disorders: Foundations, characteristics and effective practices* (pp. 261-276). Upper Saddle River, NJ: Pearson.

Wilkinson, L. A. (2010). *A best practice guide to assessment and intervention for autism and Asperger syndrome in schools.* Philadelphia, PA: Jessica Kingsley.

CHAPTER 7

TREATMENTS AND TECHNIQUES

Timothy J. Wahlberg

There is a direct correlation between someone's cognitive experience and his behavior. Anytime we impact the thinking of an individual, we impact his behavior.

This chapter explores some basic techniques and treatment strategies that can help parents and teachers work effectively with children on the spectrum.

These techniques can help you: (1) better communicate with individuals on the spectrum; (2) create an environment that is better suited for an individual with autism spectrum disorders (ASD); (3) learn how to intervene at important points to change behavior; and (4) learn how to teach individuals on the spectrum to control their emotions.

There is a direct correlation between someone's cognitive experience and his behavior. Anytime we impact the thinking of an individual, we impact his behavior. When intervention causes a decrease in linear thinking and an increase in social processing, thinking changes, and thus behavior also begins to change. This connection between experience and behavior is implied as one of the fundamental principals of the control theory.

Autism Spectrum Disorders: Inclusive Community for the Twenty-First Century, pp. 163–178

The shift from a linear world to a social world that is spurred on by treatment forces a reallocation of the focus, resources, energy, and motivation in individuals on the spectrum. They begin to develop in a more social context and, as a result, they take in more of the external environment. By managing their behavior and their thinking, we are attempting to change brain neurology and the level of brain functioning in those on the spectrum, creating more interconnectivity and the related flexibility. Individuals with autism would not necessarily choose this route on their own, so extrinsic motivation is often needed to get them to accept change and to be more social.

In the following sections, I provide some techniques and suggestions on methods to affect behavior by creating positive intervention.

VISUALIZATION

A young man named Ryan once told me that he has two sides to his brain, a good side and a bad side. He explained that there was a wall between the good and the bad sides, and when he gets upset, his brain takes a sword and jams it into the wall, puts a hole in it, and then sucks the good into the bad side. This is how he describes what is going on in his life emotionally; he uses a concrete visual image. Eventually, in therapy, we created a mental shield that stops the sword as it tries to come through the wall. Something as simple as that visualization helped him control his mind.

Another one of my clients is a big *Harry Potter* fan; when he gets upset over something, he visualizes himself casting spells that empower him to overcome his problem. You can use visualization techniques to teach a child to learn how to calm himself, such as visualizing a favorite place or activity. I often tell clients, who might be prone to nightmares or other sleeping issues, to imagine one side of the pillow as a good side, and the other as a bad side; then when they are having trouble sleeping, they can just turn the pillow over to the good side.

Visualization is an effective method for changing cognitive experience. Once individuals with autism learn that they can control their brains, therapy can be effective in stimulating other areas of change.

SENSORY BREAKS

A sensory break is an opportunity for a child to do some sort of activity that stimulates them and allows them to neurologically bridge the gap between a heightened sense of stimulation and the point at which they return to homeostasis. In most cases, this means adding stimulus, but in some cases, the child may need a break from any stimulus.

Sensory breaks can be extremely important, especially for the little ones. Children on the spectrum do say that, as they get older, the sensory issues start to diminish, and do not affect them as much. However, even though sensory channel hypersensitivities tend to diminish as children age, the feeling of being overwhelmed in a social situation may not. Children are not going to do well in any setting or environment when they are very young, unless their system is regulated. That is to say, if they are consumed with dealing with the lower level physical/sensory input, they cannot focus on the more challenging aspects of life. Even if your child is not very young, consider addressing sensory overload as a possibility to help gain some control of a difficult situation.

Occupational therapists can often help parents figure out what they need to do to help their children learn to regulate the environment, whether at home or at school. You will get so much more out of these kids if you can get them to regulate, to get the neurons firing appropriately. To do that, you can provide them with the opportunity to take sensory breaks.

For sensory breaks to be effective, we first need to teach these children to recognize when they need a break, and then how to request the break. Requesting a break may not be possible for lower functioning children, so we may need to schedule breaks. I have worked with a number of early childhood teachers and I encourage them to be consistent in allowing for breaks or movement within the classroom. This helps to regulate. Since these children (for the most part) do not recognize that they need a break, we have to provide it for them. Often, these kids do not know how to ask for what they need, especially if they are younger, so creating a simple and clear way to communicate their need for a break can be the first step in getting a child to manage himself, and can prevent a lot of difficulty.

One method is to use a break card. A break card is a communication tool between teacher and student that the student can use any time to indicate his need to engage in any activities that will promote calming himself down. A child is simply given a card that he can show the teacher as a signal that a break is needed.

One of my favorite sensory break activities is having the child do jobs around the school. Have you ever seen a janitor taking the scuff marks off the floor? He attaches a tennis ball to the bottom of a broomstick and rubs the ball back and forth across the mark. Think about the proprioceptive (the body's sense of where one's limbs are in space) feedback a child on the spectrum will receive by engaging in such an activity. They really seem to like this task; it creates an excellent sensory break. I suggest to teachers that they assign the child a certain section of the floor to clean. That's a lot of proprioceptive information.

Asking a child to deliver mail from the classroom to the office is another one of my favorite jobs for a sensory break. If there's no mail, get inventive! Take a manila envelope and put a dictionary in it. The student takes it down to the office … and do you know what the office will have to send back? Another dictionary. In some cases, all that matters is that the task gives the child a break from the stimulation. No one else in the class really knows (or needs to know) that the task is contrived strictly to create a break.

I try to make sure that the sensory breaks make the child appear as normal as possible. This serves two purposes: it helps the child to fit in to the social environment today, and it helps to train the child to select appropriate ways of calming himself in the future (for instance, when he has a job).

Quiet spots are another sensory break option. There should be a specified quiet spot in the classroom that the child can request to retreat to when she needs a break. Sometimes a child just needs time to process what is going on around her and to be removed from all the sensory stimulation in her receptive field.

Another strategy is to use color schemes like stop lights (green, yellow, and red.) Sometimes, if a child does not want to call attention to herself, she can hold a certain color pen up in the air. Green might mean "Things are going pretty well." Yellow means "I'm struggling a little bit." Red means "Something needs to happen quickly." Just getting children on the spectrum to recognize that they are nearing a melting point is a step in the right direction. A child's ability to recognize when she needs to slow down or when she needs a break reduces the behavior issues in the classroom, and, as a bonus, she does not alienate herself as much with her classmates.

Ironically, teachers sometimes complain about losing part of their teaching day to sensory breaks. This is a misunderstanding of what a sensory break can mean to a child on the spectrum. Is it not better to lose 10 minutes to a sensory break than to lose an entire day or class period to a child's being overwhelmed, being disruptive, or having a meltdown? If a child is experiencing sensory overload, what is he getting from the class? Nothing. If he loses a few minutes to gain more productive class time, then I see that as benefit. These children would learn nothing from the class time without the break.

SENSORY BREAKS FOR OLDER KIDS

One day, I was talking to a young man in my office about sensory breaks. He was a regular student in high school; he took classes all day and then spent 3 hours in football practice after school. (He never really got to play, but he loved the practices.) Then, at home, he got on his minitrampoline and jumped, every single night. I asked him how long he jumped (thinking that his day was already very full). He answered that he jumped for 2½ hours! I could not believe this. I said, "You must take breaks." He replied, "No, but sometimes I go fast, and sometimes I go slowly." I asked him what he was thinking about during that time and he said he was "processing his day."

For those of you who have been on a treadmill, you may appreciate this story. I have an elliptical machine in my basement. My first time on this machine, I set the timer for 20 minutes and started running. There was nothing to look at, no stimulation other than the running. After a little while, I felt like I was nearly done; I looked down at the timer and was shocked to learn that I was only about 3 minutes into it! I thought there was no way I could do this for 20 minutes. I will go crazy; not due to exhaustion, but to boredom. This young man was on the minitrampoline for 2½ hours, every day, and it was relaxing for him, even meditative. I asked him how long he jumped on days that he did not have school and he said 2½ hours twice a day (that's 5 hours a day)!

It has been reported in the media that one of the most successful men of our time, Bill Gates, has a room in his house that has a trampoline floor. He comes home from work and jumps on the trampoline, which I have heard helps him to process his day; it could be that this computer genius, whose quirkiness fits the profile of someone who falls on the autism spectrum, uses the trampoline to help him calm himself when he is overstimulated. It seems to be working for him—he's doing all right in life. A key to success for individuals on the spectrum is figuring out how to process the sensory world. Once they do this, there is a better chance that they can learn to relax and adapt, allowing their natural talents to surface.

SENSORY BACKPACKS

Another proactive strategy for parents is the sensory backpack. Easily portable, a sensory backpack can be filled with items that allow children to take a break and regulate themselves when they need to. Items such as a coloring book, favorite stuffed animal, video game, or iPod can be kept handy in a backpack for those situations when they are needed.

Having the necessary sensory relief for the child with autism can make life more manageable for the rest of the family. One mother reported an issue with her 12-year-old son with ASD at his brother's fourth grade Christmas concert last year. Because he did not have his sensory backpack and was unable tolerate the lights, sights, and sounds of a crowded auditorium, mom had to leave early and missed her younger son's performance. The next week, she came to therapy frustrated and disappointed in her son with Asperger's disorder. We discussed the use and benefits of a sensory backpack. Guess what happened this year? She and her son with Asperger's were prepared. As a result, the fifth grade Christmas concert went very well, and mom got to see her son perform.

Sensory breaks and sensory backpacks are effective, but we work toward the time when kids, as they grow and develop, can regulate themselves cognitively, rather than with physical stimulus. For example, using self-talk and/or visual processing to control their emotions, thereby, being able to calm themselves with their own words and thoughts and not having to use something physical.

LEAD TIME

Even many neuro-typical individuals do not like abrupt changes in their routines or schedules. When they have time to think and plan for a change, it is much easier to manage. Individuals with ASD are the same way, but to a greater extent (times 10). So another important day-to-day strategy for working effectively with individuals with autism involves providing them with notice in advance of upcoming activities or changes in routine.

This advance warning, or lead time, allows the individual time to process the information at her own pace and to prepare for what is coming up. Telling an individual on the spectrum on Wednesday that he will be going to grandma's house on Saturday is an example of lead time. The child has time to process the fact that his routine on Saturday is going to change. Even if he likes going to Grandma's house, it is a change, and therefore he has to adapt.

While it may take an extreme change (such as moving or losing a job) to create anxiety in neuro-typical individuals, for individuals with ASD, even a slight change may create that same heightened anxiety. Something as simple as moving the furniture in the living room can do it. Remember the young man who started therapy because his parents moved the couch to make room for the Christmas tree? Again, individuals with ASD want to control their surroundings, and thereby reduce anxiety and unrest in their system. Change creates something unexpected or out of the ordinary.

A word of caution regarding lead time. It is not always helpful to provide too much lead time if the child does not like the activity that is planned. Sometimes, for activities that create a great deal of stress (for example, a visit to the dentist), lead time only serves to create more anxiety, and can cause added stress or sleepless nights until the day actually arrives. In such cases, less lead time can reduce stress for all concerned—

the child and, especially, mom and dad. One sleepless night is much easier to manage than 2 weeks of sleepless nights. So, lead time needs to be balanced with practical considerations.

FIRST/THEN TECHNIQUE

Boundaries work best when the child knows clearly what is expected and what the payoff is, what is in it for them if they comply. This is what the first/then methodology creates. For example, *first* you take out the garbage and *then* you can do what you want. First you do your homework and then you can play on the computer. First you call your grandmother and then you can have your favorite snack.

Even though boundaries exist everywhere, there are no specific instructions as to how to deal with them. This is not spelled out and not intuitive if you are on the spectrum. Both the rules and the exceptions need to be clear. So, you can also say, "Here are the expectations (boundaries) you need to follow in order to get what you want." For example, you explain to your child, "You need to read for 30 minutes every night. If you do, then you can use your cell phone on the weekends. If you do not follow these expectations you will lose the privilege to use the cell phone entirely." This not only creates a clear boundary, but it also allows the child to make a decision about the choices he makes, and the outcome of his choices. Given these boundaries, the child can choose either a good outcome or a bad outcome because both outcomes have been spelled out. This sidesteps the potential loophole in the executive functioning that does not allow him to project the outcome for himself.

ADJUST BOUNDARIES WHEN NECESSARY

Sometimes the rules and boundaries need to be modified to make them more adaptable for the ASD individual. The best teachers that I work with are very structured and consistent while at the same time less rigid than the ASD individual. Let's say that the teacher has a behavior system that takes away tokens that are earned throughout the day. A child who starts with 10 tokens can lose a token for some negative behavior. If the child on the spectrum can either not understand the loss of something that was hers, or cannot handle losing something without a meltdown, the teacher may need to modify the plan to have the child earning tokens but never losing them. This is exactly why I advocate earning privileges rather than losing them. The child may be able to accept, or deal with, not earning a token at some point in her day because she did not follow the rules, but that is very different than taking away something that was already hers—an action that might elicit a very negative, if not dramatic, response.

Another example of modifying boundaries may be to tell a child on the spectrum that he can complete a portion of his chores and then take a break before completing the balance of his chores, versus insisting that he needs to do all of his chores before he can do what he wants (setting the boundary). Maybe this child can only handle two chores and then he legitimately needs a break before completing the other two chores, whereas his siblings can be held accountable for all four chores before they receive any reward. As a parent or teacher trying to motivate a child to learn or follow rules, you may have to adjust the boundary because of what or how much these individuals can handle.

Another example of modifying a boundary would be if a parent's expectation is that the child will spend the entire afternoon with the family on Thanksgiving, but the child can only handle short stints with the family. Mom and dad may need to adjust their expectations in order for their child to be successful that afternoon. The exception that they need to make for their ASD child will most likely be different than for their other children, if they have other children. The other children may experience no distress from being with the family for the entire afternoon without a break. When modifying boundaries to help your child achieve success, it is important for everyone (parents, siblings, educators, fellow students, etc.) to be flexible and adaptable.

MAKE CHOICES MORE CONCRETE

Decision making can be difficult, if not impossible, for those on the spectrum. They can be "frozen" at times, and can have difficulty seeing the pros and the cons of a situation. Creating a list of the pros and cons can help someone with ASD take a concept that is abstract and make it more concrete in order to process it. For example, someone on the spectrum who is trying to decide if she should apply for a job she saw online can make a list of pros and cons and then evaluate the fact that six pros are more than two cons, therefore she should send in an application for that job.

Whenever the decision-making process can be made more concrete, the likelihood that the individual with ASD will make an appropriate and informed choice increases.

CHECK IN TO DETERMINE "WHERE DID I LOSE YOU?"

Sometimes you can be moving through a conversation and suddenly realize that the individual with ASD has not processed the conversation to the point that would be expected normally. She got lost or got stuck earlier in the conversation. Here is an example of what that looks like. As a graduate student, I was doing therapy with a man with autism. We were sitting in a room with an observation window (like the ones in interrogation rooms), through which my professors and peers could observe us. One day, the professor asked if the man understood what I was explaining to him. I told my professor that I had asked him numerous times if he understood, and he had always replied, "Yes."

Finally, my professor told me that the next time he responds, "Yes," to ask him to explain it back to me. So, the following day, I was doing therapy and my peers were watching me through the one-way glass. I asked the man, "Do you understand?" and I got the expected "Yes" answer. I followed up with, "Can you explain it to me?" He responded, "Nope." I remember feeling everyone looking at me through the glass, and thinking, "How could I have been wrong all this time!" I was embarrassed by my mistaken perception that he had understood what I was saying.

At the time, I did not understand why he would say he understood me when he clearly did not. He probably said that to shut me up or to get me to move on, either of which would have cut down on the social interaction, putting an end to his discomfort. This type of behavior is very common.

The image of a tree is a good visual to use to describe how we follow along in a conversation, and what happens when we lose someone in a conversation. Imagine starting the conversation with a broad statement—that is like the trunk of the tree. As the conversation continues, the conversation gets more specific, which is like traveling along one of the limbs of the tree. Then, the conversation progresses to the branches and eventually ends up at the leaves, which represent the most specific information. When an individual on the spectrum gets sidetracked during the conversation, he ends up on a totally different limb, branch, or leaf.

Sometimes, an individual on the spectrum can get caught on a word or phrase that is used during a conversation and get stuck on that word even though the conversation continues. I remember losing a man in conversation and, once I realized this, I asked at what point I had lost him. He replied that when I mentioned the word hammer, it made him think of the hammer he had received for Christmas when he was 5 years old. He went on to say that the recollection of his first hammer led him to recall building a birdhouse with that hammer. This is a completely different train of thought than the discussion I was having with him. He had detoured to a totally different location on the tree.

The way to effectively work with someone on the spectrum is to stop and ask him to explain what was just said to him. In essence, to determine, "Where did I lose you?" By identifying where the individual is stuck, it makes it possible to help him piece together the information you are delivering so that he can understand. This may require listing the logical steps in a progression, providing other data as evidence, slowing down, or presenting the information in another way.

TEACH THEM TO DO IT "JUST BECAUSE"

I have already emphasized the importance of learning to do things just because. This is an especially difficult concept for spectrum individuals since they want to know the why for everything. Often, the reasons that intrinsically motivated people do things will not be the same reasons that make sense to kids who are extrinsically motivated. The best example of extrinsic motivation in our world today is money, but some things in life must be done without getting paid—like brushing your teeth or taking a shower.

When we talk to these kids and tell them, "Well, you know you might get an F in your English class," their response is, "Okay. I don't care. I don't really like English." A grade, in most cases, is not motivating for them at all—they are not intrinsically motivated.

With kids on the spectrum, we need to become more businesslike, providing concrete and specific motivators, such as computer time, alone time, their favorite meal, etc. Even five minutes of free-choice time can be used as an effective motivator. This concrete reward transforms something that they do not want to do into a choice that makes sense to them. Remember the little boy and the social studies questions? The other 24 students in his class answered those questions just because they were asked to do so, but he needed something else.

It is not wrong that these kids require a different type of motivation. (It is a lot more work for a parent or teacher.) Often, we struggle to understand this aspect of their personality because we assume something should be intrinsically motivating when it is not. So, if you find yourself wondering why a child would not do something that obviously needs to be done, ask yourself if they have any extrinsic motivation. To a child on the spectrum, doing something just because is like working for free. Does anyone want to work for free? Probably not. Extrinsic motivation is not bad, it is just different. Understanding that and teaching a child to work around their need for a concrete reward is important to long-term functionality. Learning to do something just because is a very important life skill.

PRESENT INFORMATION IN A LINEAR FASHION

A similar technique that I use is piecing information together. Children on the spectrum always ask why, as in, "Why do I have to do this?" When they ask this question, it may be because they cannot see the connection between something they are being asked to do and an outcome that benefits them. For example, if a child who does not want to write his English paper asks, "Why should I?" I will ask him, "Well, what do you want to do for a living?" He may reply that he wants to test video games for a profession. So, I will ask him, "What do you need to do to get there?" He might reply, "I have to go to college." I then ask, "In order to go to college, what do you have to do?" A typical answer is, "I have to pass high school." "How do you pass high school?" He concludes, "Well, I guess I have to write that paper." This scenario describes reaching a goal in a linear fashion.

Those on the spectrum cannot piece things together unless we show them the logical steps in the progression. Now, that does not mean they will do all of their homework without question, but if you do not make it concrete by pointing out the connection in that linear fashion, it may not make any sense to them at all. This process has a similar effect of providing extrinsic motivators, but it works by projecting the outcomes so the child can see what is in it for them.

PLAN AHEAD

When my three daughters were very young, I would take them to the Rain Forest Café as a special treat. In order to maximize the possibility of success, I had a very specific way of handling the situation. We would start our day by eating an early breakfast so that we could arrive at the Café around 11:00 a.m., when it opened. That way, we did not have to wait to be seated.

The café is located in the local mall. So, I would tell my girls, before ever leaving for the restaurant, that there would be no shopping. I set up their expectations in advance. I let them know that we would only be going for lunch and then coming straight back home. I would also tell them that we would not be buying anything at the Rain Forest Café gift shop before or after lunch. I was very explicit and thorough in my explanation of what "no shopping" meant. I did give them each five coins to throw into the alligator's mouth prior to eating lunch.

While we were driving to the café, we would discuss my expectations of how they would act at the restaurant, as well as what we were going to order for lunch, so when we got there, we did not need a menu. In order to get served faster, I would order the food as they were showing us to our table. I asked the waitress to bring the bill with the food, so there would be no wait when we were done eating. We would eat, pay the bill and be on our way in 20 minutes. Why did I do it that way? To maximize the possibility of a successful outing. We always had a good time!

Now, that type of plan is not perfect; there can always be something that comes up. One year, I thought my plan was running like clockwork when one of the girls asked to use the restroom. Since I was a dad out on my own with three young daughters, I took the girls into the men's room with me to use the bathroom. It was a slight detour in my plan, but it was easy to pull off because of all that I had set up prior to going on the excursion.

Planning ahead works well with all children, but especially with those on the spectrum who are much more successful if they have a clear and accurate idea of what is coming up. By explaining expectations in as much detail as possible, you are setting up for success.

PROMPTING PRIOR

Motivating a child by rewarding him for the desired behavior, rather than punishing him for the undesired behavior, works as long as the prompting is prior. That means, spell out the boundaries in advance. For example, "If you complete your homework, you can use the computer for 15 minutes." Not clearly spelling out the conditions for earning the reward before it is too late for the child to make an informed choice will likely elicit responses such as, "I did not know that," or "That is not fair," or "You never said that." Again, you may have felt that you did not need to spell it out because, perhaps, it was implied in the situation. But, as a result of his executive functioning difficulties, the child was not able to connect the undesired outcome to his behavior. That chain of events was not even on his radar screen.

To be effective, we need to be proactive and we need to react before we get angry. If my own children are acting up, eventually, it will drive me to the point when I am going to do something about it. When my three girls start to get surly, I will remind them that they are heading down a path that is going to get them in trouble and I will say to them, "If you keep this up, this is what the outcome will be."

Sometimes, my oldest daughter preempts trouble with her sisters by walking away; that is executive functioning. She can see that the situation is heading toward trouble and she makes a good choice not to be there when it arrives. Individuals on the spectrum do not draw conclusions that way; they do not have the foresight to make a good choice based on outcome. So, as parents, teachers, and therapists, we need to help them make better choices by presenting data in a way that makes sense to them and prompting them before they actually get in trouble. By projecting possible outcomes for them—by telling them what will happen based on their choices—you can help them choose the direction in which to proceed and the result they wish to create.

Motivation is a key factor that we sometimes overlook because we might assume that the motivation in these individuals is intrinsic. I am not saying that there is no internal motivation that drives a child on the spectrum, but it is different than for children not on the spectrum. That is why being proactive and prompting prior works for them.

Now, the key is finding out what motivates your specific child. What will make her want to work? I have found that the most effective motivator is the child's time.

MY TIME AND YOUR TIME

My time and your time is a very straightforward concept. It is a social skill. I talk, then you talk, then I talk, then you talk. If you always dominate the conversation, then you will not have very many conversations because no one will want to talk to you. What my time and your time means is doing something and thereby earning something.

Parents may punish their kids by taking away television or computer privileges. My preference would be to turn it around and make it pertinent to the child. Tell him that if he does what he is supposed to do, he will earn 2 hours of television or whatever else he may want to do. That is exactly what we did with the boy who asked about the social studies questions at the middle school. When that boy asked what was in it for him if he answered the five questions, the teacher told him he would get 5 minutes of free time at the end of the school day to do what he wanted to do. My time earns your time.

REWARD SPECIFIC BEHAVIOR

Years ago, when I started running groups for individuals with ASD, I wanted to teach children and adolescents on the spectrum the importance of asking questions of others based on what they said in conversation. In group, I would ask each child to "check in" and then I would try to get the others in the group to ask questions pertaining to what each said during check-in. Keep in mind that there are prerequisite skills that need to be in place before this can be accomplished, such as sitting without behaviors and listening to others. In one group, I had trouble getting them to ask questions of each other. I would say, "Tom, why don't you ask Pete about the trip he said he went on last weekend." Tom would say, "I do not care about Pete's trip over the weekend," which is a very common response for someone on the spectrum.

I decided to encourage the boys in this group to ask questions by providing external motivation; I promised them that I would have a pizza party for whichever of my groups asked the most questions during their group session. This particular group asked 180 questions in 45 minutes. It was humorous because, once they got into it, they would ask someone a question and then immediately look at me and say, "That is a question, Dr. Wahlberg, and it is worth a point." This is not a natural or intrinsic way to facilitate social interactions, but pizza worked as a motivator for these boys. Ultimately, it created habits that turned out to be good habits for inspiring questions in my group. Providing pizza as an incentive motivated them to do what they did not want to do until it became a comfortable behavior that could be replicated socially.

ENCOURAGE THE "NOT-HAVING-TO-LIKE-IT-JUST-DO-IT" ATTITUDE

Sometimes, parents will ask me, "Do I have to reward or bribe my child to get him to do anything that I want him to do?" I start by explaining that, to change their child's behavior over the long term, they may have to reward many things that they want their child to do in order to create good habits. Once those habits are formed, however, they can slowly start to modify the rewards for desired behavior to move the child more toward what would be considered normal, such as earning an allowance. Parents can also encourage their children to develop the not-having-to-like-it-just-do-it attitude that these kids will need in order to be functional in the larger world.

Building toward desired behavior without reward is the basis behind applied behavioral analysis therapy. This therapy begins with providing a primary reinforcer for every occurrence of a behavior, then reducing the reinforcement to every 10th occurrence of the behavior, ultimately replacing the reward with social praise in place of the original reinforcer.

If you feel as if you are bribing your child, consider it the first step toward teaching your child how to do things she needs to do just because. With conscious effort, it is possible to transform that bribe into an understanding that we all need to do some things that we do not like to do.

SLOW DOWN AND RESPECT THEIR TIMING

Sometimes, we do not realize how long it takes for individuals on the spectrum to make sense of the information we present. In my first office, the entire back wall was covered in drawings that my clients had drawn and stuck on the wall. I encourage my clients to write or draw at the beginning of a session because it breaks the ice a little. As it happened, the kids would stick their pictures on my wall. One by one, they put the pictures up during therapy until the entire wall was covered. I called it "the wall of fame."

One day, I was in my office trying to teach a parent to understand how much time it takes a child with ASD for processing. I could tell that her son took some time to process, and that the mom was a little bit high strung. She felt that her son could not make choices no matter what she asked him.

I asked the boy if he wanted to use a pen or a pencil to draw a picture for the wall of fame. Of course, mom jumped in with, "He cannot make decisions. He does not know how to ..." I interjected, "Hold on. Let me just do this." I put the notepad on his lap and I held up a pen in one hand and a pencil in the other. I said, "Do you want a pen or a pencil?" Literally, right when those words came out of my mouth, mom said, "Well, he would probably use the pen. He would like the pen better. Why don't you just give him the pen?"

I stopped her again, "Just hold on. Let's give him a little time." I saw him looking at the pen, then the pencil, then the pen, then the pencil. Finally, after about 25 seconds, he grabbed the pen. Sometimes, we do not understand how long it takes them to process information. Remember, when they are young, they are not going to tell you that they do not understand and that they need you to slow down to give them time. They may be able to do that when they are adults but, as children, it is probably not going to happen.

So, in my office, I talk slower and usually ask the kids to explain what they are saying, or I ask them if I'm losing them in any way as we are talking. Allowing these kids the time they need to process can really improve results.

OFFER DIFFERENT PERSPECTIVES

Teach children to look at other variables, possibilities, or perspectives. This works hand-in-hand with stopping, thinking, and problem solving. Seeing other viable options can be hard for children on the spectrum, but they need to learn how to navigate an abstract world in order to be more flexible and functional in their daily lives. Throughout this book, I have provided numerous examples for parents and educators to help the ASD children in their care to learn how to move from rigid black and white thinking to somewhere in the middle—the abstract gray. Remember, the key is consistency and clarity; these children are smart, they just see the

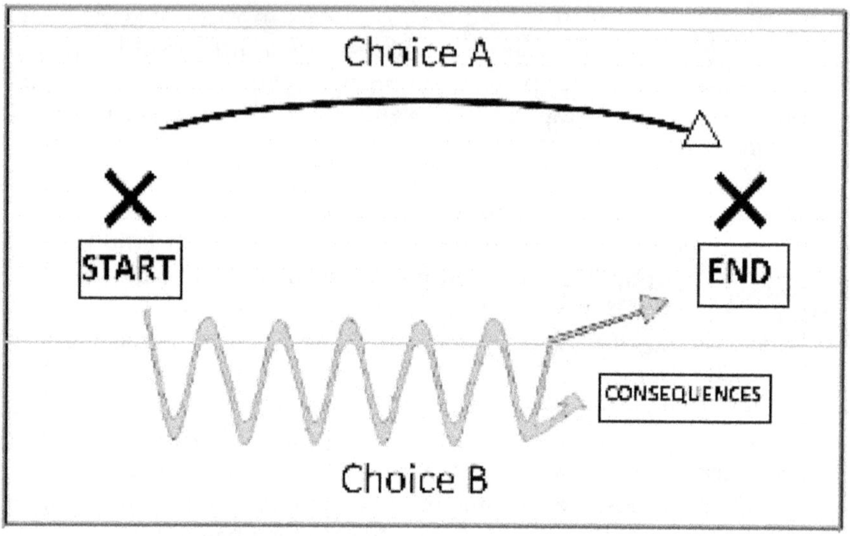

Note: When a child is required to do something that he does not want to do (e.g., homework), he can choose path A and just get it done, or he can choose path B, procrastinating and fighting/arguing, which leads to unnecessary stress. Most kids realize that they have to do homework; this figure illustrates that, either way, they will have to get it done, so why choose the more difficult path, one that could also lead to unpleasant consequences?

Figure 7.1. Making choices.

world very concretely. You can use that to your advantage by applying the techniques and treatments discussed in this chapter.

AUTHOR NOTE

This chapter is reprinted with permission from the book *Finding the Gray: Understanding and Thriving in the Black and White World of Autism and Asperger's* by T. J. Wahlberg (2010) and published by Wahlberg & Associates, Geneva, Illinois.

CHAPTER 8

STRATEGIES FOR EMOTIONAL REGULATION

Timothy J. Wahlberg

For individuals with autism, being able to recognize when they are stuck is a milestone in their growth. Once they know how to determine if they are stuck, we can teach them strategies to get unstuck.

As the control theory suggests, the bodies of children with autism spectrum disorders (ASD) are overwhelmed with the sensory environment, taking in too much sensory information at one time without an effective biological filter. Teaching a child on the spectrum how to regulate his own sensory system is one of the fundamentals in dealing with autism. Once individuals learn and apply this process of regulating their sensory systems, they then conserve neurological energy and are able to use that energy for higher level processing. Remember, these children are not neurologically hardwired to regulate themselves; this is a skill they must learn.

Autism Spectrum Disorders: Inclusive Community for the Twenty-First Century, pp. 179–194

EMOTIONAL SELF-REGULATION STRATEGIES (FINDING THE GRAY)

After a child learns to regulate his sensory system, it becomes possible for him to become aware of himself on an emotional level. It is a monumental success when a child on the spectrum realizes what he is experiencing emotionally and is able to recognize subtle changes in his emotions. This is exciting for two reasons. First, this is an indicator that the child has broken out of the black and white thinking which had previously kept him stuck because so much of the data just did not compute. He is now aware of the shades of gray in his emotions.

Second, once able to experience these subtleties in emotion, the possibility that he can make choices to move from one feeling to another appears; the door opens to growth, which was previously not possible if he consciously, or unconsciously, thought that he was a victim of his own emotional state, or that he could not control his own mind.

When a child with autism understands that it is possible for her to change emotionally, she can then learn to develop her skill in controlling her own mind. An effective way to develop this skill is to use a 0-10 point scale (or 0-3 or a 0-5 point scale for younger children) to teach them that they can actually quantify, in a black and white fashion, how they are feeling. This helps them learn to pay attention to their emotional changes as well as how to find the gray area, or middle ground, that can be elusive to them. Figure 8.1 shows a simple chart that I use to illustrate an increasing volume of emotional intensity.

The terminology that a person with autism uses to describe how he feels can be much different from the terminology someone without autism would use. Often, a person with autism may use a term such as mad or sad to describe any emotional state that deviates from feeling okay. I find that anger is one of the most readily accessible emotions for individuals on the spectrum, therefore, it is easiest for them to describe

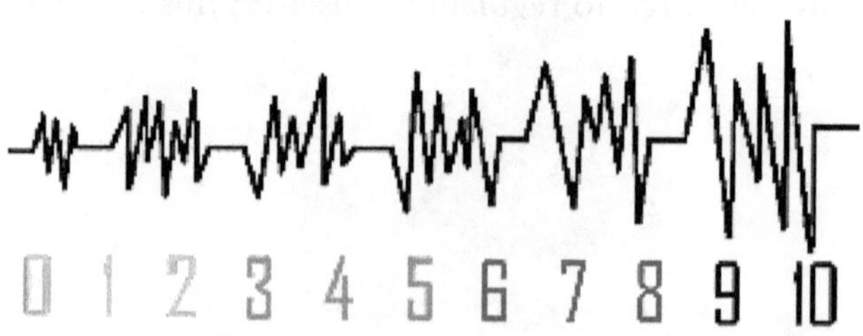

Note: A concrete visual representation like this 10-point scale can help a child on the spectrum identify and describe what he is feeling.

Figure 8.1. Point scale to measure emotional state.

and easiest for us to work with in therapy. Almost all individuals on the spectrum understand it quite well.

To help a child learn to evaluate his emotional level, I initially present a number scale to make sure that he understands what the numbers on the scale mean (which numbers are the biggest, smallest, etc.). When I feel certain that he understands the numbers on the scale, I establish the poles, that is, the 0 and the 10 in terms of anger versus no anger. I clarify that "the most anger" is either 0 on the scale or 10 on the scale. Most children see the 0 equating to no anger at all and the 10 as very angry, or rage. Others see it the opposite way. Either way can work.

Then, I ask the child (many times with the help of parents) to describe an event that made her feel the most angry she has ever felt in her life. I continue, asking for a description of an event that made her feel no anger all, or completely happy. Of course, things are not always all or none when it comes to emotions, but when setting up a scale for emotions we must define the emotional state first by designating what the extremes mean, that is, the poles (0 and 10), and then we can begin to explore the middle ground.

Let me give you an example. Recently, I was working with a young lady using this strategy. As we began, she told me that she never sees the middle between 0 and 10; she only sees things as black or white, all or none. I made sure she understood what the numbers represented on the scale. She said 0 would be no anger at all and 10 would represent the most anger she had ever felt. When I asked what event she recalled that would be classified in her mind as a 10, she said that her mom singing in the car on the way to my office was a 10. Both her mom and I felt that this did not represent a 10; the young lady did not seem that upset by the event as she described it in my office.

After some thought, her mom remembered an incident when someone had accused her of hurting one of her cats. Her eyes got really big and I could see the emotion rising in her. They both agreed, "Yes that was a 10!" I noted that incident under the 10 on the scale. Then I asked her about an event that she would see as a 0, or something she does that she likes and causes no anger. She said watching her favorite shows on TV and eating cake. So I wrote that under the 0. After this, I placed the 0-10 chart in front of her and asked her what number would represent her mom singing in the car on the way to my office. She said, "Oh, my gosh, a 3 or a 4 ... I see the middle." It was almost instantaneous. She was able to experience the moderate nature of her feelings in relation to the two extremes.

The therapeutic value of an experience like this is that you are challenging the black and white way of thinking. When the individual establishes the poles, the extremes, and then you present data that is not extreme, she is able to see that an emotion can fall between her poles. She begins to see that all experience cannot be the same. Working with this chart helps individuals on the spectrum realize, sometimes for the first time in their lives, that there is a middle ground.

Using the child's own experience, rather than words that are meaningless to her, is the key. In the future, this young lady will be able to use the scale and evaluate an event at a 10 in contrast to other situations, thus giving her an emotional benchmark. She will no longer say that every difficult experience is ranked a 10. She cannot, because that data no longer computes. Her mom singing in the car is not equal to her being accused of hurting her cats. While this strategy is an effective way to begin to erode black and white or all-or-none thinking, and this 0-10 chart exercise enables these children to see a middle ground that was previously nonexistent to them, every child is different. Not every child has an immediate shift like the young lady in my example above.

For children with autism who are nonverbal, or who are very young, we can quantify their emotional state with concrete visual aides like a thermometer that moves up and down, with the color red representing the changes in emotional state. I met a family recently that used volcano pictures. The first picture had no lava. The lava from the volcano increased until the volcano had completely erupted. Similarly, one can also use pictures of the child very upset at one end of the scale and the child happy at the other end. Keep in mind that the poles need to be established based on the child's actual experience, not on emotional language that might not be meaningful (i.e., happy or sad).

Another child with whom I worked liked electricity, and he used a visual that involved surges of electricity, with the strongest surge representing the most anger. I have used Figure 8.2 for nonverbal or younger kids.

There are programs designed for little ones with autism that use visual systems to teach them about emotional states; one example is "How Does Your Engine Run?" We just need to be careful that the younger children are able to understand what our language means, for instance, "running fast," or "running slow," or "running just right." How do we know that they understand what these phrases mean? This is why asking the child to describe an event and share his own experience becomes so important in providing a baseline to understand how that child makes sense of the scale.

Once we can get kids on the spectrum to acknowledge their own emotional states, we are then able to teach strategies to monitor and manage those emotions. We can help them learn to recognize when they start to feel themselves becoming upset, (e.g., angry, sad, hungry, etc.) and how to address the issue before they are off the charts emotionally. At that point, it may be too late to do anything preventative, so you may just have to wait out the emotional storm.

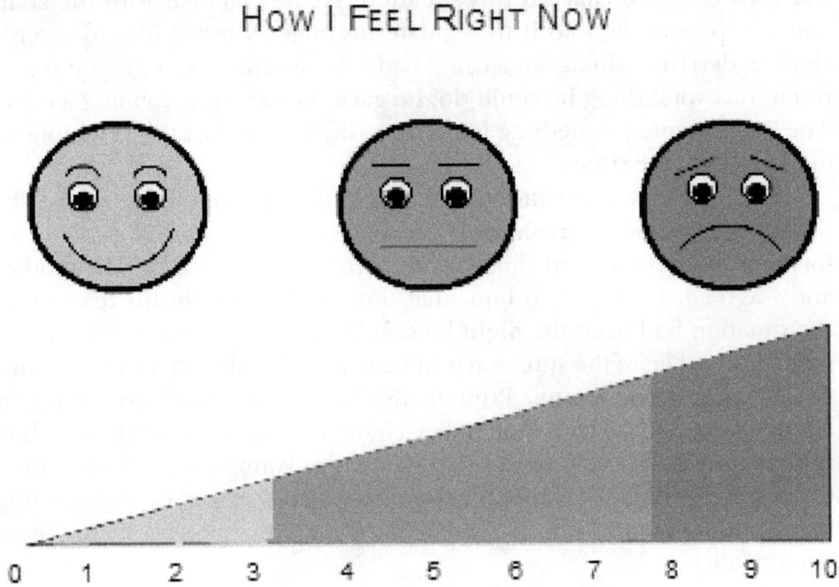

Note: This diagram can be used for younger or nonverbal children who have difficulty expressing how they feel.

Figure 8.2. How I feel right now.

The same 0-10 scale I just described can also be used to prepare an individual with ASD prior to entering into a situation that may be challenging for her to handle. Using this scale can help the child identify where she is emotionally, which could reduce a great deal of emotional discomfort in the midst of the situation.

MANAGING THE TENDENCY TO OVERREACT

This same technique, identifying and measuring emotions through a visual tool, can be used to manage a tendency to overreact to any situation. I worked with a young man whose mother said that he overreacts to the slightest things at home. When I asked for an example, she described an incident that had occurred on the previous night when she asked her son if he had remembered to brush his teeth. He was not in any trouble; she just asked. The mom explained to me that he had forgotten, but she expressed concern that his emotional response was very intense. He had a terrible meltdown.

I used the 0-10 chart in this situation. He was familiar with the chart and had previously used it to regulate his anger. I asked him to use the chart to describe "doing something bad." So, in this case, a 10 would represent the worst thing he could do; he gave the example, robbing a bank. The 0 represented something good he could do, and he said, "Helping an old lady cross the street."

When I put the chart in front of him and asked him what number he thought forgetting to brush his teeth represented, he looked at the chart for quite some time, and finally said, "Probably a 1 or a 2." His mother and I agreed. I then asked him what number he thought his reaction to the situation had been the night before. He admitted it was a 10. He was starting to evaluate the situation and how he responded in terms of both a good and bad continuum. Prior to this point, he viewed everything as either all good or all bad. Remember Figure 8.1 depicting black and white thinking? With the help of this 0-10 scale, this young man was beginning to see the possibility of something between the two extremes. Recognizing that a middle ground (the gray area) exists is a prerequisite to being there emotionally.

CALMING DOWN IS A CHOICE

I like to teach individuals on the spectrum that they are able to not only recognize changes in their emotional state, but that they also have a choice about how they respond. They can choose to calm themselves down, or they can choose not to. If they choose to calm down, they can use their strategies to do so. Strategies may include things like taking sensory breaks, using the sensory backpack, counting to 10, doing breathing exercises, using positive self-talk, and so on. I find it is not so much about what strategy they use as it is about recognizing the change in emotion and realizing that they have a choice about getting upset or controlling their emotional state. Once that happens, any strategy they use can be effective.

Figure 8.3 shows the choice they can make to calm themselves.

I tell the individual that Figure 8.3 represents his brain and the line coming from the top of the brain represents when he starts to think about something that may be upsetting. When he gets to the middle of the Y, or the crossroads, he can make a choice about which way he wants to go. I usually put the 0-10 Figure 8.1 above Figure 8.3. So, on one side you have no anger and on the other side you have a high degree of anger. I tell the individual that he can choose to not get angry and use strategies to calm himself. I list possible strategies on Figure 8.3 where the numbers 1-4 are shown.

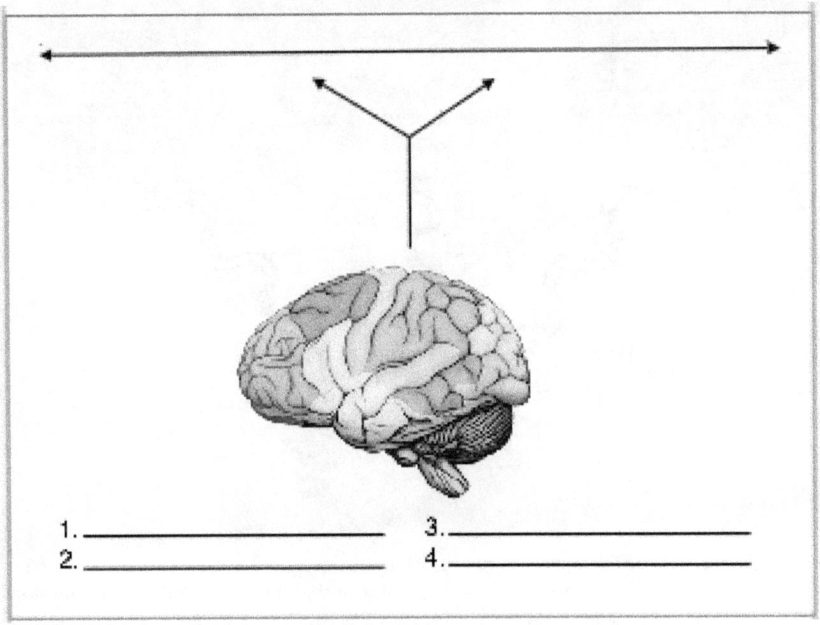

Note: By listing possible strategies that might help a child calm down, the individual learns to understand that he can make positive choices to prevent anger from escalating.

Figure 8.3. Strategies to help calm the brain.

You can use this concept to help teach a child to control his emotional states, from anger to anxiety, as well as to help him focus and learn appropriate responses to uncomfortable or difficult situations. The goal is to help the child avoid the auto-escalation that can happen when he associates other memories.

AUTO-ESCALATION/ASSOCIATING MEMORIES

Children on the spectrum are not hardwired to avoid being upset; their systems seem to naturally get sucked into uneasy feelings or unrest. Remember that they are visual thinkers. Often, when they begin to feel an emotion, they very quickly get a visual of events they have experienced in the past that elicited the same feeling. This compounds the emotion they are currently experiencing and leads to a seemingly automatic escalation in feeling. This may be the reason that an autistic child can go from 0 to 10 on the anger scale very quickly. Figure 8.4 illustrates the connection.

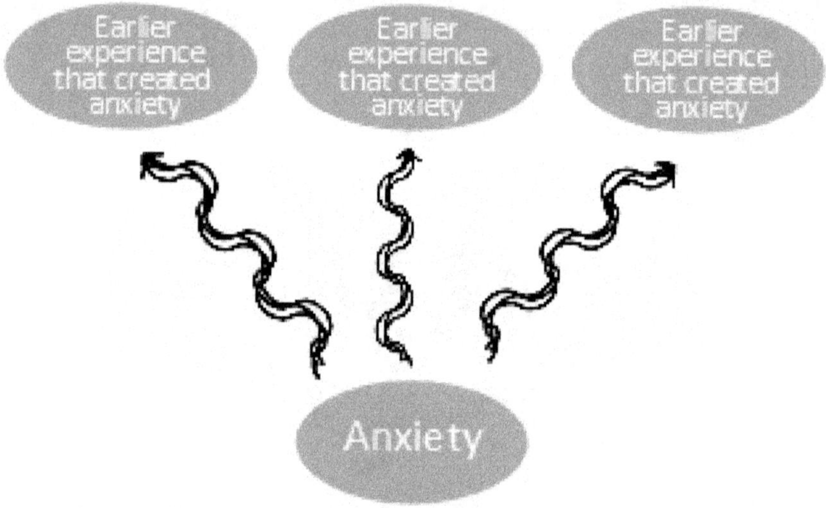

Note: People on the autistic spectrum are visual thinkers; an event that upsets them can trigger thoughts of past events they have experienced that have caused the same emotion. They remember and visualize these past experiences, which creates more anxiety. The problem is then compounded because they not only feel the current emotions, but they relive the earlier events.

Figure 8.4. Anxiety triggers from past experiences.

Figure 8.4 helps me to explain to parents how individuals on the spectrum tap into a wellspring of anxiety. All of the prior incidents may not be connected in any other way, except that they created a certain feeling. When the child experiences that same feeling again, the emotion intensifies because it brings back the memories of when she felt that way before.

Those of us without ASD can tune this out; we do not think about all other events that elicited the same emotion. While we are able to manage this type of mental association, children with ASD do not have a filter that says, "Don't go there—think about something different." There is a snowball effect; once the ball starts rolling it just keeps going, and these children can wind up inordinately distressed because of the memories of a previous experience.

If, at that critical moment when their minds begin to go down this path and they become agitated, they can apply some simple strategies, they can break the escalation pattern and calm themselves. Strategies such as using a visual system, writing an outline of steps to follow, or recalling memorized lists are very effective calming tools in this situation.

Trying to create those tools in the moment is very unsuccessful, so they need to be ready in advance. Most children with ASD need help to develop a list of options from which to draw upon when they need to calm down. Keep in mind that their neurological systems do not do this naturally, so they need to be taught. For little ones, under the age of 5 or 6, who are not yet reading, we use pictures. Creating that picture list will probably require input from parents or teachers in addition to information from the young child.

It is so important that we help them learn to break the pattern of getting angry and going immediately from 0 to 10. As you can imagine, controlling anger is a life lesson that increases functionality dramatically. These visual tools, when they are working effectively, remind the child to catch himself before he escalates to an extreme. With this awareness, children with ASD can start the process of calming down before it's too late, and they can effectively stop the auto-escalation.

I teach kids to identify the critical point at which to use these strategies in order to calm themselves. By recognizing when they start to get emotionally charged, they can apply these tools when they are at 5 or 6 on the scale, rather than waiting until they are at 10. Remember the earlier description given by a man with autism who explained how difficult it was to change his train of thought once his mind started to go in a certain direction? Being able to call a time out in that compulsive emotional landslide is a very useful skill, one that will dramatically improve the child's flexibility and functionality.

BREAKING THE CYCLE

Another strategy that I use when individuals on the spectrum are getting stuck, or fixated, on something is one I call "breaking the cycle." I teach these individuals to stop themselves from perseverating (obsessing) on a topic by doing something that distracts them from their obsessive thoughts. I use the Figure 8.5 to help them visualize what I am talking about.

The goal is to empower individuals on the spectrum to learn to control their emotions. These individuals typically strive to control situations; Figure 8.5 allows them to identify how they control their thinking and hyperfocus in a way that will help them become more functional. In the middle circle, the individual writes what he might be obsessing about. In the outer circles, he writes the strategies he can use to break that obsessive thought or cycle. This chart should be prepared when the child is calm—in therapy or at home—and reviewed or practiced often enough so that

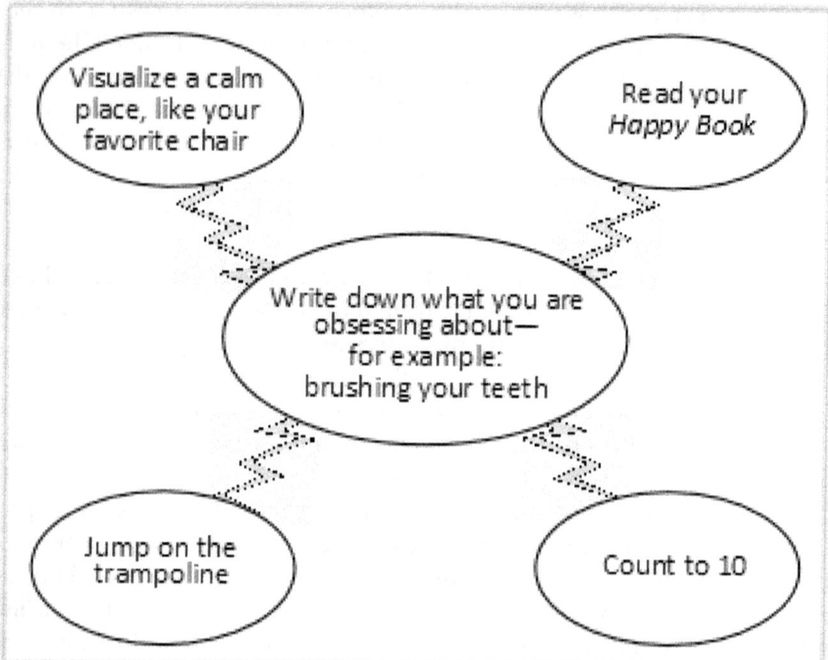

Note: This chart helps children to identify strategies they can use to calm themselves when they begin to get obsessive about something. It is a good idea to work on this chart when the child is calm.

Figure 8.4. Breaking the cycle chart.

when a situation arises, he is capable of using the practiced strategies to break the cycle.

In many cases, individuals on the spectrum seem to need another person to break the cycle (usually the mom). They are unable to calm themselves on their own, unless they are taught how to do so. A common pattern is to push mom to the point at which she gets really mad, which seems to break the cycle. It is as if the child on the spectrum realizes that mom is officially done and, interestingly enough, the cycle stops. Sometimes they get angry if she cannot fix the problem with which they are struggling.

I frequently see the mom act as the lightning rod for an individual on the spectrum. The controlled emotion needs to vent and individuals on the spectrum want to do so in the safest environment, which is home. They keep it together in school, and when they get home the emotion is expressed in full force, and usually the mom is the one who attracts that energy.

The same pattern occurs when it comes to doing homework. In some cases, individuals on the spectrum are stuck, unable to organize themselves enough to do homework on their own. They can only do homework if someone is sitting with them. This chart helps them to break the cycle and to be able to self-organize.

STRATEGIES TO AVOID GETTING STUCK

For individuals with autism, being able to recognize when they are stuck is a milestone in their growth. Once they know how to determine if they are stuck, we can teach them strategies to get unstuck. First, they need to be calm. Until they are in a state of calm, there is no point being in a classroom, or engaging in social situations, since, at that moment, they cannot process or absorb what is going on because they are too distracted by the stimulus around them.

Without some intervention, individuals with autism can get stuck thinking about negative events and spiral downward emotionally without being able to let it go. It is crucial that they learn to recognize changes in their emotional state before they are at the end of their scale. When an individual is at the intense end of the scale, it is very difficult (if not impossible) to change his thought process. These individuals can also easily get stuck in not doing things that they are asked to do, such as chores or homework, for example. They just do not want to do the activity (times 10), and they get stuck, unable to move themselves forward.

Here is a typical scenario where the individual is stuck: A young man with Asperger's disorder was recently in my office because he really struggled doing assignments for which he could not see the relevance. When I met him, his grades were C's and D's, although he is a very bright student. The first fall we worked together, he was able to dramatically improve his grades because he decided to do the work. He ran into trouble in the spring, when he had a literature class; he decided to skim the 400-page book instead of reading it and to ignore the assigned study guides because they were not going to be graded. However, the teacher did encourage the class to complete the guides because students would be allowed to refer to them during the test.

Well, needless to say, the test did not go very well for this young man; he was totally unprepared. We spoke about what happened and he was sure it would never happen again. When school started the following term, there was another book to read and more study guides to be completed. Once again, these study guides were not going to be scored, but could be used for the test. Guess what happened? He did not complete the study guides. His father was livid and fumed, "How could he have not learned his lesson?" I explained that he was stuck at the point of not doing something that he did not want to do since it was not graded. He could not get himself to do it. This is a perfect example of how individuals with autism behave; once their brains start in a direction, it is difficult to stop the momentum or change direction. Doing something in a different way is extremely difficult, if not impossible, for them.

To help that young man overcome being stuck, I had him write himself a script to read each night before he does homework. This is what he wrote:

> How to Get Unstuck Paper:
>
> Think about something positive/some kind of reward/something to look forward to after I get this task accomplished. Also, think: "how will this benefit me in the long run?" If it's studying for a test, I will get an A, which will get me a better grade in class, which will increase my GPA, which will help me get into college, which will help my education and get me a job, which is what I will do for a decent part of my life.

OTHER STRATEGIES TO MANAGE EXTREME BEHAVIOR

Given the tendency for individuals with autism to wear their hearts on their sleeves (that is, to be very blunt about what they are feeling), it is not a difficult stretch to understand that their behavior can also be perceived as blunt or extreme. From the outside, they seem either okay or very bad. We do not often see a middle range of emotion in them. Parents usually describe a lack of emotion which, in this context is a good state. That absence of emotion is contrasted with upset, which can manifest as yelling, aggression, tantrums, or even rage. Both the child and his parents can benefit from the ability to recognize subtle changes in emotions before it is too late, and have a plan available to interrupt the pattern. Below are additional options for intervention:

PRACTICE IN ADVANCE

Sometimes an individual with autism will describe a situation that creates such turmoil and duress for him that he feels he cannot be effective at using the scale technique, or any other, in the moment. Many of the situations that threaten to feel overwhelming involve social interactions. My experience suggests that if the child is concerned that he will be overwhelmed by a situation, he is most likely correct. Intervention needs to focus on practicing the situation in advance, in an effort not to end up trying to do it in the moment. This is most effectively done in a place that is nonthreatening, such as at home, in a therapist's office, or at school.

With practice, an abstract unknown becomes more concrete and, therefore, more manageable. Unfortunately, it is impossible to predict the future, so this advance practice cannot cover every possibility for whatever events they might encounter. Remember the young man who was practicing a phone call to join in a group? When the receptionist asked him to "Please hold," and that response was not one of his anticipated scenarios, he was unable to continue the call.

The act of practicing is important. In my groups, we practice small talk, which can be problematic since most social interactions do not follow the same pattern every time. For example, slang can make the exchange confusing. I treated an adult who drove his own car, lived alone next door to his sister, and had a job as a maintenance man at a toy store. He expressed his confusion one day over a common greeting, asking me, "Why would someone say, 'What's up?' " He went on to say that he answered with, "The lights, the ceiling tiles" Unable to grasp the meaning of this colloquialism, he wondered why a person would ask him such a thing.

This same young man was on his way home from his maintenance job when his favorite car got a flat tire. He liked his car because of the "hum it made as it drove across the road." Unfortunately, when he got that flat tire, he pulled into a Cadillac dealership and ended up driving away in a brand new Escalade. Why? Because the man at the dealership told him that he needed a new car and he took that literally. There lies the difficulty for someone with a social disability in a world that, unfortunately, has many predators (not that all car dealers are predators).

In addition to all the other stumbling blocks, the individual's need for additional processing time may impact how a social interaction goes. Practice may help reduce the processing time in an actual situation. Although practice can be a very effective strategy in many circumstances, it cannot cover the myriad number of possibilities in any one social encounter. Here is another strategy that can truncate the number of possibilities and help the individual with ASD manage the direction of a social interaction—using written messages.

PREWRITTEN MESSAGES TO EDUCATE OTHERS

Under duress, it may be more effective to utilize a strategy that does not involve the individual with ASD having to explain herself verbally or calm herself down (which may be impossible in that moment). This strategy would require educating those involved in the situation about what the individual with autism is experiencing and why. This can be very helpful in steering an encounter to a successful conclusion.

For example, individuals with autism may come into contact with police officers, for whatever reason. Many neuro-typical people are uncomfortable around law enforcement officials; think about how it feels when a police car is behind you while you're driving. For an individual with autism, this can be stressful times 10. If the individual with autism happens to be an adolescent, he may fall victim to a certain stigma attached to teenagers in general. That might be even further compounded by the fact that adolescents (who are discovering a sense of autonomy and feeling as though they are adults) think that they understand how the world operates. Now we have all the makings of a potential problem.

If a police officer approaches an individual with autism and begins to talk to him, the stress of this could cause the teen to go into shutdown mode and render him unable to respond to the officer. How do you suppose this looks to the police? The individual may even smile due to nervousness, which might be perceived by the officer as arrogance or rudeness. Obviously, if the police officer misinterprets the response of the individual, the situation could escalate.

If this individual with autism could hand the police officer a prewritten note that read:

> Hi, my name is Tom Smith and I have Asperger's disorder. I often get very nervous in social situations and have trouble coming up with words to say and to communicate what I am thinking and feeling. It takes me a few minutes to process what is going on when I am nervous. Could you please allow me a few minutes to communicate with you what I am feeling and thinking? If you have questions could you please call my mother, father or doctor at the following numbers? Thanks for your patience.

This could potentially diffuse a situation that could get very serious very quickly, especially if the police officer begins to get physical and the individual begins to resist or fight back.

Here is an example of an interesting encounter with the police that stemmed from the innocent, yet quirky, behavior of one of my clients. I had just started working with a young man who was driving to my office by himself. He was obsessed with hitting the exact speed limit each time he started driving from a complete stop. He would start at 0 and expect to hit 45 miles per hour immediately when starting out. If he felt that he was over or under 45, he would completely stop his car and start over.

One day, on his way to my office, he did this stopping and starting maneuver. Another driver phoned the police, and an officer was dispatched to pull him over. Once pulled over, my client became overloaded and felt like the officer was taking too long to handle the situation, so he began to drive away. Needless to say, the officer did not respond very well to this obvious sign of disrespect. He actually dove into my client's car and turned it off. What do you suppose happened when he touched my client? To make a long story short, this young man ended up strapped to a gurney and taken to the emergency room.

If this young man had presented a prewritten statement to explain his situation to the officer, the ensuing events might have gone easier on everyone concerned. He needed to learn to manage his emotions in order to handle situations such as this. What we worked on therapeutically was how he could calm himself down when he felt stressed. Once I taught him how to regulate his emotional state, he was better able to manage himself in situations where he felt uncomfortable or uneasy.

I also know of parents who carry prepreprinted cards similar to business cards explaining that their child has autism. Then, if a disturbance occurs in a public place, the parent can easily and efficiently explain to others that their child has special needs and is not being mistreated.

INTERVENING AT THE POINT OF AN EMOTIONAL MELTDOWN

I often get asked how to intervene when a child is at a 10, at the height of a tantrum. The unfortunate reality is that there is little we can do once kids get there, so preventing them from getting there is the best strategy. If they do end up in a meltdown, all we can do as parents, therapists, or educators is to keep them safe from physical harm and get them to a place where they can calm themselves down. Once they are at a 10, they often do not want to use "any stupid strategies," so we need to wait it out. That is why I advocate recognizing and managing emotional states before the children hit extremes. Prevention is the best strategy to avoid meltdowns.

DEVELOPING THEIR ABILITY TO READ THE EMOTIONS OF OTHERS

The same qualities that make it tough for people with autism to read their own emotions also make it difficult to read the emotions of others; it is a skill that usually needs to be taught. This is an area where visual tools can be very effective. First, with the help of a number scale, a child can learn to identify the intensity of her own emotions (1-10 for older kids, 0-5 or even 0-3 for the little ones). Because many of these children seem to go from 0 to 10 with no stops in between, practicing this technique also helps them to see the middle of the emotional range. Then, once they understand how to use this tool to identify their own emotions, they can use it to help them begin to read the emotions of other people.

One other tool I use in treatment for younger kids is a "Happy Book." This is a book that the child has put together with pictures or visuals that make her happy and distract her from whatever is going on. I usually use a scrapbook that has one picture per page. Often these pictures include family pets, photos of trips or activities the child has enjoyed, video games, cards, or her favorite drawings. The interesting thing about black and white thinking is that one cannot feel like a 10 and a 0 at the same time. If children learn to control their brains in a way to focus on things that they like (analogous to 0 on the scale), they cannot feel like a 10 at the same time. When they are somewhere in between, it is good because it is manageable. You can talk and deal with a child who is at a 5 as opposed to a 10; a child can process and make sense of things at a 5, where he is seemingly out of control at a 10.

PROVIDING MOTIVATION: "WHAT'S IN IT FOR ME?"

Motivation is always an integral part of every intervention for a child on the spectrum. Remember that children on the spectrum need to be extrinsically motivated. Again, to someone with ASD, it is all about, "What's in it for me?"

Many individuals do not see anything wrong with their behavior or the way that they handle their emotions, so they will not change on their own. Taking action because they know it will help them requires intrinsic motivation. Even if they know a strategy helps them, they may not use it. Therefore, we need to provide motivation to coax them to use the strategies. Motivation is always a key factor when trying to modify behavior of someone on the spectrum.

AUTHOR NOTE

This chapter is reprinted with permission from the book *Finding the Gray: Understanding and Thriving in the Black and White World of Autism and Asperger's* by T. J. Wahlberg (2010), and published by Wahlberg & Associates, Geneva, Illinois.

CHAPTER 9

COPING WITH OTHER LIFE ISSUES

Timothy J. Wahlberg

I will tell you, with a child on the spectrum, you have to pick your battles. You cannot deal with every issue at once. You have to stay focused on what is most important.

Because of the complexities of any human relationship, it is no surprise that individuals with autism spectrum disorder face many challenges when trying to build and maintain friendships. These challenges are diagnostic and clinically significant for them and, again, this is part of what separates those on the spectrum from those not on the spectrum.

FRIENDSHIP AND RELATIONSHIP CHALLENGES

When evaluating a child, I look for signs that peer relationships are a challenge. Does the child go to birthday parties? Does he get invited to the homes of friends for play dates and overnights? Is he able to manage group interactions and play? Is she always picked last for team events, or excluded from group activities? Does she have trouble in school with projects that require group participation?

Autism Spectrum Disorders: Inclusive Community for the Twenty-First Century, pp. 195–209

Individuals on the spectrum will often interact reasonably well with older individuals and younger individuals, but they will struggle with social interactions involving peers. A child on the spectrum who is playing ball with a bunch of other kids may find it difficult to adapt to special rules because, in her mind, "this isn't the way the game is played." In other words, the child may not be flexible enough to adopt adjustments to the rules in order to be part of the group.

For example, let us say that there are not enough players to field two separate baseball teams. The individuals playing may decide that because there are not enough players, they are not going to have a right fielder. So, they adopt the rule that if you hit the ball to right field, you are "out." The child on the spectrum may have an issue with this change to the rules. If she is playing with a group of older children, the more mature kids may just acquiesce to the child on the spectrum to keep the peace. If there are younger children playing, they may just agree with the older child on the spectrum because she is older. The age difference makes it possible for the child on the spectrum to control the rules or the situation. The problem occurs when her same-aged peers (who do not agree with the child on the spectrum) are neither willing to acquiesce nor make an exception. In many cases, the child on the spectrum will quit—she will not play because she cannot be flexible enough to accept the new rule that hitting the ball to right field will result in an out.

Another social difference that I sometimes see is that boys on the spectrum like to hang out with the girls, and girls on the spectrum like to hang out with the boys. This may be because boys on the spectrum tend to be uncoordinated and do not generally like or play sports, whereas girls on the spectrum sometimes really like rough and tumble play and do not do well chatting with other girls. This reversal of the typical roles is an interesting phenomenon. It is not necessarily a bad thing, however, it can have negative ramifications. If, for instance, a child does not establish a core group of friends of the same gender, it could create a social void for the child. I encourage kids on the spectrum, especially those who are extroverted, to build friendships with other kids who are of the same gender.

With all the social difficulties that children on the spectrum experience, friendships are almost always a challenge. This challenge is one that some children simply do not have the desire or motivation to work through, thus many children with autism end up spending much of their time alone. Parents should encourage their children by setting up play dates. As with anything you plan for these black and white thinking kids, provide a structured and specific schedule for how the play date will unfold. For example: from 1:00 to 1:20, the children will play a board game; from 1:20 to 1:30, they will have a snack; from 1:30 to 2:00, they will play on the swings; at 2:00, the other child will go home. As your child becomes accustomed to having other children over, you can increase the time.

DEALING WITH SIBLINGS

Parents sometimes find it difficult to manage different limits with different children in the same family, especially if they are younger and do not yet understand the autism. Once the siblings reach age 8 or 9, they are more able to understand the special needs of a sibling on the spectrum, and that can make it easier to explain why you require something different (often perceived as more) from them than from the brother or sister with autism spectrum disorders (ASD). Once again, fair is not equal.

I will tell you, with a child on the spectrum, you have to pick your battles. You cannot deal with every issue at once. You have to stay focused on what is most important, or you will lose your control and, in the process, make things more difficult for your child.

I have a client whose family owns a vacation home where several families congregate regularly. Several of the mothers in this group have established the rule that there is to be no eating in the game room. They did this to reduce the mess that they have to clean up at the end of the weekend. They can enforce this with their children because they can get their children to eat at the table with the family, without risking that the child will not eat at all, or that an emotional explosion will disrupt the entire weekend. The mother whose 13-year-old son has autism chooses not to enforce that particular rule; instead, she saves her effort for more important battles with him, such as his taking medication, attending school, doing homework, or showering everyday. Sometimes, the rules and boundaries need to be modified to make them more adaptable for the individual with ASD.

Balancing family needs is tough in the best of situations. When one (or sometimes more than one) of the family members is on the spectrum, the resulting stress increases accordingly. Like other major issues, autism impacts the entire family dynamic and, thus, every individual in the family. Often, siblings need counseling for issues that arise from living with a brother or sister who has autism. Slanting everything to accommodate that individual's needs and neglecting or downplaying the needs of a more self-sufficient child could possibly set up a codependent pattern that could lead to long-term difficulties for the siblings.

As important as it is to tailor expectations of your child with ASD, it is equally important to consider the needs of your other family members.

Be sure to schedule time to spend with each child individually doing something special that the child really enjoys.

Again, I cannot stress the importance of educating all members of the family about autism. Teach young siblings early on why fair does not always mean equal.

VIDEO GAMES AND "SCREEN TIME"

Parents often ask me why their child is so captivated by video and computer games. This question comes up all the time, so, if you are a parent wondering about it, you are not alone. These electronic games offer children on the spectrum a very unique interplay between themselves and the world.

When you consider the linear thinking of an individual on the spectrum, it makes sense that video games fit that type of thinking. Playing a video game creates a black and white world, one that is completely pattern-driven; there is little, if any, abstract thought required. The computer-generated character shooting at you steps out from behind the same door every time. If you break a rule, what happens? If you step in front of a bullet you die; this will happen each and every time the game is played. Even better, if you do die, with a press of a button you can quickly start another game, every single time. If things are not going your way, *beep*, start over. You die, *beep*, start over. You make a mistake, *beep*, start over. So, for an individual on the spectrum, playing the game makes sense; it provides a structured experience that is comfortable and predictable.

One of the first video games was PacMan; playing PacMan was a huge fad when I was growing up. In grade school, I remember my buddy telling me that PacMan was at the arcade and I had to go see it. So, I went to the arcade and played PacMan. I did not play it very often because I was not very good at it. I remember one time, watching this older girl play; she was probably on screen 47. At that level, the game is moving so fast that I could not even keep up with how she was maneuvering PacMan. I asked her how she did that, and she said, "Don't you have the book?" I thought, "The book to tell me how to eat dots? I don't need that." The book she was talking about showed the pattern to follow on each screen so the ghosts would not eat PacMan. She did not see the ghosts the way I saw them when I played. She was just following the patterns she had learned: "I have to go down, I have to turn there, and then I have to go around here." The screens were flying by and she was just sitting there, talking to me and playing the game. I was happy if I made it to the third screen with no distractions.

Video games give children on the spectrum a way to control the environment. The better a player gets at the game, the more success he experiences, and the higher his score becomes; there is a direct correlation between the score and how long one lasts in the game. What is interesting is that these games serve very similar interests for children who do not have autism spectrum disorder. Researchers have found that many troubled youths play video games as a way to make sense of the world; the rules are consistent.

Every video game that exists is patterned (even the interactive ones). The interactive ones are more complex because there are two people involved, but they still work on a patterned format. The interactive games are mostly shooting games now—I guess that is what kids like. So, if I am playing a shooting game and I start with Level 1, I am going to have to go into a building and there will be two guys there that I will have to shoot. Every time I go to Level 1, there will be two guys that I have to shoot. Now, if I go to Level 2, there are three guys. Every time I go to Level 2, there will be the same three guys.

Now, I could change the dynamic of the game by having my partner play with me, but there will still be two guys in Level 1 and three guys in Level 2. Do you suppose that is appealing to kids on the spectrum? Yes, and why? Because that is a world that makes sense to them; it is a world that's not gray. I am behind this rock and I step out. I wonder what is going to happen to me? I will die. I will try it again. I wonder what is going to happen now. I die. And you know what? This is awesome! Every time I turn this on, the same thing happens. In real life, I walk out my front door into the world and it is different every day. Well, not in the video game. Video games create a world these kids would love to live in because it does not get any more linear than that. It is very easy for them to memorize and to focus, so that eliminates a lot of psychological noise in their world.

I remember watching one boy play with his little brother. I think they were playing a game with the character "Mario," and they had to find stars and secret passages. The boy was 4 years older than his little brother who had autism. He said, "Now, Stevie, where's that star?" "Go up, go over, go down, climb that ladder." "Oh, yeah. Thanks." This kid had played it the same amount of times and was 4 years older, but Stevie knew where everything was. It was just amazing that he knew that level of detail. Because this is an environment that can be very comfortable for individuals on the spectrum, many of them enjoy it.

I was speaking to one young lady in my office recently about how the brain works and video games. Let me tell you, there is a big difference between girls on the spectrum and boys on the spectrum regarding video games. I am not saying that the girls do not like the computer, but I rarely have a girl on the spectrum who says, "I LOVE to play Mario Brothers. That's all I want to do." I am not saying this is always true, but the girls have a tendency to focus more on trying to establish friendships and on boys. Girls have to figure out what they are going to do with their time, their energy, and their focus. Boys tend to focus on the video games. I have boys who will literally play video games, if given the opportunity, 10 to 12 hours per day.

Video and computer games can also calm the autistic player by allowing him to tune out external sensory stimuli. However, playing is not always relaxing because the child can become very stressed if he cannot beat a particular level or must stop playing the game in order to eat dinner.

Although these electronic games often serve the purpose of calming and entertaining the child while allowing him to control the environment and giving him a sense of accomplishment, they also allow the child to avoid social interaction. As with anything, there needs to be balance.

HANDLING HOMEWORK AND HANDWRITING HEADACHES

Homework is a common problem for students with ASD. Think about the amount of stress in their day; it is so hard for them to simply get through the day, let alone handle the added stress of homework when they get home.

Homework presents a number of problems for these kids. Usually, they come home from school mentally drained, and they do not have enough energy to do homework; they are simply too tired. Encourage your child to take a break after school with some type of physical activity. This is good advice for any child, but especially for a child on the spectrum.

Also, these kids think that they should not have to do school work when they are not at school. Their black and white thinking predisposes them to an aversion to homework. Add to that the executive functioning and organizational difficulties from which they suffer; it is a very complex process to be organized enough to know what assignments are required and when those assignments are due, and to bring home all the materials needed to complete each assignment. Given these factors, it is easy to see how the difficulties caused by autism add up to a recipe for failure when it comes to homework.

We have already described how children can maneuver to fall between the cracks; they tell a parent that homework is at school and tell teachers that the homework is at home. For many parents with kids on the spectrum, this situation is very confusing and frustrating indeed. Homework does not even come home. It is nearly impossible to help a child complete homework or hold a child accountable for assignments that cannot be identified or accomplished without the proper materials. Many kids do this intentionally to manipulate the situation at home and, thereby, avoid working on their assignments. I see this all the time.

With their lack of intrinsic motivation, these kids know that their parents care much more about the homework than they do. I have seen this become a trap for many parents who, in an effort to teach their child how to do homework and assist him in staying on track at school, end up taking on the responsibility of the work, which is just the way their spectrum child wants it.

One day, in a discussion about homework, a student asked me, "Dr. Wahlberg, how many hours do you work a week?" I told him, then, he followed up with the question, "Okay, what do you do when you get home?" Well, I told him that I check e-mail, eat, and go to bed. He then said to me, "Well, I go to school 36 hours a week, which is pretty much my job. Then, after school, I have to go home and do more work. And I don't even get paid. See, Doctor, you at least get paid!" That was his perspective, and it seems to be common. For individuals on the spectrum to do homework, they need to know what is in it for them. They most likely will need extrinsic motivation. This requires the first/then linear processing. First, 20 minutes of homework, and then 20 minutes of time on the computer, and so on.

In addition, when a child on the spectrum has done his work, he thinks, "done is done," regardless of the accuracy, quality, or level of completion. Asking him to redo it to improve its quality is a concept that is not even on his radar. Since he may not have cared about doing it in the first place, he thinks that he has already made a gargantuan effort, and reworking it is utterly unthinkable. Besides, these children typically do not care about the grade, so providing extrinsic motivation is the only way to get homework of any quality done.

Another issue that relates to homework and warrants mentioning is handwriting. Almost all of the kids I have worked with who are on the spectrum have difficulty with handwriting. Handwriting includes doing homework assignments, especially English, but also copying from the black board, taking notes, and so on. Typing or drawing may not be a big problem, but the act of writing, of actually forming the letters with a pencil or pen, may be a cognitive act for a child on the spectrum, rendering it nearly impossible for them to write and listen at the same time. This makes taking notes in class (or relying on notes taken in class for studying) disastrous!

If a child with ASD has handwritten something, and it is not up to the teacher's standard, and the child is asked to rewrite it, he is probably thinking something like, "Are you kidding me? That was so painful there is NO WAY I will rewrite it. There is nothing you could do to me that would get me to do that. You could threaten to take my computer away and I wouldn't redo it."

This can become exasperating for teachers and parents alike. One parent told me that she knew her child could write legibly, but that often the child's handwriting would get messier and the child would refuse to do it. I use this analogy to explain this very situation: Imagine lifting weights at the gym. People usually begin by lifting maybe 25-50 pounds, which is manageable for most. Then, your gym trainer asks you to lift 100 pounds; it is harder, it takes more effort, but it still may be manageable. After a while, you are asked to lift 200 pounds; you struggle with fatigue, sore muscles, and frustration. Would you want to go back to the gym the next day and be asked to lift even more weight?

Now, imagine that just functioning every day—getting through daily tasks—is like lifting that 100 pounds. For most of us, we get through the day a little fatigued maybe, but not exhausted. For children on the spectrum, however, just getting through daily tasks is like lifting 200 pounds; at the end of the day, they are exhausted. Handwriting, for a child on the spectrum, is like lifting 250 to 300 pounds. They have great difficulty writing longhand, which is further complicated because they are not motivated to do it.

One child described it to me by saying that his head and hand each had a brain, and sometimes the brain in his head would tell the brain in his hand to do something, and it would do something different. Imagine the focus it would require to write if you felt that your hands and your brain were at odds. Suffice it to say, handwriting is a major challenge to almost all kids on the spectrum.

Giving individuals on the spectrum options other than writing by hand can make a big difference to their success. Simply reducing the amount of handwriting required will make a difference (e.g., multiple choice questions versus short answers). A few strategies that will ease the writing process for those on the spectrum include: allow them to type on a computer; provide them with notes for the class rather than requiring them to take their own; or provide voice recognition software so they can dictate their assignments. Remember, communicating to the teacher what they know in their heads is what is important, not how that information gets delivered.

Many teachers argue that the child will need these skills in the future to be successful in a career. My response is always, "There is no way that he will choose a career that will require him to use those skills." My focus is always teaching the child how his brain works and giving him strategies for compensating in areas that are a challenge.

BEWARE OF TRANSITION TIMES

In addition to the lead time and processing time that most people on the spectrum experience, another time issue arises for people with ASD when it comes to change and transition. Remember, the stress we feel when things are changing is multiplied times 10 in someone on the spectrum. New routines, new requirements, and new patterns can be very challenging for kids with spectrum disorders; we need to prepare them before a change is going to happen and then allow them the time they need to adjust to that change. Whether they are going to experience a shift in routine or a move to a new environment, they need time to acclimate, to adjust their thinking.

This is most obvious in school-age children at the end of the school year. Even though a child might hate school, she may have trouble adjusting to summer vacation because of the change in routine. This difficulty with change can make the transition from grade school to middle school, or from middle school to high school, a particularly challenging time.

MIDDLE SCHOOL

Middle school is one of the most difficult times for a child on the spectrum. Like all other children their age, individuals with autism experience a developing sense of autonomy and independence during these years. They are trying to fit in, thinking about dating, and learning about sex. Most preteens and teens learn these things from their peers or by trial and error. Individuals on the spectrum go through all the same emotional changes without access to a network of friends for support and information. As a result, they learn critical life lessons from television, movies, and the Internet (all of which may be inaccurate at best).

Some research suggests that most of what we gain from grade school and middle school education is social. It is about fitting in, socializing, and processing. Some argue that the majority of educational skills carried over into adulthood—basic reading, writing, and math skills—are learned in kindergarten through grade three.

I could say to anyone reading this book, "Let's go back in time." I have all the testing materials from your second semester as a junior in high school. I am going to give you all those tests you took then. How would you do? Probably not very well. That does not mean you did not do well in high school.

Have you ever played, "Are You Smarter than a Fifth Grader?" My kids usually win against me. I did just fine in fifth grade, but what did I learn, if I did not retain all of the information that I studied back then? I learned how to function socially, how to fit it, how to do things I did not want to do, and how to respect authority.

In general, what most people learn in school is how to navigate the social environment. Teachers cringe when I say this, but it's not about textbook education for these kids—it is about fitting in, it is about socializing, it is about processing information, and it is about learning to be flexible. Those are some of the lessons we need to teach individuals on the spectrum to help them to be functional.

The student who does not want to write an English paper will probably never be required to write an English paper for a job; I can almost guarantee it. Remember the young man who earned a score of 32 on his ACT college entrance exam but was not very functional at work because he turned in employees who bent the rules? He is going to have a job as a chemical engineer and has learned to be more flexible and not to worry so much about others.

During the middle and high school years, parents need to watch out for the "alone time" issue. Spending too much time alone, while it may be relaxing to a child on the spectrum, can be deleterious. Children who are spending time alone are not learning to be social; they are not becoming more flexible by playing video games all day. In fact, they may be going backwards in these areas of development.

Unfortunately, individuals who isolate themselves may struggle with finding jobs and learning independent living skills. Where do you suppose they will end up living? So, it is important that alone time be balanced by activities that stretch the child to learn social skills and interpersonal communications. As I mentioned earlier in this chapter, parents must encourage their child to spend time with friends, especially if the child is introverted. You can use the first/then technique here; first you spend time with friends, then you can spend equal time alone.

BULLYING

Bullying is a big concern for kids on the spectrum. Their odd behavior and lack of social skills often make them targets for bullies at school. The bullying seems to peak in middle school, especially during unstructured time without adult supervision, such as in the gym locker room. I find that, generally, boys tend to seek out others to bully, and girls tend to exclude other girls (obviously not in all cases). Individuals on the spectrum can also misinterpret what is being said to them. Middle schoolers often call each other names in a joking way, although it may not be perceived as such by those on the spectrum.

Bullying is also a big issue on the bus, again because of the lack of adult supervision. For kids who are bullied, this creates a very negative perspective concerning school. It can keep them up at night and create somatic issues with stomachaches, headaches, and so on. They really do not want to go to school. The best thing to do with bullies is also the hardest for kids on the spectrum to pull off—that is, to ignore them. Bullies are good at being persistent, and often individuals with ASD cannot ignore them. I find it easiest to teach these children to try to control themselves when they are being bullied, to acknowledge the bully with a comment like, "Whatever," and to move on. This way, the bully realizes he has been heard, and he sees that it is not bothering the student, which, hopefully with time, leads him to move on.

In some cases, gym classes or the bus ride may be too much for a child, so a different option can greatly reduce stress for the student on the spectrum. However, care should be exercised when creating alternative programming. Substituting writing a research paper on racquetball may not be an appropriate alternative to gym class because kids on the spectrum do not like writing and may see this as a punishment.

A couple of years ago, I wrote a letter to excuse a young man who was miserable in his physical education class. The next week, he was almost dancing when he came to my office, he was that excited. He reported that the bullying was gone and, best of all, he got to use the gym period as a study hall, which meant that he did not have as much homework! It was a double win—what a change in his life.

Interestingly, when things improve in their lives, kids seem to experience less bullying, even if the actual level of bullying has not changed a great deal. This happens because when they are feeling good, their good box is much larger and, therefore, they are much more accommodating of those around them. In this way, the child's experience of bullying can be used as a barometer for his overall state of mind.

OVERLOAD

Overload happens frequently to kids on the spectrum when they are in a school environment. In reaction to feeling overwhelmed, they express behavioral extremes: overt acting out or shutdown. The kids who are overtly acting out are the easier kids to deal with; those who shut down into their own little world are much harder to reach and much harder to motivate. They seem to have pictures, movies, or songs playing in their heads; it is very easy for them to escape inside themselves, letting their minds go where they want to go.

Sometimes overload occurs in reaction to dealing with circumstances that are gray (i.e., not black and white). I worked with a young man whose high school Spanish teacher would randomly call on students to answer the homework questions. He always had his homework done, and he always knew what he was doing, but the second he walked through those doors, he would feel overloaded to the point where he could not process what was being said in the class and he could not respond. So, our therapeutic approach was to take something that was gray, and causing serious distraction, and try to make it more black and white. I asked the teacher, "Is there any way that, if you are going to call on this boy, you could tell him the day before which problem you were going to ask him to answer?"

One day, she explained to the boy, "Okay, tomorrow, I'm going to call on you for question number 3. I won't call on you for anything else we do in class, but I will call on you for number 3. Is that okay?" That approach was still stressful for this young man but, at least when he walked through the classroom doors, he knew what was expected of him and, most importantly, when he would be called on. If a child on the spectrum feels that a situation is going to be random, and he does not know what is going to happen, his anxiety increases and this can cause him to hit overload.

If I announced to an audience, "Someone has a sticker under the seat, and whoever it is has to join me on stage for a chat. We might talk about some personal issues, but I won't embarrass you too much." How many people would think, "Oh, I hope he's not serious?" Then, each person would feel under his or her chair and think, "Whew! I don't have a sticker so I have nothing to worry about. I can't wait to see what happens because it's not happening to me!" That sense of stress and panic begins to describe what occurs all day long to kids on the spectrum.

Usually, school itself is not so bad because it is consistent. Classes start at the same time, lunch is at the same time, the teachers are the same every day, and so on. However, there are inconsistencies at times. Remember, in middle school and high school, when you had a substitute teacher? What was that like? In my school, that information spread like wildfire. Everyone wanted to know what class the substitute was teaching and tried to find out as much information as possible, because it was perceived as a kind of free class.

I really liked when I had a substitute teacher for band period. I normally played the trumpet, but when we had a substitute, I took advantage of the opportunity and played the drums, which was not possible when we were in our regular routine. I could not wait to play the drums. That is what some individuals who do not have autism feel—the excitement of a new experience. Imagine how individuals who have autism feel. It is completely opposite. "I have to go home today." "Why?" "I have to go home today because we have a substitute teacher seventh period. It is not the regular band teacher." What is left unsaid is, "I don't know what to expect, or what will happen, so I can't handle it."

Why does the perspective change so much for children on the spectrum? These children do not like substitutes because they know the band teacher (how he talks, the language he uses, his expectations) and they know his routine (always exactly 10 minutes for warm-up, etc.). A substitute teacher changes the routine and that is a stressor for them. Neuro-typical kids, however, probably think that having a substitute is fun. Remember the rule of thumb—in many cases, what creates positive excitement for the neuro-typical kids creates stress for children with ASD.

APPEARING DIFFERENT IN THE CLASSROOM

Many individuals with ASD do not want to appear different; expecting them to raise their hands and ask for help is unrealistic. Neuro-typical kids know how to adapt by watching and learning from other students. Individuals on the spectrum do not have that skill and so are often left on their own. The important thing about getting these children to ask for help is that we do not want to draw a lot of attention to them. That is why I encourage teachers to walk around the classroom when they give an assignment, to see if anyone has any questions. I recommend that the teacher ask several students, "Could you please tell me what you are supposed to be doing?" By asking a few of the students, including the child on the spectrum, if they are clear on what they need to be doing, the teacher does not single out any one particular child.

The child might respond, "Yes, we're supposed to be circling the verb." Now, will anyone be able to tell who the child on the spectrum is? No. There will probably be five or six other children in class who do not know what is going on either. But the difference with those kids is that they know how to fake it, or to ask a peer. They look onto someone else's paper to compensate or ask someone else in class what to do. Children on the spectrum do not know how to do this. The walking around technique is a good strategy because the teacher can make sure the students understand the assignment, and the students will be motivated to answer without being put on the spot.

Working with educators, I have had children put on the reward system just for listening to the teacher. So, every time the teacher approaches the student and the child can repeat what the teacher said, the child can earn some "your time" at the end of the day. See how that works? I reward children for listening to a teacher whom they do not want to listen to, because they would rather go into their own little world which is so much more interesting and comfortable than the world we are forcing them to be in. This is much more effective than penalizing a child for bad behavior.

DATING

Dating is a challenge for kids on the spectrum; they talk about dating and they work through dating issues just like everybody else does. As I have mentioned, I facilitate quite a few social groups in my practice. When the kids are younger, the boys and girls meet in separate groups, but when they reach college age and become adults, I integrate them.

The girls in my middle school Asperger's groups all talk about boys and dating. None of them have really dated, but they talk about it. It is not as if there is not an interest. It is not as if they do not want to be social. It is just a challenge for them. We work on getting over that social barrier; I teach them how to be social.

A few years ago, a young man joined the boys high school group and said that he needed help meeting a girl whom he liked; he wanted to ask her to an upcoming dance. He asked the guys in group for ideas on how he could go about meeting this girl. It was very interesting to hear four guys give their thoughts on meeting girls when none of them had ever done it before. I remember one young man said, "You put your arm on the locker next to her and lean over and give her a kiss on the cheek." Maybe he saw an old episode of "Happy Days" and was referring to how the Fonzie character acted. I was quick to explain that this would not be such a good idea.

Needless to say, we came to the conclusion that he should start by waving to her and eventually just say, "Hi" and introduce himself. We practiced this in group and he did it. He made first contact. With time, and with practice in group, he asked her to the dance, and she said yes! He was like a hero in group; I thought the guys were going to carry him off on their shoulders when the session ended.

He did come in with one issue as the dance approached; he said that he did not know how to dance. One of the guys said, "Make sure you only dance the slow dances because if you dance the fast dances you will look like a dork." (I am not sure where he got this information, but maybe he's not so far off).

Well, the young man said "okay," but he was worried because he did not know how to dance slow dances either. The individual who made the recommendation said, "Stand up and I will show you." I could not believe it! Both young men stood up and began slow dancing in my office! The one said to the other, "Put your hand here, move your feet like this, etc." Of course, he had never been to a dance, but somehow he knew how to dance anyway. These two did this dancing demo in front of the three other guys in group. Guess what they were doing? Taking notes. They were asking questions and trying to learn the slow dance steps. The young man with the date went to the dance and was successful and said that he had a good time; once again he achieved hero status in the group.

He came back a few weeks later, and one of the guys asked him how things were going with the girl from the dance. He responded with, "I hate her." I remember thinking, "Oh, no, what could have happened?" Many thoughts raced through my abstract brain. He explained that he was at a church group and this girl was there. He was standing in a group of young adults right next to her and she did not say, "Hi" to him. I asked if anything else had happened and he said, "No." I asked for more information, and he said that he had planned out what to say to her but, in the plan in his head, she needed to say, "Hi" first to initiate the conversation. I asked him, "What if she felt the same way? Maybe she went home and said to her dad, 'Tom was standing right next to me and never even said hi!'" He replied, "I never thought about it in that way, but I still hate her." He simply could not get over the fact that she disappointed him because she did not say hello first. He did learn how to deal with this issue in future interactions by being more flexible and adjusting his expectations but, once again, the linear thinking of autism took its toll in this social interaction.

Sometimes issues arise when an individual on the spectrum hyperfocuses on a girl, for example, memorizing her schedule in order to see her during the day, which might appear to others as if he is stalking her (this is more obvious if the girl happens to be popular). Part of the problem is that these kids do not blend very easily and often get caught watching or following the girls they like. They need social instruction in order to fit in.

Group sessions fill a critical need for young people who struggle with social acceptance. The group therapy helps them build confidence in their social skills, and, for some, it is the only place where they feel comfortable enough to share their experiences.

AUTHOR NOTE

This chapter is reprinted with permission from the book *Finding the Gray: Understanding and Thriving in the Black and White World of Autism and Asperger's* by T. J. Wahlberg (2010) and published by Wahlberg & Associates, Geneva, Illinois

ABOUT THE EDITORS

Julie A. Deisinger, PhD, is the department chair and an associate professor of psychology at St. Xavier University, Chicago, IL. She is a licensed clinical psychologist in the state of Illinois. Dr. Deisinger has more than 20 published book chapters and journal articles on ASD and other psychopathology issues. She has presented on ASD topics at local clinical and educational associations. Dr. Deisinger is a practicing clinical psychologist who specializes in treating ASD clients and families. Her academic specialty is teaching courses in psychopathology, stress management, substance abuse, and adult development.

Sandra Burkhardt, PhD, is a full professor of psychology at St. Xavier University, Chicago, IL. She is a licensed clinical psychologist in the states of Illinois and Indiana. Dr. Burkhardt has published nine books and many book chapters on topics such as sexual abuse of children, curriculum for sexual abuse of children with disabilities, autism, issues, practices and concerns in special education, intervention techniques for individuals with exceptionalities, special education administration, and effective education for learners with exceptionalities, and current practices on learning disabilities. She has given more than 30 ASD presentations at state, national, and international conferences. Dr. Burkhardt is a practicing clinical psychologist and a diplomate of the American Board of Professional Psychology, who specializes in assessing and treating children and adults with autism. Her academic specialty is teaching psychology courses in psychopathology, counseling methods and intervention, and child development.

Timothy J. Wahlberg, PhD, is the clinic director at Prairie Clinic in Geneva, IL. He is a licensed clinical psychologist and a certified school psychologist in the state of Illinois. Dr. Wahlberg has extensive clinical experience from his work in public schools, a community mental health center, psychiatric facility, and private practice. He established and directs an innovative community clinic that serves individuals with ASD and their families. Dr. Wahlberg has authored two books on ASD and has many book chapters and journal articles on ASD and neurological impairments. He has given numerous presentations and workshops on ASD at regional, state, and national conferences. Dr. Wahlberg has consulted with many public schools regarding effective ASD intervention.

Anthony F. Rotatori, PhD, is a full professor of psychology at the St. Xavier University, Chicago, IL. He is a licensed clinical psychology in the state of Illinois. Dr. Rotatori has published 28 books and more than 100 journal articles on topics such as autism, assessment in special education, childhood obesity, behavioral weight reduction with special populations, history of special education, sexual abuse, and issues and perspectives in special education. He has given more than 70 state, regional, national and international conference presentations on special education topics. Dr. Rotatori is a practicing clinical psychologist who specializes in the treatment and intervention of individuals with developmental, cognitive, and autistic disabilities. His academic specialty is teaching courses in assessment, behavioral modification , health psychology, and the psychology of children with exceptionalities.

Festus E. Obiakor, is a full professor in the Department of Exceptional Children, University of Wisconsin-Milwaukee. Dr. Obiakor is internationally known for his scholarship in multicultural special Education. He has been a distinguished visiting professor at three universities and has served as a consultant to numerous universities. Dr. Obiakor is a prolific scholar who has published more than 25 books and authored or coauthored more than 70 journal articles. He has given more than 100 conference and workshop presentations at state, regional, and national conferences on topics of diversity and special education. In addition, he has been editor for a number of special education and teaching journals. Dr. Obiakor has written on topics ranging form multicultural special education, issues and perspectives in special education, autism, behavioral disorders, current perspectives in special education administration, and learning disabilities. His academic specialty is teaching courses in introduction to special education, multicultural special education and curriculum methods.

www.ingramcontent.com/pod-product-compliance
Lightning Source LLC
Chambersburg PA
CBHW051151180926
51611CB00001B/22